SPEAKING TO BODY AND SOUL

 PIETIST, MORAVIAN, AND ANABAPTIST STUDIES

EDITED AND TRANSLATED BY
KATHERINE M. FAULL

# SPEAKING TO BODY AND SOUL

Instructions for the Moravian Choir Helpers, 1785–1786

The Pennsylvania State University Press
University Park, Pennsylvania

Library of Congress Cataloging-in-Publication Data

Names: Faull, Katherine M., editor, translator.
Title: Speaking to body and soul : instructions for the Moravian choir
    helpers, 1785–1786 / edited and translated by Katherine M. Faull.
Other titles: Pietist, Moravian, and Anabaptist studies.
Description: University Park, Pennsylvania : The Pennsylvania State
    University Press, [2017] | Series: Pietist, Moravian, and Anabaptist
    studies | "This volume consists of the translation of 214 pages of German
    manuscripts, dated 1785–86, held at the Moravian Archives in Bethlehem,
    Pennsylvania. The manuscripts, titled 'Instructions for the Choir Helpers,'
    are copies of originals held in the Archives of the Unity of the Brethren
    in Herrnhut, Germany."—Preface. | Includes bibliographical references
    and index.
Summary: "An annotated and translated collection of instructions on
    religion, health, sexuality, and family life from the eighteenth-century
    Moravian Church"—Provided by publisher.
Identifiers: LCCN 2016045291| ISBN 9780271077673 (cloth : alk. paper) |
    ISBN 9780271077680 (pbk. : alk. paper)
Subjects: LCSH: Theological anthropology—Moravian Church—
    Early works to 1800. | Human body—Religious aspects—Moravian
    Church—Early works to 1800. | Pastoral care—Early works to 1800. |
    Moravian Church—Doctrines—Early works to 1800. | Moravian
    Church—Liturgy—Texts—Early works to 1800. | Moravian Archives
    (Bethlehem, Pa.)
Classification: LCC BX8571.3 .S64 2017 | DDC 284/.6—dc23
LC record available at https://lccn.loc.gov/2016045291

The Pennsylvania State University Press is a member of the Association of
American University Presses.

It is the policy of The Pennsylvania State University Press to use acid-free
paper. Publications on uncoated stock satisfy the minimum requirements of
American National Standard for Information Sciences—Permanence of
Paper for Printed Library Material, ANSI Z39.48–1992.

This book is printed on paper that contains 30% post-consumer waste.

# CONTENTS

ILLUSTRATIONS

This volume consists of the translation of 214 pages of German manuscripts, dated 1785–86, held at the Moravian Archives in Bethlehem, Pennsylvania. The manuscripts, titled "Instructions for the Choir Helpers," are copies of originals held in the Archives of the Unity of the Brethren in Herrnhut, Germany. They contain detailed advice to the counselors of the men, women, and children in the Moravian congregations throughout the world on how to address potential concerns about the condition of one's body and soul. These pastoral issues were discussed in the monthly Speaking, a regularly scheduled dialogue between the choir helper (counselor) and member to determine whether the individual could be admitted to Holy Communion. These materials are a unique resource for scholars in the fields of religious history, gender studies, intellectual history, and colonial American church history. Whereas many scholars have concentrated their investigations of the nature of the cultural interpretations of the body during the Enlightenment on the study of sickness and psychosis, these manuscripts can provide detailed insights into an interpretation of the body that sees it as a holistic system that must be cared for as the vessel for the spirit. This care of body and soul was, however, also a response to a time of crisis within the Moravian Church, as its members negotiated the tempting new intellectual and spatial territories of the time: European Enlightenment thinking and the North American colonies.

The instructions are able to bring together in a particularly Moravian way what were still in the eighteenth century considered to be the separate realms of mind and body. They achieve this through a spiritualization of the corporeal, effected through what today might be called a "talking cure." By means of regular and persistent religious conversations in the Speaking, Moravian men and women were offered spiritual guidance on topics as far ranging as the physical manifestations of puberty, attraction to the opposite sex, frequency of sexual intercourse, nursing, and bereavement. In the Speaking Moravian men and women were provided with a regular opportunity to examine their bodies and their souls and trace the connection between the two.

The documents make up an important part of the history of the Moravian Church or, as the church is known in German, the Herrnhuter or *Brüdergemeine*.[1] From their founding in 1722, the Moravians were remarkable for their positive evaluation of the body and held that the natural manifestations of masculinity and femininity were integral elements of spiritual consciousness.[2] This positive evaluation of corporeality within Moravian theology and practice also drew fierce criticism to the group. From the eighteenth century to the present, a sex-positive theology, coupled with the hyperrealistic linguistic and artistic depictions of the crucified Christ that peaked in the 1740s, gave rise to virulent attacks on the practices of the Moravian Church.[3] The intertwining of faith and the body, and its concomitant spiritual and religious enactment in the Moravian Church, persistently challenged the parties of both reason and religion.[4]

Within the field of Moravian historical studies, archivists and scholars have known of the existence of these manuscripts for some time, but the church discouraged their publication for more than two centuries because they contain passages that were considered to be inflammatory and likely to draw attacks from outside the Moravian Church. But with the growth of the field of Moravian studies and its critical stance toward the construction of Moravian history and identity, a new generation of archivists and scholars recognizes that these manuscripts contain rare insights into the application of Moravian theology to the practical concerns of the body in the eighteenth century. These documents, the contents of which were highly confidential and passed on only by permission of the overall administration of the church, contain explicit and detailed instructions on how to apply Moravian theology

---

1. The term *Gemeine* is complex and can be translated in a variety of ways into English. It can refer to a local congregation of the Moravian Church and also to the Moravian Church overall. It can also refer to both at the same time. Although some authors prefer to leave the crucial term untranslated, in this volume I have decided to translate the term depending on its particular usage in context, as either "congregation" (local) or "church" (general).

2. Recent examinations of Moravian notions of masculinity can be found in Faull, *Masculinity, Senses, Spirit*, especially the chapters by Faull, Peucker, and Atwood. See also Miller, "Moravian Familiarities"; and Faull, "Moravian Mission Field." For a broader context, see Broomhall and Van Gent, *Governing Masculinities*, especially Van Gent, "Side-Wounds, Sex, and Savages," in Broomhall and Van Gent, *Governing Masculinities*, 189–208. Jensz also addresses this issue briefly in her monograph on the Moravians in Australia in the nineteenth century; see *German Moravian Missionaries*, 91.

3. As almost proof positive of the new critical stance of the Moravian Church toward its own history, see the groundbreaking book *Time of Sifting* by the archivist of the Northern Province of the Moravian Church in North America, Paul Peucker.

4. Such violent reactions to the theology of the Moravian Church can be found in Zinzendorf, *Antizinzendorfiana*. This volume contains much of the original polemical literature against the Moravians. Fogleman's *Jesus Is Female*, and even his most recent *Two Troubled Souls*, have continued the tradition of sensationalizing Moravian practices.

not only to the spiritual but also the physical well-being of men, women, and children.

## Methodology

This book has been a long time in the making. Almost twenty years ago, as I was finishing my book on Moravian spiritual memoirs (*Lebensläufe*), the late archivist of the Northern Province, Vernon Nelson, slipped a folder containing the manuscripts onto my desk and suggested I might find them an interesting read. I did. For me they opened up what I think of as the other side of memoir. The question I had asked myself repeatedly when translating the memoirs was how did these women from all classes and cultures reach a point of self-awareness to write (or dictate) their spiritual and physical life stories? The instructions provided me with an answer. Within the eighteenth-century Moravian Church, the practice of speaking about the self's body and soul was fundamental to the creation of both a group and an individual identity. Speaking, investigating, questioning, and relating the experiences of the body and the soul to a confidant all constituted a central moment in Moravian lives. This awareness shone through in the memoirs.

## Organization of the Volume

This translation is organized as follows: after a more general introduction that speaks to the origin, purpose, and relevance of the instructions, the translated texts follow and are divided according to choir: single sisters, single brethren, married persons, and widows. Each set of instructions is preceded by a short introduction that points to the distinctive qualities of that particular set of documents. To maintain the style and particular terminology of the source documents, I have consulted extant English-language versions of the instructions, albeit from a slightly later date. So, for example, even though the sets of instructions for the choir helpers of both the single sisters and married persons from Gracehill (Northern Ireland) stem from 1819, they still contain terminology in English that is useful in finding an equivalent for German terms: I have also developed a glossary of terms particular to the Moravian Church in the eighteenth century (and some still exist today) to help in the understanding of structures of stations within each choir. To minimize annotations I have placed most notes on terminology in the glossary.

## ACKNOWLEDGMENTS

In 2002 I was fortunate to receive a Collaborative Research Grant from the National Endowment for the Humanities, which helped to fund the transcription and translation of the instructions. I would like to thank my collaborators, Kate Carté Engel and Jeannette Norfleet, for their assistance in this process. Tom McCullough, the assistant archivist of the Northern Province, was invaluable with his help finding manuscripts and paintings. Paul Peucker, archivist of the Northern Province, was a meticulous reader of the draft translations, and I owe so much to his compendious knowledge of the Moravian Church. I would also like to thank Craig Atwood for his unwavering intellectual support of this project, his invitation to give the Moses lectures at the Moravian Theological Seminary in 2011, and his encouragement, especially in the last phases of the publishing of this work. Deepest gratitude also goes to my children, Udoka, Amaka, and Nnamdi, who have made my life so full of joy and meaning. I dedicate this book to them.

Sections of this book appear in modified form in previously published work: Katherine Faull, "Girl Talk: The Role of the 'Speakings' in the Pastoral Care of the Older Girls' Choir," *Journal of Moravian History*, no. 6 (Spring 2009): 77–99; Faull, "The Married Choir Instructions (1785)," *Journal of Moravian History*, no. 10 (Spring 2011): 69–110; and Faull, "'You Are the Savior's Widow': Religion/Sexuality and Bereavement in the Eighteenth-Century Moravian Church," *Journal of Moravian History*, no. 8 (Spring 2010): 89–115.

# INTRODUCTION

## The Moravian Church

Since the eighteenth century, many members of the Moravian Church have claimed the origin of this Protestant group to be in the Unity of the Brethren, or Unitas Fratrum, a Protestant church founded in 1457 by followers of Jan Hus (1373–1415), the Czech religious reformer.[1] Within the dominant historical narratives of the Moravian Church in North America, Moravians link these early Protestants with what is known as the Renewed Church. Their emphasis on primitive Christianity, manifested in an emphasis on scriptural authority, the integration of spiritual and social life, and the use of women to give pastoral care to women is particularly important for this volume's focus on the pastoral care of the members of the congregation.[2] For the early Moravians, public and private worship was in accordance with scriptural teaching and modeled after the apostolic church; above all else, living a godly life was an essential part of faith.[3]

By the closing years of the seventeenth century and the beginning of the eighteenth, the early groups of brethren were almost completely decimated. Small pockets of secret communities were said to exist in Poland, Moravia, and Bohemia, but they seemed to be on the brink of extinction. It was at this

---

1. For a fuller treatment of the Unity of the Brethren, see Říčan, Crews, and Molnár, *Unity of Brethren*. For a history of the Renewed Unitas Fratrum, or Moravian Church, see Hamilton and Hamilton, *Moravian Church*; for a more specific examination of Herrnhut and Bethlehem in the eighteenth century, see Gollin, *Moravians in Two Worlds*; and Smaby, *Transformation*. For a broader economic history of Bethlehem, see Engel, *Religion and Profit*. An extremely useful collection of original materials can be found in Hahn and Reichel, *Zinzendorf*. For a complete bibliography of Zinzendorf's works, see Meyer and Hahn, *Bibliographisches Handbuch*. For an overview of Moravian historiography, see Atwood, "Ancient Unity."

2. See Atwood, *Czech Brethren*.

3. For an extended examination of the Unitas Fratrum in Poland during this period, see Ptaszyński, "Between Marginalization and Orthodoxy."

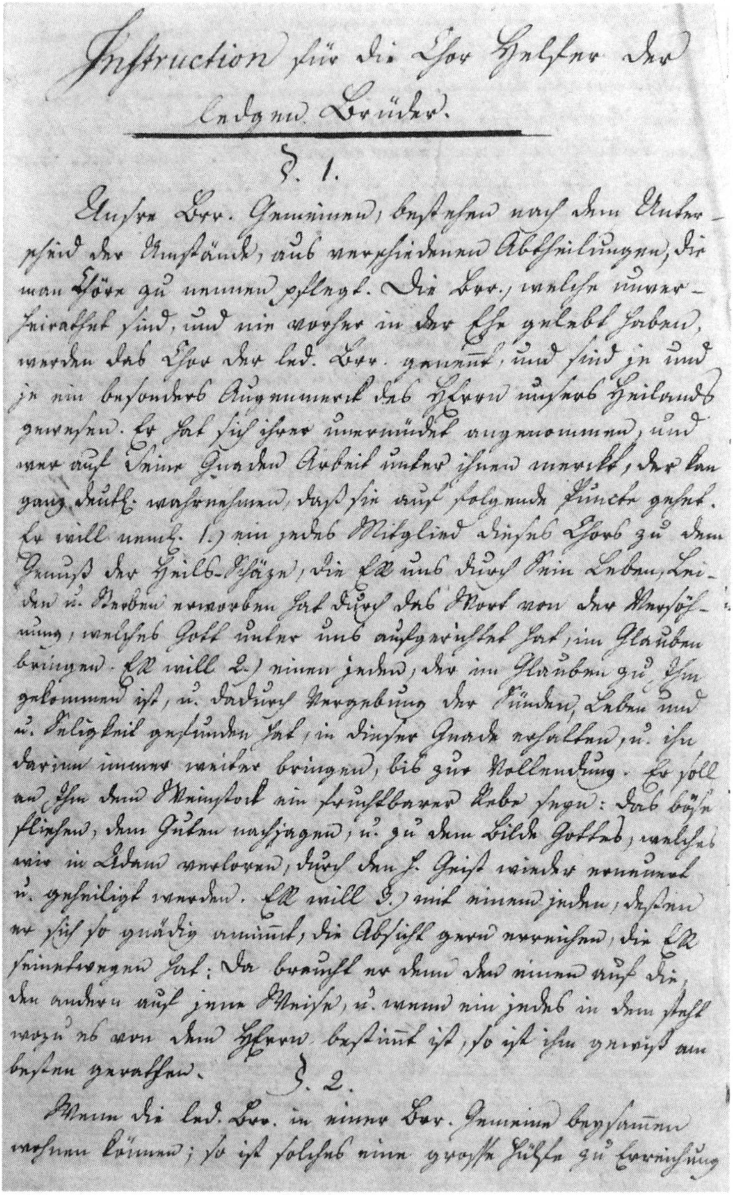

Instruction für die Chor Helfer der ledigen Brüder.

§. 1.

Unsere Brr. Gemeinen, bestehen nach dem Unterschied der Umstände, aus verschiedenen Abtheilungen, die man Chöre zu nennen pflegt. Die Brr., welche unverheirathet sind, und nie vorher in der Ehe gelebt haben, werden das Chor der led. Brr. genannt, und sind je und je ein besonders Augenmerk des Herrn unsers Heilands gewesen. Er hat sich ihrer unermüdet angenommen, und wer auf Seine Gnaden Arbeit unter ihnen merckt, der kan ganz deutl. wahrnehmen, daß sie auf folgende Puncte geht. Er will nemlich 1.) ein jedes Mitglied dieses Chors zu dem Genuß der Heils-Schätze, die Er uns durch Sein Leben, Leiden u. Sterben erworben hat durch das Wort von der Versöhnung, welches Gott unter uns aufgerichtet hat, im Glauben bringen. Er will 2.) einen jeden, der im Glauben zu Ihm gekommen ist, u. dadurch Vergebung der Sünden, Leben und u. Seligkeit gefunden hat, in dieser Gnade erhalten, u. ihn darinn immer weiter bringen, bis zur Vollendung. Er soll an Ihm dem Weinstock ein fruchtbarer Rebe seyn: das Böse fliehen, dem Guten nachjagen, u. zu dem Bilde Gottes, welches wir in Adam verloren, durch den h. Geist wieder erneuert u. geheiligt werden. Er will 3.) mit einem jeden, dessen er sich so gnädig annimmt, die Absicht gern erreichen, die Er hineingelegt hat: Da braucht er denn den einen auf die, den andern auf jene Weise, u. wenn ein jedes in dem Stück wozu es von dem Herrn bestimmt ist, so ist ihm gewiß am besten gerathen.

§. 2.

Wenn die led. Brr. in einer Brr. Gemeine beysammen wohnen können; so ist solches eine große Hülfe zu Erreichung

*Fig. 1* The first page of the "Instructions for the Choir Helpers of the Single Brethren." Courtesy of the Moravian Archives, Bethlehem, Pennsylvania.

point that Count Nikolaus Ludwig von Zinzendorf (1700–1760) entered the history of the Moravian Church.

Zinzendorf was born in 1700 in Dresden, the capital of Saxony, and was a descendant of Protestant Austrian nobility. He was raised by his grand-mother, Henriette Catharine von Gersdorff, after his father's death and his mother's remarriage. His grandmother, an educated and talented woman, exercised great influence on the politics and pietism of the day.[4] Philipp Jakob Spener, August Hermann Francke, Karl Hildebrand Canstein, and Paul Anton, the major proponents of the Halle school of Pietism, were all welcome guests at her castle of Großhennersdorf. Zinzendorf was educated at Francke's school in Halle and in 1716 sent to the University of Wittenberg, the bastion of Lutheran orthodoxy, to study law, although his interests and passion grew more and more to be the study of theology.

Zinzendorf's theological and intellectual debt to the traditions of German mysticism and Pietism is important to understanding the system of Moravian pastoral care described in this book. His reaction to the orthodoxy of Wittenberg's Lutheranism caused him to embrace the visual emphasis of mysticism, as manifested in the work of Gottfried Arnold, Paul Gerhardt, Franz Buddaeus, Madame Guyon, and François Fénelon. Zinzendorf also owed much to the theology of the Pietists Philipp Jakob Spener and August Hermann Francke, with their emphasis on the development of a personal relationship with Christ.

In the 1720s Zinzendorf allowed a small group of refugees from Moravia to establish a village on his estate. These religious refugees wanted to revive the church of their ancestors, the Ancient Unity. But not only these early Protestants came to Zinzendorf's estate in Saxony. The village also attracted Christians from all over central Europe who wanted a more intense life of faith. Lutheran, German Reformed, and various types of Pietist believers were united into a *Brüdergemeine*, or congregation of the brethren. The village was named Herrnhut (God's Watch), and under Zinzendorf's leadership it became a Christian community. Many distinctive Moravian practices developed in this early period, such as the choosing of Daily Texts for each day of the year, the drawing of the lot to determine God's will in the decisions of the church, and the choir (*Chor*) system.

These early Moravians in Herrnhut held that ordinary men and women, regardless of race and social class, could be chosen as leaders and priests—a belief highly controversial to the authorities of the time. Moravians of mixed

---

4. See "Gersdorff, Henriette Catharine Freifrau von," *Deutsche Biographie*, accessed June 29, 2016, www.deutsche-biographie.de/gnd120296233.html.

social rank and racial origin lived together in community and called one another brother and sister. From the very outset in Herrnhut, women (most notably, Anna Nitschmann, 1715–60) were allowed to hold leadership positions, even those of deacon and presbyter. As can be seen from the documents translated in this volume, women provided pastoral care to women, single, married, and widowed. Even children were deemed to lead spiritual lives and had their own choir and worship services. But all these practices gave rise to much criticism from outside the church.[5]

Another organizational principle that shaped life in Herrnhut and later Moravian congregations was that of the choir system. To promote Christian growth and spirituality, most congregations were divided into choirs of children, older boys, older girls, single brethren, single sisters, married persons, widowers, and widows. The single brethren, single sisters, and widows lived, worked, and worshipped together in their respective choir houses. This well-planned and practiced homosocial structure has long been considered to be the linchpin of the religious group's success in the town congregations and missions of both Europe and North America. Within the choirs, each member of the church had his or her specific place that was determined by sex, marital state, and age. Multiple daily services were held within the choir. During the earliest period of the Bethlehem congregation, known as the General Economy (1742–62), even married couples lived with other members of their choir and not their spouses.

The Moravian choir structure was based on the notion that creation, redeemed by Christ, was divinely blessed; thus, Zinzendorf maintained, the natural order constituted the best way for the mutual development of piety. In his *Berliner Reden* (1738) Zinzendorf stated, "the difference in class, temperament, life, age all make an immediate difference to the way in which the individual serves the Savior."[6] Indeed, in 1751, August Gottlieb Spangenberg, Zinzendorf's successor, went so far as to describe the choirs as "Propheten-Schulen," schools of prophets.[7] In keeping with this notion, the choirs developed into the hallmark of Moravian life on all the continents of its activity in the eighteenth century.

---

5. For a popular summary of the history of the Moravian Church, see "Brief History" on the Moravian Theological Seminary website. There are many descriptions of the founding of the Moravian Church in print: Atwood, *Community of the Cross*, and Sommer, *Serving Two Masters*, are two good examples.

6. Zinzendorf, *Berliner Reden*, qtd. in Uttendörfer, *Zinzendorfs christliches Lebensideal*, 16.

7. "Die Chöre wären nicht anders anzusehen, als Propheten-Schulen, in denen so wenig licentia, als audacia statt finden kan." Spangenberg, "On the Oeconomie," UA.

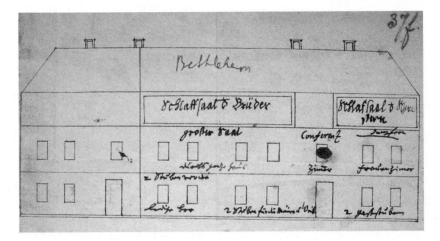

*Fig.* 2    This early sketch of the *Gemeinhaus* in Bethlehem clearly shows the separate sleeping quarters of the married brethren and sisters on the third floor. Courtesy of the Unity Archives, Herrnhut, Germany.

The choir system originated in Herrnhut in February 1728, when a group of unmarried men moved to their own dormitory to worship, live, and work together.[8] In 1730 the unmarried women, led by fifteen-year-old Anna Nitschmann, made a similar move and founded the first single sisters' house. Eventually, there existed choirs of boys, girls, single men, single women, married men, married women, widowers, and widows. Those choirs that could support themselves financially were able to enjoy living in their own separate structure, but others, mostly the widows and widowers, could not. This abundance of distinct groups of the faithful gave rise to a multiplicity of religious services, as each group celebrated its own Communion and foot-washing (*Pedilavium*) rituals. The choirs also instituted more informal forms of worship, such as the love feast (*Liebesmahl*), singing meeting (*Singstunde*), and choir quarter-hour (*Chorviertelstunde*) service.[9]

The Speaking (*Sprechen*)—a monthly conversation that the choir's spiritual counselor, known as the choir helper (*Chorhelfer/Chorhelferin*) or sometimes as the laborer (*Arbeiter*) or laboress (*Arbeiterin*), held with each member of the choir—aided in the maintenance of faith. These spiritual conversations with choir members focused on the state of each individual's body and soul.

8. See the introductions to the "Instructions for the Choir Helpers of the Single Brethren" and "Instructions for the Choir Helpers of the Single Sisters."

9. Explanations of these terms specific to the Moravian Church can be found in the glossary.

In the Speakings the choir helper carefully guided conversation through the matters of the body and soul to probe whether there might be any impediment to celebrating Holy Communion. The instructions contained in this volume were intended as a guide for the choir helper in this process. In accordance with Zinzendorf's understanding of the "natural order," the Speakings between a choir helper and a teenage girl (greater girl) differed substantively from those with a newly widowed woman or a single brother or a single sister. And, as we see from the texts that follow, in all these life stages, the instructions assume one underlying principle: Christ's incarnation blesses the corporeality (inclusive of sexuality) of all humans.

From early in the history of the Moravian Church, each member participated in the Speaking prior to Communion, a conversation designed to invite individuals to reflect on their own spiritual and secular path.[10] Initially, according to historical accounts, Zinzendorf himself counseled the men and married couples in Herrnhut, and within the single sisters' choir Anna Nitschmann counseled the single sisters, despite her young age. But as the Moravian Church grew and new congregations were formed around the world, the office of choir helper was established for the choirs of the single brethren, single sisters, married persons, and widows and widowers. Office holders were privy to the most intimate details of individuals' lives: their spiritual and emotional state, their physical condition, and for the married persons, even their economic status or health. As confidants, choir helpers had to be persons of the highest integrity, with the ability to keep confidences and the discretion to avoid prying too deeply into the private emotions of individuals (doing so might cause resistance). They needed to be tactful and possess a friendly and trustworthy demeanor that invited the interlocutor to "open a window in their breast."[11]

The efficacy of the Speakings was directly related to how they took place, both structurally and theologically. Living within the choir system reinforced the message that an individual's life of faith mattered to the community and thus should be scrutinized by another. Indeed, the most problematic choir for the Moravian Church was that of the married persons, in that the members (a) looked first to their marriage partners as interlocutors and (b) practiced the most intimate part of Zinzendorf's sex-positive theology. The

---

10. The earliest specific mention of the Speaking is in David, *Beschreibung* (1735). A brief reference can also be found in Dober, *Verfassung*, where he states, "Before Communion Day all persons are accounted for by the laborers examined, and their condition reported to the Pastor" (131).

11. Spangenberg, "Chor-Helfer der ledigen Brüder," § 10.

regulation of sexual intercourse in fact proved to be the bone of contention that eventually caused the demise of the Speakings.[12]

The manner in which this sacralization of the sexual was to be experienced was the central topic of the Speakings. As Jesus was born of Mary, a woman's body is blessed and to be treated with respect; as Christ's mother nursed Him, so a nursing mother is to be treated; as Christ was born of a woman, so the "monthly cleansings" of women should be venerated; as Christ was circumcised, so the single brother should treat his male organ with respect. As the Eternal Bridegroom of *all* Moravians, male and female, the single brethren were to look to Christ as a model of masculinity. Married brethren were to conduct marital relations as Christ's viceroy, in His place.

Zinzendorf introduced another dominant and controversial practice to the Moravian Church during the eighteenth century, perhaps following Martin Luther—that of the drawing of the lot.[13] The lot played a crucial role in the lives of those ministered to through the Speakings, especially the single brethren and single sisters. In the eighteenth century Moravians made frequent use of the lot in an effort to determine the will of God in any situation in which the right course of action was not clear to them. The lot was usually drawn after a prayer, and then slips of paper, usually containing Bible verses, were drawn as an answer to the question at hand: affirmative, neutral, or negative. Deferring to the will of God was based on the conviction that Christ, who since 1739 was a chief elder of the church, could thereby make His will known. As the instructions for the single sisters and brethren show, the lot was frequently drawn when making decisions about marriage between a single brother and a single sister.

These practices were not limited to the congregation village of Herrnhut. Moravian town and mission settlements were quickly established in Germany, North America, Greenland, and the Caribbean. This impetus toward the worldwide spread of the Moravian Church lay in Zinzendorf's early days, when he, still a student at Francke's *pedagogium* in Halle, had met his first

---

12. Such problems can be seen in, for example, Fogleman, *Two Troubled Souls*, where the reader is presented with the life stories of two married European Moravian missionaries, Maria Knoll and Jean-François Reynier. The troubles to the souls of this couple include the nature of their marriage, the demands of their religion, and the challenges to their faith by what they encounter in their work in the mission field. Fogleman's book is a tour de force of historical research of the early eighteenth century, with one exception. He fails to address a central feature of Moravian life, one that would have factored into Knoll and Reynier's crisis; namely, this couple—as with all Moravians, married and unmarried—would have been counseled by a choir helper whose responsibility was their pastoral care.

13. For an extended discussion of the lot, see Sommer, *Serving Two Masters*, 86–109.

missionaries, who had returned from the Danish colony of Tranquebar, today Tharangambadi, in the Indian state of Tamil Nadu. At this time Zinzendorf also most likely read Falckner's *Curieuse Nachricht von Pennsylvania*, which described the attractions of the North American colonies.[14] From his contact with the Halle missionaries who had been in Tranquebar, Zinzendorf was well aware of the problems Protestant missionaries had already encountered in their contacts with other cultures. The refusal of some missionaries to mix with the non-Christians or to live at their level of poverty was, for Zinzendorf, contrary to the spirit of Christ. Missionaries and non-Christians alike, he claimed, should both show deference only to the invisible Savior. For Zinzendorf, to convert the non-Christian was to extend the Kingdom of God and also create another individual instance of Christ in the world.

Zinzendorf's particular understanding of mission policy meant that baptisms, whether in the Caribbean, North America, or Greenland, were performed individually or in small groups and not en masse. The individual's path to salvation was charted by means of frequent Speaking with spiritual helpers, usually from the same national or language background as the candidate. Within the home church as well as in the missions, this meant that each convert was a member of a small group of persons (referred to in the instructions as bands, classes, or societies) who came together regularly in the evenings to discuss their spiritual growth, exchange confidences about their personal problems, encourage and forgive one another, and help one another toward Christ.[15] This emphasis on the individual connection between missionary and convert, as well as the importance of shared ethnicity, would have significance for Moravian missionaries in their exchanges with indigenous men and women throughout the Moravian missions. And the Speakings were an important part of this relationship.

After Zinzendorf's death in 1760, this complex network of congregation towns, missions, and settlements throughout what has been called the "Moravian Atlantic" was left in the hands of Zinzendof's "lieutenant," August Gottlieb Spangenberg (1704–1792). Spangenberg was a very different sort of man and theologian from the count. Although having been initially an adherent of Gottfried Arnold and other Separatist groups, Spangenberg was later considered to be profoundly practical and pragmatic and as such the ideal guide for the Moravian Church through its initial mission efforts, its

---

14. Falckner, Falckner's *"Curieuse Nachricht."*

15. For a more detailed examination of the Speakings in the mission field, see Faull, "Speaking and Truth-telling," in Lempa and Peucker, *Self, Community, World*, 147–67. For a more general overview of Moravian theology, see Atwood, *Community of the Cross.*

building of North American congregations, and the realignment of the church after Zinzendorf's death. As Craig D. Atwood has argued, scholars in the nineteenth and twentieth centuries have actually considered Spangenberg to have had a more lasting impact on the religious thought, praxis, and modus of the Moravians than Zinzendorf, especially in North America.[16] Spangenberg's best-known work, the *Idea Fidei Fratrum* (1779), translated by British Moravian bishop Benjamin Latrobe in 1784, contains within it a sober and far more orthodox account of Moravian piety than is found in Zinzendorf's writings.[17] But within Spangenberg's volume we can also find many of the notions of pastoral care that are then elaborated on in the instructions and enacted within the choir houses across the Moravian world. This is no surprise, as the principal author of the instructions was Spangenberg himself.

### The Speakings

The Moravian system of pastoral care was designed to ensure that every Moravian engaged regularly with a member of the community whose role it was to identify troubled souls, listen to their doubts, prepare them for Communion, and thus alleviate their paths through life. But as the social structure of the choirs changed, it became harder and harder to enforce the regulation of interior and intimate life. The Speakings, as conceived by Spangenberg, should consist of a discussion of the individual choir member's previously conducted process of close self-examination of the soul. As Spangenberg noted at the 1775 synod, "the Speaking that takes place before Communion should not be taken for the actual examination which actually should occur beforehand."[18] In other words, the Speaking was not an examination of the brother or sister by the choir helper but rather an opportunity for each individual to speak with the choir helper about how he or she had examined themselves in conversation with Christ, their "invisible friend." This conversation, referred to repeatedly within the Moravian memoirs, was the necessary precursor to a successful Speaking with the choir helper.

The notion of Christ as interlocutor prior to the actual Speaking is long lived within the Moravian community, as we find in the minutes of the Provincial Conference held with the laborers of the Moravian Church in Great

---

16. Atwood, "Spangenberg."
17. See Atwood, "Apologizing for the Moravians."
18. "*Incidenter* wurde angemerkt," UA, 461.

Britain in 1795. The minutes there record the explicit statement, "No communicant should imbibe the idea that self-examination is less necessary when there is Speaking, or more, when there is none: because our conversation with our Savior can never be supplied by the activity of any human being." In their conference the choir laborers within the British Moravian Church elaborated on this idea with these words:

> If Brn. and Srs. come to Speak with their laborers, glad to have a bosom-friend, appointed by our Savior himself, with whom they are indebted to converse in a confidential manner, and desirous to obtain the aim of Speaking with their respective laborers: then none will have occasion to lament that the Speaking does not answer the purpose. This regulation in the Unity of the Brethren is both a privilege and a duty. And the whole Prov. Conference is so fully convinced of the essential blessings to be derived from it, that we resolved, that whoever neglects coming to the Speaking (to be Spoken with) previous to the H. Communion without mentioning before the Communion some urgent (sufficient) reason for this neglect, is to be informed that he or she cannot be admitted to the Communion for that time.[19]

Despite both its prevalence and importance for the spiritual life of the members of the Moravian Church as a practice in Moravian pastoral care, the Speaking has hardly been discussed in the secondary literature. The only scholarly investigation in English of this particularly Moravian practice is a doctoral thesis in which the author's main focus is the possibility of reintroducing the practice into today's church.[20] In German, a recent study by Christine Lost on the Moravian memoir (or *Lebenslauf*) briefly discusses the practice of the Speaking as the author examines the role of communication in the Moravian Church.[21] Developing her earlier work on the role of education in children's development in the Moravian Church, Lost sees Moravian pedagogical philosophy as imbued with a thoroughly holistic thinking about children and discusses the various means the Moravians implemented to bring children into fellowship with their peers to, among other things, provide the opportunity to record and also to hear autobiographical reflections in letters, memoirs, and diaries. According to Lost, these oral and written

---

19. Minutes, September 30–October 13, 1795, Provincial Helpers Conference, UBSC, 20–23.

20. Lloyd, "Speaking." Lloyd is clearly an advocate of the practice of the Speaking, even though, as he reveals, there was abuse of the practice in the mission field, where all too frequently the Speaking became a means to elicit money from communicants before they were allowed to take Communion.

21. Lost, *Leben als Lehrtext*, 10–11.

forms of communication, in conjunction with the gender-specific structures of the community through the choir system, underscored the Moravian notion that the human being is *not* divided into realms of mind, body, and spirit but rather consists of a holistic unity. The Speaking served a similar function; alongside the letters, memoirs, and diaries identified by Lost, it constituted a central form of communication within the Moravian communities and served as a crucial factor in the process of shaping Moravian conceptions of self, spirituality, and identity.[22]

The power of the instructions stems from those passages that focus on specific instances of the intersection of care for the body and soul, and these instances might have caused the most contention within the Moravian choir system in the eighteenth century. Indeed, the demise of the Speakings in the early nineteenth century was directly linked to the perceived intrusion of the Moravian Church, and specifically the helpers of the married persons' choir, into the most intimate realm of human coexistence, the marriage bed.

## The Instructions

The Speakings were part of life in the Moravian congregations from the very beginning of the church. The efficacy of such spiritual conversations was best implemented within the Moravian choir structure, because that structure was intact and regulated. In the post-Zinzendorf era, however, the general reevaluation of the theology and praxis of the Moravian congregations brought with it the perceived need for a new definition and codification of Moravian practice.

In the period after 1760, as recent scholarship on the fascinating post-Zinzendorf era of the Moravian Church has discussed, Spangenberg and other leaders felt the need for the outward promotion of a new Lutheran orthodoxy, coupled with a retrenching of earlier emancipatory tendencies in gender politics. This redefinition brought with it a less than liberal turn for Moravian theology.[23] But composed within this climate of a new conserva-

---

22. Lost identifies three distinguishing marks in Moravian methods of education: (1) the unifying idea of body, soul, and spirit; (2) the consideration of the developmental stages of each individual; and (3) an agreed-on process of education within the Moravian community. See "Kinder in Gemeinschaft bringen," in Neumann and Sträter, *Kind in Pietismus*, 95–110.

23. See Atwood, "Apologizing for the Moravians," one of the most recent examinations of Spangenberg, whose life, thought, and work truly deserve more research. To mark the three-hundredth anniversary of Spangenberg's birth, papers from a special conference in Herrnhut were published in German in *Unitas Fratrum* 61/62 (2008). For a discussion of the redefinition of the role of women in the church, see Smaby, "Lust for Power," in Gillespie and Beachy, *Pious Pursuits*, 162; and Peucker, "Selection and Destruction," 185. See also Smaby, "Only Brothers," in Strom, Lehmann, and Van Horn Melton, *Pietism in Germany*, 133; and Peucker, "Gegen das Regiment."

tism, the instructions themselves reflect an interesting amalgam of Zinzendorfian sex-positive theology and Spangenbergian orthodoxy. As external contributing factors to the drawing up of the principles and instructions, we can certainly count the death of Zinzendorf and the confusion caused by the Seven Years' War in Europe and North America (1755–64). But Spangenberg also recognized the pressing need to closely examine and codify the choir system.

The primary and secondary sources make it clear that in the 1760s the choir system faced a range of challenges: social, ideological, and financial. According to Elisabeth Sommer, in her comparative study of Herrnhut and Salem, North Carolina, the post-Zinzendorfian era posed challenges to the authority and discipline of the Moravian community. Whether it was in regard to the lot or the regulation of sexual conduct, the Herrnhut and Salem records show a significant growth in expulsions from the congregations for the single brethren. Changes in notions of reason, free will, and increasing economic opportunities in North Carolina, as well as what Sommer calls the "Second Generation" problem, all fueled the push to undermine the strict rules that governed life in the congregations. Troubles, especially in the single brethren's choir, to which the instructions allude consisted of members opting to not attend morning devotions but rather act in a disruptive fashion. There were also disciplinary issues where single brethren frequented taverns, arranged secret meetings with single sisters and young women from outside the congregation, and went shooting in the surrounding countryside rather than attend services.[24] The disciplined life of the first-generation members of the Moravian congregations was being disrupted and challenged from within and outside.

In North America the great distance from the European centers of the Moravian Church further exacerbated these internal problems. The dissolution of the General Economy in Bethlehem in 1762 and the chaos leading up to the Revolutionary War made the imposition of order from Herrnhut very difficult. As noted in the minutes of the 1775 synod, the physical distance between the U.S. settlements and the central point of Herrnhut led to concerns about the faithfulness with which the choirs in North America were functioning. With the dissolution of the General Economy, the education of children had moved to the parental home, with the concomitant loosening of oversight as to what the children were actually being taught.[25] Furthermore,

---

24. Sommer, *Serving Two Masters*, 61–85.

25. On the Revolutionary War and the move of children out of the choir houses and into the parental home and the subsequent problems, see Gollin, *Moravians in Two Worlds*, 10; and Smaby, *Transformation*, 113.

the disbanding of the choir houses for the married men and women and the establishment of family households created a rival source of knowledge and experience about the relationship between the body and the spirit. As the education of children moved into the parental home, the need for clear guidance in the practice of the Speakings increased, as did the difficulty of monitoring the practice of Moravian sexuality. Clearly, when children and adults spent their lives in the formalized and ritualized physical and spiritual space of the choir and its house, the need for codified spiritual instruction was not as overt, but as the individual choir members moved into the economic and social structures of the family economy, the importance of instruction in one's spiritual life was heightened.[26]

Spangenberg recognized the dangers of an unregulated domestic space. In the introduction to the instructions, he records, "At that time it was already known what sort of harm had often resulted from awakened women engaging in confidential discourse with men concerning their internal and external circumstances."[27] Bethlehem and the other North American congregations were considered to be the primary locations where this "damage" might occur. For one thing, the Revolutionary War had a significant effect on the social organization of Moravian settlements. American soldiers were billeted in Moravian towns, soldiers slept in dormitories once intended only for young men, communication between settlements (a crucial part of maintaining the Moravian spiritual community) was disrupted, and Moravian householders were separated from the centers of their religious life.[28] The disruption of Moravian lines of communication, whether physical or metaphysical, was a cause of great concern to the Unity elders back in Germany, particularly the suspicion that North American Moravians might be moving away from the principles of the German church. To clarify and codify pastoral practice within the choirs, the post-1760 synods turned to the compilation of a set of principles (the *principia*) for each of the choirs, and then the composition of instructions to the choir helpers of each of the choirs, who would see that these principles were upheld.

Thus the 1764 synod of the Moravian Church, the first after the death of Zinzendorf, was opened by Spangenberg, who expressed a burning desire to examine and clarify what he considered to be the defining element of the Moravian communities around the world and their lives of faith, namely, the choirs. He declared, "Now we must consider what in the future is the gra-

---

26. On life as liturgy, see Atwood, *Community of the Cross.*
27. Spangenberg, "Helpers of the Single Sisters," MAB, 1.
28. See Levering, *History of Bethlehem,* 426–535.

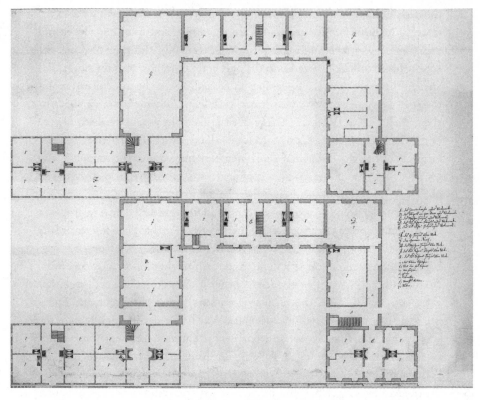

Fig. 3   This floor plan of the Church Street complex in Bethlehem shows the carefully regulated spaces for each of the choirs. Courtesy of the Unity Archives, Herrnhut, Germany.

*Unity Archives*, Herrnhut, TS Mp.216.15

Legend

A   *des* Gemeinhauses erstes Stockwerck (first floor of the Gemeinhaus)

B   *des* Flügels am Gemeinhaus erstes Stockwerck (first floor of the wing of the Gemeinhaus)

C   *des* Mädgenhauses erstes Stockwerk (first floor of the girls' house)

D   *des* ledigen Schwestern Flügels erstes Stockwerck (first floor of the single sisters' wing)

E   *des* ledigen Schwesternhauses erstes Stockwerck (first floor the single sisters' house)

F   *des* Gemeinhauses 2ter Stock (second floor of the Gemeinhaus)

G   *der* Gemein-Saal (the congregational Saal)

H   *des* Mädgenhauses 2ter Stock (second floor of the girls' house)

J   *des* ledigen Schwestern Flügels 2ter Stock (second floor of the single sisters' wing)

K   *des* ledigen Schwesternhauses 2ter Stock (second floor of the single sisters' house)

a   *das* kleine Säälchen (the small Saal)

b   *Saal* der ledigen Schwestern (Saal of the single sisters)

c   *Vorhäuser* ([entrance] halls)

d   *Gänge* (corridors)

e   *Cabinetter* (cabinets [small rooms])

f   *Vor[r]aths-Kammern* (pantries)

g   *Stuben* (rooms)

cious will and counsel of our dear Lord in the matter of our Congregation's Choir Houses and of bearing witness; and in general in internal and external consideration of our whole constitution and leadership."[29]

The 1764 synod discussed at length the need for a body of men to compose the principia and issued the call for Spangenberg to occupy himself for the next five years with the composition of the detailed instructions that would guide the monthly Speakings. The codification of what had, from the beginning of the community, been an informal and very personal spiritual conversation between either Zinzendorf himself or his close circle of leaders was considered paramount due to the vast criticism the community was subjected to from outside. At the synod Spangenberg specifically expressed his concern about contact between the sexes, whether married or single, during the monthly Speakings: "Not in regard to one or the other specific person, but generally, I have been very concerned for several years that one must be more convinced of and concerned about the necessary separation of the sexes and the careful prevention of any unnecessary intercourse and conversation between brethren and sisters, whether they are single or married."[30] One of the most effective ways to control contact between the sexes was through the regulation of same-sex gender groupings such as those found in the Moravian choirs. It is then no surprise that at these synods held in the two decades following Zinzendorf's death, committees of choir helpers compiled the principles of the choirs, followed by Spangenberg drawing up the instructions for the choir helpers. As the minutes of the 1764 synod state,

> A brother noted at this whether or not it was the problem that our brethren and sisters did not have enough repetition of and clarification of those things that belonged to the order of the church and choirs and the correct principles from which they came. For, if things were right with the hearts [of the brethren and sisters] otherwise, then wouldn't they adhere to everything with pleasure. And (as another brother noted) if one thought, that people who have lived in the church for 10, 12, or 20 years, could not lack correct principles, from experience one could find many examples that there were some people who definitely did lack them, and that for this reason one should never tire

---

29. Minutes, 1764, General Synod, Marienborn, UA.

30. "Es hat mir schon seit etlichen Jahren nicht in Rücksicht auf die oder jene Person, sondern überhaupt sehr angelegen, daß man von der nöthigen Separation der Geschlechter und von der sorgfältigen Verhütung des nicht unvermeidlichen Umgangs und Conversation zwischen Brüdern und Schwestern, sie mögen ledig oder verheiratet seyn, mehr überzeugt seyn und darüber halten möchte." Minutes, 1764, General Synod, Marienborn, UA, 1507.

of teaching them these and making the rules that came out of them more pleasant.[31]

Thus, a lack of clear principles of each choir, especially for new members, was considered to be contributing to the discipline problems. This discussion was taken up again five years later, at the 1769 synod at Marienborn, and focused on the desirability of having written principles that would delineate exactly the intention of the Savior for each choir.

Consequently, ninety men and women from Europe decided and delineated the principles and the bylaws of these groups of brethren and sisters, defined by age, sex, and marital status. The committee of choir helpers that had been constituted already at the 1764 synod was then sent away to think about these principles, and their deliberations were approved.[32] In the minutes to the 1769 synod, we find the following description of the principles: "The central principles of the church and Choirs . . . we must defend with our bodies and souls. These all revolve around one central point: the sanctification of the body and the soul by means of Jesus's incarnation and death. They vary only in the way in which they are applied to the various sexes and classes, but must have only this one purpose—the main principle must operate with all the children of God, whether in the Diaspora or in the congregation.[33]

While the principia revolve around the central idea of the role of Christ in the life of the individual and the relationship of the former to the corporeality of the believer, Spangenberg spent the next five years, until the 1775 synod, occupying himself with the composition of specific instructions to the choir helpers. He was commissioned to compose the "Instructions for the Choir Helpers" of those groups that would guide the pastoral counseling of every man, woman, and child across each continent where the Moravians were active, from the end of the eighteenth century into the beginning of the nineteenth.

---

31. "Ein Bruder merckte hiebey an, obs nicht daran fehle, daß unsern Geschwistern die sachen, so zur Gemein- und Chor-Ordnung gehören, und die richtigen Principia, woraus sie entstehen, nicht genugsam wiederholt und klar gemacht würden; denn wenns nur sonst mit dem Herzen seine Richtigkeit habe, so würden sie sich mit freuden zu allen bequemen. Und ob man wohl (wie ein anderer Bruder bemerckte) denken sollte, daß es Leuten, die 10, 12, 20 Jahr bey der Gemeine sind, an richtigen Principiis nicht fehlen könnte; so habe mans doch aus der Erfahrung, daß es manchen nur zu viel daran fehle; dahero man nie müde werden müsse, ihnen solche beyzubringen, und die daraus fliessenden Ordnungen angenehm zu machen." Minutes, 1764, General Synod, Marienborn, UA, 1533.

32. The principia are contained within supplement 3 of the minutes of the 1769 General Synod, Marienborn, UA.

33. Minutes, 1769, General Synod, Marienborn, UA, app. 3, p. 821.

The text of the instructions is written in an open and frank style that is remarkable for its simplicity; however, the text is also quite categorical in its assertions about the workings of Christ within what would seem to be the most practical and corporeal of concerns. The pervading tone is one not of stern self-castigation but rather of love and compassion. Spangenberg describes how all human existence, all our worries, pains, aches, and illnesses, imagined and real, can be understood within a framework of contemplation of Jesus's suffering and sacrifice for us. He compares all pain, physical or emotional, to that of Jesus on the cross; he assures the reader that all anguish can be alleviated by Jesus and all physicality understood in the context of service to God.

It is important to realize that the choir helpers who read these instructions were not expected to give prepared answers to commonly posed questions or situations. Rather, they were to provide a theological context in which to redirect the bodily concerns of the individual to a focus on Christ. For example, the onset of menstruation, a traumatic moment in the life of any girl, is interpreted as the passage of the girl from childhood to the state of virginity and, as one of the virgins (*Jungfrauen*), the girl is to dedicate herself to the Savior. Spangenberg writes, "the choir helper will take the opportunity to talk with them sincerely and to explain to them that, due to this circumstance and their physical condition, they are now to be counted among the virgins. Because of this important change, therefore, they should place themselves very especially in the care of the Savior, the true physician for body and soul, and should implore Him to sprinkle them with His blood and to bestow on them and preserve in them a pure heart, directed to Him alone."[34] If the girls can maintain this relationship with the Savior, a relationship that looks to Him as their healer, they will be able to understand their physical changes in the light of Christ's suffering. This interview, occasioned by the girl's first shedding of blood, is concluded with the laying on of hands and a blessing.

One of the dominant themes in all the sets of instructions, whether to the single sisters, the single brethren, the married persons, or even the widows, is the topic of how marriage was to be understood within the Moravian Church. Both the instructions for the single sisters and single brethren contain sections on how the choir helper should prepare the brother or sister for marriage; the actual mechanics of intercourse are discussed by the choir helpers of the married persons after the marriage ceremony. But the helpers of both the single sisters and the single brethren performed the preparatory work of

---

34. Spangenberg, "Helpers of the Single Sisters," § 23.

molding both male and female virginity to the service of the Savior, ensuring that both man and woman become a "fruitful branch on the vine."

In this way, Spangenberg's instructions are not just about the spirit. They are also about the body. Contemporary scholarship on the history of the human body during the European Enlightenment has all too frequently employed the lens of cultural theory. Literary critics have used the methodological approaches of literary anthropology, body theory, feminist and gender theories, and queer theory as tools to redefine the modern human body to show how eighteenth-century notions of corporeality view the body as a theoretically and culturally constructed matrix.[35] Basing their arguments on eighteenth-century literary, cultural, political, and medical texts, authors cited range from Johann Wolfgang von Goethe, Karl Philipp Moritz, Heinrich von Kleist, and Immanuel Kant. To date, only a few scholars have published archival material from the eighteenth century to reveal the patient's perspective on the connection between body and soul. For example, in her groundbreaking work, *The Woman Beneath the Skin*, Barbara Duden analyzed a doctor's notes on the perceptions of rural peasantry in early eighteenth-century Germany of the symptoms and cures of their diseases.[36] Unfortunately, there has been, to date, a dearth of primary materials that reveal what critics claim is the modern turn to a connection between "soma" and "psyche."

In the last half of the eighteenth century, the medical system that still dominated the Moravian communities was a late Aristotelian, Galenic humoral system, as best described in Christian Richter's volume *Die Höchstnöthige Erkennnis des Menschen vom Leibe*. Moravian leaders and bishops, such as Zinzendorf and Johannes Ettwein, and the congregation *medici*—such as Adolph Meyer, John Friedrich Otto, and his brother John Matthew Otto, the physicians working in Bethlehem in the congregation's first forty years—sought out this popular manual for its advice on maintaining the flow of the *motus vitales* around the body.[37] Vestiges of this notion of the flow are present in the instructions to the single brethren and the single sisters.

---

35. See Jones and Porter, *Reassessing Foucault*. See also Porter and Hall, *Facts of Life*; Porter, *Disease, Medicine, and Society*; Fox, Porter, and Wokler, *Inventing Human Science*; Porter, *Rewriting the Self*; Gilman, *Disease and Representation*; Gilman, *Making the Body Beautiful*; Tobin, *Doctor's Orders*; and Tobin, *Warm Brothers*.

36. Duden, *Woman Beneath the Skin*.

37. Rau and Myers, "Physicians of Early Bethlehem"; R. Wilson, "Moravian Physicians," in Gillespie and Beachy, *Pious Pursuits*, 65–82. Blockages to the *motus vitales* flow, caused by imbalances in the humors, manifested themselves in the imagination, reason, and fantasy as well as in fevers, lethargy, and skin lesions. Common treatments included bloodletting, herbal infusions, and cupping and were all designed to get the body back into balance. Manuals of medicinal botany instructed the

Furthermore, these documents and the Moravian theory and praxis of the body and its relation to the soul fit squarely into the contemporary eighteenth-century notions of sexuality, marriage, and concepts of sexual difference. In them, we can see, as Thomas Laqueur has famously argued, the shift from a concept of the sexes as complementary (that is, of one origin but manifesting in opposing ways) to dimorphous (manifesting as having two completely different origins).[38] Furthermore, the well-known eighteenth-century debates on the scourge of masturbation are clearly played out in the instructions, especially those to the single sisters and single brethren.[39]

In the pages that follow, we can find evidence that supports and also interrogates these debates on the body and soul in the eighteenth century. For example, the single sisters' choir helper must take great care that the greater girls (the girls in their teenage years) are not permitted to form friendships that are too close, nor should two girls be allowed to be alone together, and they should be ready to answer questions about their "flow." For the single brethren, the choir helper's scrutiny is directed toward nightly emissions and their source. Are they a result of diet and appetite or of more illicit fantasies? The instructions provide us with original source material that adds to the corpus of material that helps us to understand how the early modern body became modern.

The importance of the Speakings to the maintenance of faith within the Moravian Church in the eighteenth century, both in Europe and North America, and the complexity of relationships between the choir helpers and those they counseled—the married and unmarried men, women, and children—cannot be underestimated. The enormous corpus of autobiographical material that exists within the collections of Moravian memoirs provides ample evidence of commonly occurring crises that required the assistance and intervention of a choir helper in the maintenance of proximity to God. For example, Brother Nikolaus Lorenz Bage (1732–1789) reports consulting and conversing with multiple people through his *Erweckungsprozess*, or spiritual awakening. He writes of how he vividly sees his spiritual state before him but is unable to tell either his schoolmaster or his parents about this crisis. Only after he is accepted into the boys' choir in Herrnhut and is under the

---

layperson how and when to collect the appropriate herbs, as each needed to be prepared according to the nature of the plant. For example, some herbs needed to be collected at the full moon, as this was considered to be the time at which their healing properties were most concentrated. Thus, they all had to be prepared according to their natures to help the flows and balance of the human body. See Richter, *Höchstnöthige Erkenntniß*, 681.

38. See Laqueur, *Making Sex*, especially "Destiny Is Anatomy."

39. For a comprehensive history of the medical debates on masturbation, see Laqueur, *Solitary Sex*.

spiritual care of the choir helper, Brother Metschel, do the Speakings finally allow him to perceive that he can receive forgiveness with the words of the hymn, "O You Precious, Worthy Bridegroom."[40] Valentin Führer (1724–1808), the later innkeeper and toll collector on the Lehigh River, writes of his own spiritual crisis, which occurs in 1747, a year after having been accepted into the Bethlehem congregation; again, his perceived distance from the Savior is overcome through the Speakings with his choir helper. In her memoir, Anna Boehler (1740–1809) tells of the same kind of spiritual paralysis. But rather than leading her to her choir helper, this crisis causes Boehler to avoid her. She writes in her memoir how a spiritual crisis in her seventeenth year gripped her, but she refuses help from her choir helper and continues to suffer greatly. Not until she is in the single sisters' choir (which would have been when she turned eighteen) does she explicitly refer to gaining confidence in her choir helper and seeing their honest relationship as a "blessing."[41]

This pattern is repeated in the memoirs of both men and women. Again and again we see the path of life described as oscillating between a distance from and proximity to God, and the conversations with the choir helper, the regular Speakings, and the self-examination that needs to occur prior to the monthly pastoral conversations repeatedly bring the interlocutor back to God.

## Instructions in the Missions

This book provides a modern English translation of the instructions and reveals the frank and surprising detail with which these conversations went into the physical and spiritual state of the interlocutor. This frankness is perhaps most clearly seen in the discussion of sexual intercourse. The frequency, manner, and reason for intercourse became part of the practiced theology of the Moravian Church. This, for the married persons' choirs, became the greatest bone of contention, most especially within the mission field. For, in addition to opening up the discourse of the Speakings in the town congregations, the instructions also help reveal the substance and nature of the Speakings between the Moravian missionaries (male and female) and those in the missions: Native Americans and enslaved Africans in the Caribbean and Suriname. Whereas the extant diaries of these missionaries (almost exclusively written by men) do include mention of Speak-

---

40. Bage, memoir, MAB.
41. Anna Boehler, qtd. in Faull, *Moravian Women's Memoirs*, 71.

ings and visits among the native peoples, with the instructions, we can begin to reconstruct what those conversations might actually have contained.

By the time the instructions were composed, in 1785, the Moravian Church had been running missions for more than forty years. The spread of these worldwide missions gave the church cause to rethink the universality of its concepts of sexuality and the body. As A. Gregg Roeber has argued in his exploration of the reevaluation of marriage in the Lutheran and Reformed churches, occasioned by their missions to India, their crisis was in part brought about not so much by political and economic revolutions but by the encounter with social structures very different from the church's own, above all in the mission movement.[42] Here Roeber claims that the mission movement of the 1740s brought about a call for a "new life," not only for the converted but also for those converting. And this new self-understanding was needed, especially within the realm of marriage.[43]

This need also revealed itself within the Moravian Church in that the expansion of the Moravian worldwide mission brought with it also a need to formalize the pastoral care of its adherents. Simultaneous with the composition of the 1786 "Instructions for the Choir Helpers for all the Congregations in Europe and North America," Spangenberg drew up a set of instructions and an official statement (*Gutachten*) on the problem of marriage within the "Heathen" congregations.[44] Based on fifty years of experience in the missions and the changing concepts of what constitutes the political state (most likely occasioned by the revolution in North America), the 1786 *Gutachten* makes the strong statement that the assumptions about the possibility of regulating the frequency and form of sexual intercourse within the European and North American congregations did not hold for the "heathen." As we will see in the section on the married persons' choir instructions, the sex-positive theology of Zinzendorf that made possible such a radical reshaping of the intimate realm was considered impossible to regulate for the newly converted. Whether in the choice of partner (governed in congregations by the use of the lot) or in the timing and nature of intercourse, this 1786 statement argues firmly that the sexuality of populations who had not grown up under civic laws (*bürgerliche Gesetze*) could not be regulated. It would then seem that the regulation of the intimate realm in Moravian congregations was dependent, to an extent, on an external, well-organized, and policed Christian state (*Christlichen Staat*), where laws against adultery and divorce existed.

---

42. Roeber, "Waters of Rebirth."
43. See Roeber, *Hopes for Better Spouses*.
44. "Gutachten des Unitäts-ältesten-Conferenz" and "Instruction zum Gebrauch," both in MAB.

This difficult balance between the external societal and political forces and the internal need for a different order also contributed to the demise of the Speakings overall. The difficulties (alluded to earlier) that were inherent in administering the Speakings in the North American context because of their perceived intrusion into the structures of authority within the patriarchal family led those congregations, in 1818, to ask that the General Synod abolish the Speakings in North America.[45] The request was refused at that point.[46]

## The Manuscripts

As stated in the preface, the documents translated here are to be found in the Moravian Archives in Bethlehem, Pennsylvania. They are copies of the original German manuscripts held in the Unity Archives in Herrnhut, Germany. There we find instructions for the single brethren (Spangenberg's handwriting), the single sisters (unknown handwriting), the married persons (Spangenberg's handwriting), and the widows (Spangenberg's handwriting), all dating from 1785. The handwritten circulated copies of these documents are translated in this volume. There are no extant instructions for the children or for the widowers. But older boys and girls are included in the instructions for the single brethren and single sisters after they have left the children's choir and have been accepted to partake in Holy Communion. The four sets of instructions are of varying length: seventy-one pages to the helpers of the single sisters' choir; sixty-six pages to the helpers of the married persons' choir; forty-one pages to the helpers of the widows' choir; and thirty-six pages to the choir helpers of the single brethren. The reason why the instructions to the single sisters are almost twice as long as those to the single brethren is not explicitly stated.

---

45. Hamilton and Hamilton, *Moravian Church*, 233.
46. Hutton, *History*, 467.

# 1

## THE SINGLE SISTERS' CHOIR

### Introduction

The instructions for the single sisters are the longest of the collection: they consist of seventy-one pages of manuscript, divided into fifty sections. The overriding intent of the instructions is that the choir helper of the single sisters understand that "experience teaches that, just as there are various illnesses of the body, so there are different conditions of the heart for persons belonging to a choir" (§ 10). And, indeed, the instructions are careful to delineate these illnesses of body and soul and provide the choir helper with guidelines on how to speak to the single sisters about these most intimate of concerns.

The instructions begin with a short history of the single sisters' choir and the justification for the creation of the office of choir helper to the single sisters. Women should take care of women: their *Seelenarbeit* (care of the soul) is acknowledged as a central part of the work of the office from its very establishment. And, if any of these souls are not tended, "harm would extend to the whole church" (§ 1)[1]

The first ten sections explain how the choir helper is chosen for her thorough knowledge of her own spiritual state (Anna Nitschmann acting as the example par excellence) and her ability to work with others. She is called to her position by the Unity Elders' Conference in Herrnhut, from whom she receives her set of instructions when she is approved. In her own home congregation, whether in Germany, England, Ireland, Pennsylvania, or North

---

1. "Weil, wenn dieses verwahrlost würde, der Schade sich nothwendig aufs Ganze erstrecken würde" (§ 1).

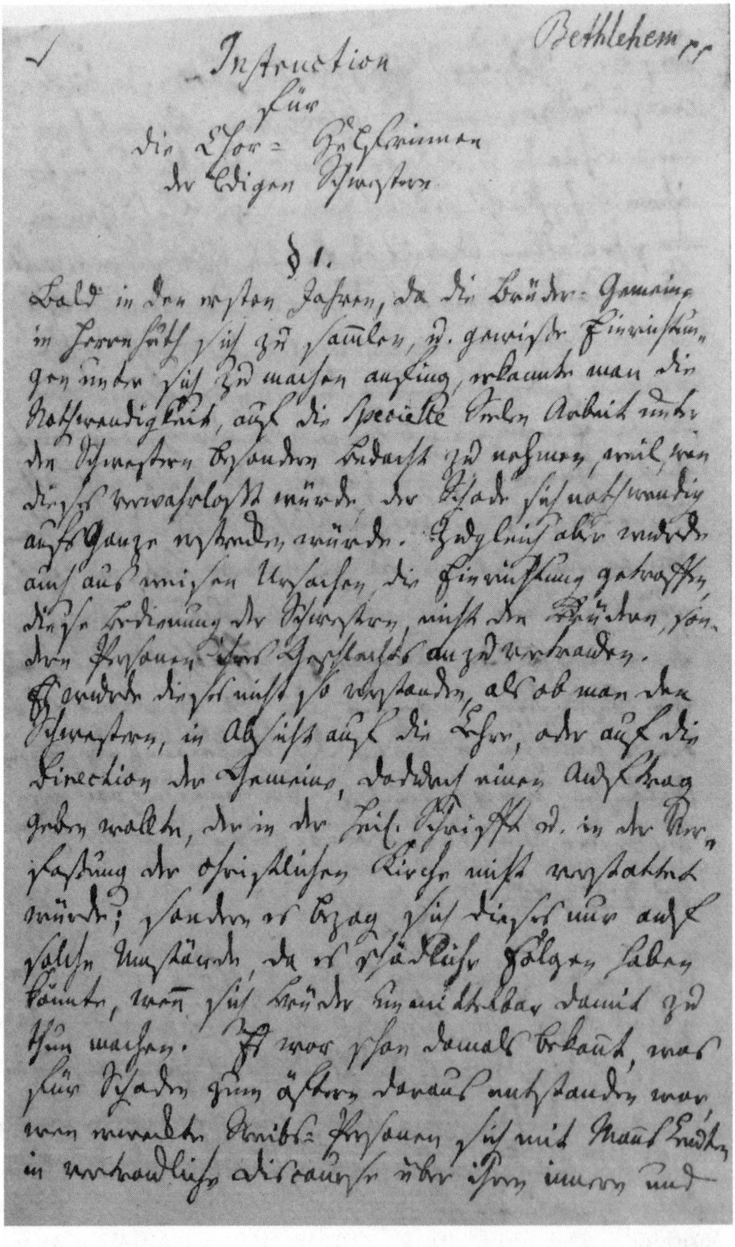

Bethlehem

Instruction für die Chor-Helferinnen der ledigen Schwestern

§1.

Bald in den ersten Jahren, da die Brüder-Gemeine in Herrnhuth sich zu sammlen u. gewisse Einrichtungen unter sich zu machen anfing, erkannte man die Nothwendigkeit, auch die specielle Seelen Arbeit unter den Schwestern besonders bedacht zu nehmen, weil, wenn diese verabsäumt würde, der Schade sich nothwendig aufs Ganze erstrecken würde. Gleichwohl aber wurde auch aus weisen Ursachen die Einrichtung getroffen, diese Bedienung der Schwestern nicht den Brüdern, sondern Personen ihres Geschlechts anzuvertrauen. Es wurde dieses nicht so verstanden, als ob man den Schwestern, in Absicht auf die Chor, oder auf die Direction der Gemeine, dadurch einen Auftrag geben wollte, der in der heil. Schrifft u. in der Verfassung der christlichen Kirche nicht verstattet würde; sondern es bezog sich dieses nur auf solche Umstände, da es schädliche Folgen haben könnte, wenn sich Brüder unmittelbar damit zu thun machen. Es war schon damals bekannt, was für Schaden zum öftern daraus entstanden war, wenn verehlichte Weibs-Personen sich mit Mannsleuten in vertrauliche discourse über ihren innern und

*Fig. 4* The first page of the "Instructions for the Choir Helpers of the Single Sisters." Courtesy of the Moravian Archives, Bethlehem, Pennsylvania.

Carolina, she is a member of the elders' conference, where she is to comport herself with simplicity and discretion. She is, however, also expected to contribute to the discussions of the members of the congregation.

In a larger choir, the choir helper would have assistants to help her in the administration of pastoral care, and these individuals could be assigned the task of conducting "conversations" with the individual sisters or also in groups, called "classes" or "bands." Furthermore, in larger choirs, the tasks of the choir helper and choir warden are to be kept separate (the latter taking care of the practical, physical, and economic concerns of the choir). The choir helper is instructed to work with "one heart and soul" (§ 6) with the warden but also to stay out of the business of running the choir. At times single sisters might come to the choir helper with concerns and complaints about the warden, and then the choir helper is to listen sympathetically, at the same time remembering that she and the other officers of the choir work together and support one another and that each office can provide information to the other about the inner and outer condition of the individual sisters.

The instructions show that women's leadership and speech are still encouraged post-1760 in the administrative structure of the congregation, but within clearly prescribed limits.[2] The choir helper reports primarily to the congregation helper and ultimately to the Unity Elders' Conference in that she prepares regular reports on the spiritual condition of the choir and its members. She must also be fully aware of the directions and stipulations that the Unity and the synods have passed regarding her choir.

Some of the most striking passages in these instructions occur in sections 10–15, where Spangenberg's psychological portrayal of the single sisters can be most clearly perceived. In section 10 Spangenberg writes that it is the task of the choir helper to get to know the *Herzenszustand* (or heart's condition) of each sister as well as possible and that the choir helper has to pay attention to each individual sister's physical and spiritual condition. Crucial also is the recognition that "the souls of sisters are of such a nature that they can easily be moved. A touching discourse or beautiful expression in a verse can make so deep an impression on their spirit that they are carried away by it and can imagine they have now discovered the foundation on which their heart can take repose, but in the end it is only a fleeting stirring of the spirit" (§ 10).

Thus, the heightened sensibility of the earlier part of the century, one that had lent itself so well to the aesthetics and spirituality of the blood-and-

---

2. There were, for example, no female signatories of the instructions for any of the women's choirs, although one suspects that Spangenberg's wife, Martha, had a hand in the more delicate sections on menstruation and the flows; see Smaby, "Lust for Power," in Gillespie and Beachy, *Pious Pursuits*, 159–75.

wounds theology of the 1740s, is now firmly rejected as a model of appercep-
tion or religious consciousness in the latter quarter of the same century.
Rather, a Moravian single sister's spirituality should be one established on a
"firm foundation" and a personal relationship with the Savior that is rooted in
a consciousness of grace and forgiveness. The choir helper will weep and pray
with her wards, but she also will be vigilant against excessive worldliness.

Sections 16–28 deal primarily with the bodily concerns of the prepubescent
and adolescent girls. How should the choir helper field questions about the
facts of life? How should she guide girls through their *bedenkliche Jahre*, their
years of trouble? How should she explain the growing manifestations of wom-
anhood? How should she prepare the greater girls for admission into the single
sisters' choir?[3] How should the single sisters be prepared for marriage?

One of the major concerns of the instructions for the single sisters is the
question of marriage. To be prepared for marriage in a Moravian sense, as the
helpmate (*Gehülfin*) of a brother, the single sister had to be spoken with and
educated in the theory and discourse of Moravian sexuality. The actual
description of sexual intercourse and its practice within the church was
reserved for the helpers of the married persons' choir to share after the marriage ceremony.[4] But the helper of the single sisters' choir performs the preparatory work of molding each sister's virginity to the service of the Savior.

Choir helpers not only are responsible for the care of the souls in the choir
but are also central to the process of accepting single sisters into the congregation and into Holy Communion. The instructions make careful distinc-
tions between those women who had been raised in the Moravian Church
and those who were petitioning to join from the outside. Different concerns
are at play here about the way in which the women have attained some awareness of themselves and their sins. Those who have been raised within the
spiritual and physical space of the Moravian Church have already been counseled in the accepted forms of religious expression and spiritual consciousness. Those who come from outside relate to the choir helper their life story;
they are then cordially interviewed about their previous circumstances to
allow them to "mention things that they otherwise would be too timid to
disclose." The choir helper should not force the conversation but rather is
instructed that "one should wait for another opportunity, while seeking to
preserve the trust of their hearts" (§ 13).

Entrance into the older girls' choir happens as the girls reach their twelfth
year, usually on March 25, at the choir festival of the girls (§ 18). At the

---

3. For a far more detailed examination of these issues, see Faull, "Girl Talk."
4. See Faull, "Married Choir Instructions."

Speaking before their admission, girls are required to reflect back on their childhood years and recognize that this time was now behind them and that they were now entering the *bedenkliche Jahre* (difficult years) of puberty that signal the beginning of their lives as virgins to Christ. The instructions stress the importance of teaching the older girls about the physical manifestations of puberty slowly and individually, maybe once they have come to the helper to ask questions about or to express their dislike of the changes in their body (see § 20). These physical changes, the growth of pubic hair, for example, are to be understood as how "the wise Creator has so ordered it" (§ 22). As mentioned earlier, the start of menstruation marks the passage from childhood to the state of virginity. The instructions direct the girls to maintain their dedicated relationship with the Savior that sees Him as their healer. This relationship will enable them to understand their physical changes in the light of Christ's suffering.

Choir helpers must be prepared to lead the older girls through these difficult years, recognizing that the natural proclivity to sin reveals itself increasingly in the human soul and body (§ 24). The instructions also warn the choir helper that the time spent in the older girls' choir coincides with the time in which they often withdraw and do not want to speak with their choir helper. The experience of puberty can manifest itself as a time of increasing confusion and an ever-increasing distance from Christ. The instructions advise the choir helper to seek out specifically those girls who seem to be in spiritual difficulties and who do not want to speak with her. The choir helper must try especially hard to regain the trust of the girl. At the same time, these years can be a period during which the girls became self-absorbed with their own perceived sinfulness, signaled by physical manifestations such as an increased flow of monthly "bleeding" (*Schärfe des Geblüts*) or discharge, called the "whites" (*weißer Fluß*). If the choir helper notices such a withdrawal, she is to try to discuss the physical and medical reasons for the symptoms that could cause stirrings (*Regungen*) and to explain to the girl that this is what she is feeling. These symptoms can of course also be the result of "impure imaginings and fantasies in the soul . . . that arise from a forbidden inclination" (§ 27), and, in this case, the choir helper is to guide her gently and advise her to look immediately to the figure of Jesus on the cross and be cleansed of these impurities by His blood.

It is remarkable that the instructions include a whole section on the appearance of a white discharge that could indicate either sexual arousal or just a normal part of a girl's menstrual cycle. If the girl is otherwise completely healthy then the appearance of the *weißer Fluß* is nothing to be worried about; however, if the flow becomes too heavy or replaces her monthly period, then a medical doctor is to be consulted. This doctor might well conclude that excessive "impure desires" are the cause of such a heavy discharge, and in that case it falls to the choir helper to draw on her knowledge of the girl in question to determine whether this might be the case (§ 28).

Similarly, the instructions are quite explicit about the dangers that present themselves to girls living in close quarters with one another. Section 31 attempts to counsel the choir helper in dealing with "special, warm, and close friendship[s]" that occur among a group of sisters. How is the choir helper to deal with such same-sex love between the girls? Once imputed (either by the room overseer [Stubenaufseherin]) or by other girls), the nature of the intimate relationship between two girls must be investigated through loving and gentle inquiries. The choir helper is directed to keep a vigilant eye on the younger sisters, especially as they are dressing and undressing, to ensure that they do not enter into "playful" (freyes, tändelhaftes) behavior with one another. Just as the young sister is not to treat her adolescent body in a frivolous manner, so are her relations with the other sisters to display proper decorum (§ 31).

The discussion of same-sex love or desire between the single sisters soon moves to deepening desires for the other sex and how the choir helper is to deal with this subject. First, and most important, contact between the single brethren and the single sisters is to be avoided at all costs. If a sister reveals through the Speaking that she has such thoughts about the other sex, then the choir helper is instructed not to respond in an alarmed or anxious fashion but rather offer her "sympathetic compassion" (§ 32). Spangenberg's psychological insight into the emotions of an adolescent girl is again quite remarkable. Offering sympathy and compassion, redirecting her desire away from the human object of fantasy and toward Christ, and deemphasizing sexual desire by not condemning it are all extremely effective ways to reassure the young sister that the choir helper understands her individual situation and is not there to judge her but rather to help her in her spiritual growth. Once the girl has reached a point of knowing herself, her body, her spirit, and her desires well enough, then she might be considered for a Moravian marriage.

The instructions conclude with sections dedicated to the choice of single sisters to serve in families outside the church (positions that sometimes led to problems) and also the care of the sick, the care of "difficult" sisters, guidance for sisters who are to visit other congregations, and how the choir helper should prepare herself for a move to a different congregation. Above all, life in the single sisters' choir should be considered as an idyll: singing beautiful hymns, many of which were composed by Anna Nitschmann, the single sisters live in their choir house in the "pastures of the Gospel" (§ 46).

§ 1. In the early years of the formation of the Moravian Church in Herrn-hut, as it began to organize itself, it was quickly recognized that it would be necessary among the sisters to take into particular consideration the special care of the soul (*Seelenarbeit*); for, if this were neglected, harm would extend to the whole church. At the same time, the wise decision was made to entrust this service for the sisters not to the brethren but rather to persons of their own sex. This was not to be understood that the sisters were being given an office in the choir that was not approved by the holy scriptures or in the constitution of the Christian church or in the direction of the Moravian Church; rather, this referred only to such circumstances where harmful consequences could result if brethren were directly involved.[1] At that time it was already known what sort of harm had often resulted from awakened women engaging in confidential discourse with men concerning their inter-nal and external circumstances. To prevent this, those sisters who possessed grace and gifts and who were known to their peers were selected as helpers for the special work among the sisters.[2] They served under the direction of the elders of the congregation, who managed all the work and watched over the well-being of the congregation and each of its divisions. This arrange-ment, which the Savior has acknowledged with great grace, has been recog-nized and confirmed over the years by all synods as an essential part of our congregational constitution. Thus, in the beginning of the first Moravian Church in Herrnhut, the unmarried women had their special eldress (*Ältes-tin*), who assisted them in all faithfulness and, under the direction of the elders of the church, endeavored to offer good counsel to her choir members, each according to her special circumstances.

§ 2. In 1730, however, in Herrnhut, there arose a situation that we will here note. There were single men who, according to their circumstances, decided to change their status by marrying. For this purpose, they spoke to one or another of the single women. This gave rise, as one can easily imagine, to some confusion. Accordingly, a change toward a more paternalistic (*väterlich*)

---

1. Spangenberg is careful to point out here that having women as choir helpers is not contradict-ing any scriptural interdictions against women's preaching; rather, it is a way to avoid the sexes' coming into inappropriate contact with each other. The same concern is mentioned at the beginning of the instructions to the single brethren and the married persons. On the restrictions to women's activities after the death of Zinzendorf, see Smaby, "Lust for Power," in Gillespie and Beachy, *Pious Pursuits*, 159–75.

2. The first of the selected helpers was Anna Nitschmann.

system was made in the congregation. It was difficult for the late Ordinary[3] and the elders of the church to deal appropriately with this situation simply by means of rules and regulations, but there was an even greater opportunity for gratitude to the dear Savior when this situation took care of itself over the years in conformity with the Gospel. Eighteen single sisters, whose hearts and minds were prepared for total sacrifice to their Lord Jesus Christ, formed a covenant on May 4 and proposed, by means of God's grace, to guard against ways that the church would find unseemly and to conduct themselves in a Christian manner as virgins. With heart and hands, they pledged to surrender themselves without reservation to the Bridegroom of their souls,[4] to surrender themselves completely to the guidance of the Holy Spirit, and, with regard to a change in their status, to reject any proposal they received that was not made in accordance with the customs of the church. If it should be found necessary, however, to provide a brother with a helpmate, and if, after consideration placed before the Lord, a proposal should be made to one or another of the sisters, they would to take it into consideration and make a decision, according to their conviction and according to the call that the Savior would make clear to them in their heart.[5]

Since this time, May 4 has been the annual choir festival day of the single sisters, when they gratefully remember and renew their commitment to the covenant, in which many hundreds have over time participated.

§ 3. Our dear Lord and Savior does a great work of mercy in our single sisters' choirs. It is therefore even more important that all aspects of this work be attended to in the proper way, that is, according to the mind of Christ and according to the rule of His word.

We are assured that the merciful work of the Savior and His Spirit in our single sisters' choirs is directed as follows:

(1)    He wants to bring each member of this choir in faith to the blessed enjoyment of the salvation that He has won for us in heart and soul by means of His life, suffering, and death and which He offers to us in His Gospel; that each one, as a poor but pardoned sinner, might rejoice in God, her Savior, because she has been redeemed by His blood, that is to

---

3. The late Ordinary is Zinzendorf.

4. The Bridegroom of their souls is Jesus Christ.

5. It is made quite clear that the single sisters, from the beginning of the organization of the single sisters' choir, had the opportunity to reject a proposal of marriage. According to much of the anti-Zinzendorfiana in the eighteenth century and also some recent scholarship, there is a misapprehension that sisters were forced to marry brethren that the elders and the lot had chosen. For example, see Fogleman, *Two Troubled Souls*.

say, through the forgiveness of sins. She thereby learns through simple faith to claim as her own the merit of Jesus's incarnation in the body of a virgin, whereby she also obtains the proper respect for her own station.

(2) He wants to preserve in this mercy each person who comes to Him in faith and who has thereby obtained life and blessedness and so will help her on to perfection. She should be a fruitful branch of the vine that He is, and she should flee from evil and pursue what is good, and, by means of the Holy Spirit, she should be renewed and sanctified in the image of God, which we lost because of the Fall.

(3) With each one person who belongs to Him, He wants to attain His purpose for her. To do so, He will require a different way for each person, and if each follows the calling determined for her by the Lord, things will turn out well for her.

§ 4. In a church settlement (*Gemeinort*), it is a great help in the attainment of our Lord's purpose for the single sisters to live together, because not only does this arrangement distance them from many circumstances that could be harmful to them, but it also provides them with the opportunity to be helpful and a blessing to one another in internal as well as external matters. We must therefore thank the Savior with all our hearts for the choir houses He has given to the single sisters in the Moravian Church and ask Him that they achieve their purpose everywhere. That sisters living in a choir house, or those who belong to the choir without being able to live in the house temporarily, may agree in an orderly way on external matters, and proceed unhindered, it is necessary for a sister to be present who takes a special interest in this matter, and she is called the choir warden. On the other hand, the sister who has the essential task of attending to internal matters, or those concerning the soul, for the whole choir as well as for each individual soul, is called the choir helper. Now and then it also happens, especially in smaller choirs, that one sister must perform the duties of both the choir helper and the choir warden, and in this case, she is usually given the name choir laboress. The present essay is, however, actually intended to be instructions for those sisters to whom the office of helper in their choir is assigned through the Direction of the Unity of Brethren according to the will of the Savior.

§ 5. Above all, a sister who is appointed as choir helper is expected to have become thoroughly acquainted with herself as a poor sinner, to have turned in her distress to the Savior, to have come to know reconciliation through the blood of Jesus, and that, in mercy, she has procured her portion of His costly wages for the soul and body; that she will steadily proceed with the feeling of a sinner who loved much because she was forgiven much, trusting in herself for nothing, but all the more cleaving fast to the Man of Sorrows with her spoiled childlike heart. She is expected to be faithful and painstaking in her own heart's path and to attend carefully to the voice of the Holy Spirit, who teaches, warns, comforts, helps, and strengthens us; to pay careful attention to everything, even to things that can appear insignificant. She is expected particularly to stand every day in a heartfelt and intimate association with the Savior, and first to seek His counsel concerning every circumstance, large and small, in the choir; and not to seek what she needs for her position within herself but rather daily to ask for the powerful assistance of the Holy Spirit. If a choir helper pays attention to herself in this way and steadfastly remains a student of grace, then not only will she be bright and cheerful as she attends to her position in all faithfulness and serves as a good example for others, but, from time to time, she and her choir will grow and prosper in the blessed recognition and experience of Jesus's merit and the special blessings won for the young women's choir through the merit of our Lord's incarnation in the body of a virgin.

§ 6. A choir helper also has assistants in her choir, and it eases her duties if she makes proper use of them. If she has one assistant, she should be concerned in every way not only to stand with her in cordial confidentiality and love but also to communicate faithfully with her concerning everything that happens in the choir, yet without passing on every specific confession that has been made to her, if circumstances do not require it. The assistant, for her part, must do likewise. She [the choir helper] tries carefully to prevent the thought from arising in the choir that everything must go through her hands but deems instead that whatever her assistant has to deal with will be as faithfully considered and given the same attention as that which she herself must deal with.

If one or more sisters are appointed as assistants in the choir, she will try to help them so that they gain more and more experience in the care of souls, and she will assign them the task of speaking first to one, then to other groups of sisters, before Communion. If the assistants then confidentially communicate to one another their thoughts and observations regarding what they have found during their conversations with the sisters and if the choir helper does not neglect to encourage her assistants kindly in their tasks and if she takes the opportunity to refer sisters in the choir to them, then she herself will receive more help, and the Savior will receive more proficient workers who can be employed. She should just as much desire to be of one heart and soul with the choir warden, to concern herself sympathetically with her tasks, to advise her, and, as situations present themselves, to kindly offer her a hand. This can be of great benefit to the choir. If she wanted to take an interest in external matters too often and unnecessarily, she would be a hindrance to herself in her own mission; therefore, she tries in such cases to maintain proper moderation as much as possible.

To be sure, it is reasonable for her to listen to complaints the sisters bring about the choir warden and to help them with this as much as possible. She will also wisely advise the sisters about matters that cannot be changed, and it is very important for the choir helper to try in an appropriate manner to support the choir warden among the sisters. They both deal with the house warden (*Haus-Diener/in*) every day, and if she conscientiously attends to her duties, she can be very useful to them both. For the most part, the house warden is responsible for errands in the choir. She therefore always has the opportunity to see and hear what takes place in the rooms, and a choir helper can obtain important information from her.

If the choir laborers (*Chorarbeiter/in*) suggest a sister for the position of house warden, it is especially important that they make certain she has the universal trust of the choir; the question will then be asked in the elders' conference (*Ältesten-Conferenz*) if the Savior approves her for the position. When proposals are made for the positions of room overseer (*Stuben-Vorgesetzte*) and company leader (*Gesellschafthalterin*), not only will the choir helper think about whether someone has the requisite gifts and skill; she will also take into special consideration how things stand with the sister's heart, because if something is lacking there, then gifts and skill will not be sufficient.

The choir helper will maintain a constant close connection with all these sisters, regarding their mission as well as their hearts. During conferences with the company leader and the room overseer, and in other conferences that she regularly attends, she will try to persuade each sister to state her opinion in a sincere and straightforward manner. If she can do this, she will gain a great deal. On the whole, the laborers' interaction with one another must be cordial and kind, but also honest, straightforward, and open.

§ 7. By virtue of her position, a choir helper is a member of the elders' conference in the congregation to which she belongs. Whether or not the care of her choir is immediately commended to her, as a member of the elders' conference, whose duty it is to give attention to everything that could enhance the well-being of the congregation and its members, she must for her part think about where harm can be prevented or where something useful can be accomplished. She should ask for the Savior's blessing so that out of shyness she does not keep a good idea to herself that could be useful for the congregation or her choir. However, she will do well always to explain herself with simple and discreet remarks, not to take it amiss if someone advises her concerning a matter about which she was mistaken, and to guard against falling into a particular point of view. One of her important contributions is helping to ensure that proceedings of the elders' conference are frank and candid. Of course, no mistrust can then exist between her and the other laborers. If such a feeling should arise toward one or another member of the conference, it will be discussed as soon as possible and settled in love. She will always do well to discuss in advance with the congregation helper any special concern she has to place before the elders' conference; however, in the conference she must not be reserved, just as she encourages her assistants to express their thoughts and not merely to allow things to be determined by what she says.

The choirs in a congregation maintain such a close connection that if something is lacking in one then, before one knows it, the others will suffer. Accordingly, if a choir helper becomes aware of something outside her choir that is incompatible with the order of the congregation, she will comment on it to the congregation helper, or she can mention it in the choir helpers' conference or in the elders' conference.

§ 8. The synod recommends and expects that a choir helper will maintain a confidential relationship with the congregation helper. This relationship serves as an abundant comfort and relief for her. If she has no particular concerns, it will nevertheless be good for the maintenance of the relationship if she frequently visits him and his wife and makes it her wish to stay on friendly terms with him. In this way he will not easily neglect something that needs his attention. It will also be her wish, insofar as is possible, to make the congregation helper acquainted with her sisters, and when from time to time opportunities to do so arise, she will make the most of them. She will also try to be in loving harmony with the other congregation laborers and sisters in the elders' conference. The choir will be influenced by the manner in which its laborers behave toward the other sisters, whether they are cold and unfriendly or whether they are cordial and loving to them. Now and then a choir helper will speak simply and sincerely about her heart and feelings to those brethren in the elders' conference who from time to time preach homilies to the choir or hold other gatherings. She will express her feeling concerning the present course of the choir and likewise about the special proofs of grace or particular defects that she perceives at the time and also about what matters have the greatest effect on the hearts of the sisters. Her speaking of such things has its particular blessing and usefulness, and it enables the brethren in question to be in a position of being able to talk more appropriately with the heart of the choir and to say a word to them at the right time.

§ 9. A choir helper must also consider herself a servant in the worldwide Moravian Church. According to the Savior's direction, the Unity Elders' Conference calls her to her office, and she also receives her instructions from them. Hence, it follows that she is obligated from time to time to report to the Unity Elders' Conference, and particularly to its helpers' administrative division (*Departement*), on how things stand, not only with her, but also with the choir entrusted to her care, as well as anything she finds especially noteworthy at the time. Recently, a short proposal was passed along to the elders' conference in the congregations explaining how the choir helper could best prepare her reports and what in particular she should mention in them; it will also be referred to here.[6] It goes without saying that, before she forwards such a choir report to the Unity Elders' Conference, she will communicate with the congregation helper about it and will take note of his thoughts or suggestions. Furthermore, it is expected of the single sisters' helpers as well as of all laborers in the Moravian Church that they make themselves very familiar with the Harmony of the Synods (*Synodalverlaß*) and that, through God's grace, they will be faithfully guided by the agreements and regulations stipulated therein.[7]

§ 10. What should a choir helper do if she desires to serve the choir commended to her care in a way that conforms to the purpose of her position? Above all, she must make it her concern, through the Savior's grace, to become as closely and thoroughly acquainted as possible with each of her sisters, according to the condition of their hearts. Experience teaches that, just as there are various illnesses of the body, so there are different conditions of the heart for persons belonging to a choir. Not only can it make a difference if the sisters have grown up and been educated in the Moravian Church or if they first came to the Moravian Church in their adult years, but from this there also arises a noticeable difference in whether or not souls faithfully make use of the grace given them by the Savior for their conversion and sanctification and whether or not they allow it to come to complete fruition in them. It is best if a choir helper always asks the dear Savior what

---

6. So far, no one has been able to determine what document Spangenberg is referring to in this sentence.

7. The Harmony of the Synods (*Synodalverlaß*) contains not only individual recommendations for the choirs but also the principia.

she should say and how she should advise each sister, according to her individual condition.

The souls of sisters are of such a nature that they can easily be moved. A touching discourse or beautiful expression in a verse can make so deep an impression on their spirit that they are carried away by it and can imagine they have now discovered the foundation on which their heart can take repose, but in the end it is only a fleeting stirring of the spirit. As little good as it would do for a choir helper to destroy this feeling they have experienced or to talk them out of it, it is nevertheless necessary to lead them to the recognition that the heart obtains a firm foundation only when one recognizes and feels genuine pain for one's miserable sins, hurries to the Savior, and finds grace and forgiveness for these sins in His blood and death. If she deals with persons who live without God in their hearts, who proceed in indifference and lack of self-knowledge, then it is better if she lets them feel her sympathy for their condition than if she reproaches them for it, because doing so could lead to a hardened and resentful heart. She will warn timid souls not to try to embrace things for themselves and act independently but will seek to lead them to sincere petitioning of the Savior and childlike obedience to admonitions of the Holy Spirit.

§ 11. If a choir helper observes that a sister finds her way to self-knowledge through the merciful work of the Holy Spirit, it will be necessary for her to take a special interest and to weep and pray with her. If the sister is on the point of becoming despondent, she will try unobtrusively to encourage her with heartfelt words and to help her recognize those things she has to learn about herself in the light of grace, taking into consideration that she should not be disturbed in such important hours of grace by all sorts of minor matters. At the same time, she will guard against being too active in this and will not offer untimely comfort but will instead prefer to witness the divine work of the Holy Spirit in quiet reverence. If it then becomes evident that the Savior has manifested Himself to this soul, revealing Himself to her in His reconciliation and bringing her delight in His love, then she will rightly join her in thanking the Savior. The choir helper will prefer to lead her to preserve her treasure quietly in her heart and to hold on to the Savior in lowliness and fidelity than to make something special of her or to give her preference, since this could inevitably lead to harm. Such a soul could also find herself in a state of conceit. If it occasionally takes a long while until a soul who feels self-conscious and reveals herself thus comes to the genuine consolation of grace, one must wait patiently. It is also important to examine whether there is a serious desire for peace and comfort of heart or whether there is something else that is not upright and sincere and that stands in the way of the Savior's proving Himself in grace to her.

§ 12. How should a choir helper conduct herself regarding proposals for reception into the congregation and to Holy Communion? Here there is an intention to treat differently those who were brought up in the Moravian Church and those persons coming from the outside world. In the case of the latter, we cannot think about their admission to the Moravian Church until there is reason to believe that they are certain of their gracious call to the Unity and that they are grateful to the Savior for allowing them to escape the pollutions of the world. For the former, however, we can consider it time when traces of the merciful work of the Holy Spirit are evident in their hearts and we can perceive in them a true longing for the Savior.

A person who through Jesus's grace has escaped from the world and come to the Moravian Church may not rightly be proposed for Holy Communion until such a person has left behind their corruption and its eruptions and until they enjoy blessed freedom from sin in Jesus's blood or weep for it with all their heart. On the other hand, we can occasionally propose young people for Holy Communion who have been born in the Moravian Church, even if we cannot yet find in them the complete, fundamental recognition of their misery and utter ruin but can sense their embarrassment that they do not love the Savior more tenderly, along with a desire to love Him more ardently and to rejoice more in His death. And it will be their good fortune to be admitted to Holy Communion at the time when they still have their childlike innocence; this will preserve in them a childlike trust in the Savior during their critical years[8] and will be a strong support in the face of increasing knowledge of themselves and of their innermost defects. If, however, corruption has already been awakened in them, it would be better to postpone the proposal for Holy Communion until we are able to perceive in their hearts a genuine self-understanding and a sincere longing for the Savior and for grace in His blood.

If a girl has never been to Holy Communion, the minister of the congregation will provide the necessary instruction for her, and when the time comes for her to partake of Holy Communion for the first time, several brethren from the elders' conference will speak with her beforehand. This will also happen in the case of sisters who come to the congregation as adults, when they are preparing to go to Holy Communion with the Moravian Church for the first time.

---

8. By "critical years," Spangenberg means adolescence.

§ 13. When sisters come to the Moravian Church from the world, the choir helper needs to be especially faithful in assisting them from the very outset. Although most of them will have already experienced something of the Savior in their hearts before they come, after they have spent some time in the Moravian Church, it usually happens that a new work of grace takes place in them and they begin to get to know themselves more thoroughly in their corruption. Since, as has been previously mentioned, we will wait before proposing them, this generally takes place during the time before they are admitted to Holy Communion. Here, however, a necessary distinction needs to be made. We can find persons among them who have had a solitary and virtuous upbringing and who are often more ignorant of all sorts of human circumstances than our youth in the congregation. It takes time before they thoroughly get to know the corruption that exists within them. It is easiest to become well acquainted with them by listening to them tell their life story and then in a truly cordial manner to ask more directly about their circumstances, thereby giving them the opportunity to mention things that they otherwise would be too timid to disclose.[9] One should beware of forcing anything, however, and if the desired goal is not attained in one conversation, one should wait for another opportunity, while seeking to preserve the trust of their hearts.

§ 14. It is to be noted here that when a sister has told her complete life story and spoken freely about the state of her heart, the choir helper will admit her into the covenant of the single sisters' choir. This will be for her according to the holy scriptures: as we confess our sins, so He is faithful and righteous in forgiving our sins and cleansing us from all vice. In the name of Jesus Christ, she will receive assurance that the old shall be laid aside, forgiven, and forgotten. She will promise that her desire from this time forward is to devote herself with all her heart to the Savior, to be guided in all circumstances by His word, to be led and directed by His Holy Spirit, and to preserve herself unblemished in body and spirit before Him. In this understanding, her choir helper will then wash her feet and commend her in prayer to Jesus's mercy and keeping thereafter. When we can believe that a sister has attained true grace and a new life from Jesus's death, it will be necessary to make certain that she continues as a living branch on the grapevine, remaining close to Jesus Christ. To be sure, she will become more and more aware of her human corruption and, like the truly pardoned, will grow poorer and more needy within herself, but she will also think of the Savior's words: "He who is for-

---

9. A questionnaire that acted as a guide to the choir helpers was used for this interview.

given much (and she is daily forgiven) loves much"[10] and, again, "If you love me, keep my commandments. As you keep my commandments, so you continue in my love."[11] The choir helper can and will be doubly exacting with such sisters, when she indicates to them things in their conduct that are unseemly for a member of the body of Jesus and that can offend the congregation and her choir. Such a sister should be diligently reminded of what is told about our sanctification to those who love our Lord Jesus Christ, about the purification of the soul in obedience to the truth, about divine life and conduct, and that whoever clings to the Savior is of one spirit with Him.

§ 15. This brings us to the important point especially concerning those circumstances specific to the female sex and to which a choir helper should particularly direct her instruction in these matters. It is certain that nowhere else but in Jesus's sacrifice can we find the complete, true sanctification of body and soul and that no sister can acquire a pure heart and mind until she has come as a sinner to the Savior, has experienced Him in faith as her reconciler, and has been cleansed of her sins by the blood of the Lamb. It is essential that every person, from the older children on, receive, through all grace, faithful teaching in choir matters and about the changes in human nature, so that each one for her part may learn to carry her spirit in His hands and may know how to maintain her vessel (her body and all its limbs) in sanctification and honor.

§ 16. Experience teaches us that a noticeable difference can be found already in children regarding their awareness of their human condition. When children are brought up at home by their parents, of primary importance is the care parents take, if they have children of both sexes, to treat them in such a way and to keep them apart so that they do not see and hear more than is good for their age. If parents do not do this, and if they talk carelessly in front of their children about everything that happens, then the result usually is that children begin to fall into inquisitive thoughts about many things concerning human nature, for example, how children come into the world, why one looks different from another, and so forth. It can often do great harm if a choir helper or other sisters who take an interest in the children make indiscreet inquiries to find out what or how much they know about these things. It is therefore necessary to exercise great care in this matter, and one must never ask children the sort of questions that give rise to

---

10. Luke 7:47 (King James Version).
11. John 14:15 (KJV).

thoughts they haven't had before, thoughts which will arouse their curiosity. But if it should turn out that children are no longer uninformed or begin naively asking about these things, it is best to answer them simply and according to the Bible. If, for example, one should ask where children come from, we should answer them with David's words: "You, Lord, drew me from my mother's womb."[12] In this way one leads them back to our dear Savior, who was born of His mother Mary, and so forth.

If a young girl sees her little brother's different body parts and asks why her body doesn't look the same as his, one should explain that the Creator has made human beings in this way from the beginning and that He has His own judicious reasons for doing so. We should not forget to recommend to children that they not talk with other children about these matters and that they should not consider this as foolishness, because the Savior will take offense if we do not show proper respect for things that He as Creator has put in order.

§ 17. If the children in our schools ask such questions, unless they are extraordinarily intelligent and thoughtful children, it is better to advise them that they are presently not able to understand this and would comprehend it more fully when they are older. When children come into our schools from the world, it is wise to try to find out how far they are beyond the usual innocence of children, and accordingly one should give attention to their conversation and association with other children. In general we must take care that children who live and sleep together in the children's schools do not do harm to one another. For this reason, no two should be left alone in the privy or allowed to go anywhere alone into a quiet corner. The sisters who are with them must constantly keep a watchful eye on them when they sit close together at the table or when they go for a walk and want to go off by themselves under the pretext of playing. Should a child lie in her bed at night in a disorderly manner, an opportunity will be found to admonish her about it.

A choir helper will do well from time to time to talk about these matters with the children's teachers (Kinder-Schwestern), and particularly with the single persons' attendants (ledige Wärterinnen). She should urge them not to deal with the children in any improper manner but rather to serve them reverently, because otherwise on such occasions something false (unecht) can stir in a sister, and such a way of dealing can make an unfortunate impression on the children and in time lead to bad habits.

---

12. Ps. 22:9 (KJV).

§ 18. When girls have reached their twelfth year, they are admitted into the greater girls' choir, and this usually takes place on March 25, at the girls' choir festival. At the Speaking held with such girls before their admission, it will be sincerely recommended to them that they now reflect on their childhood years once more before the Savior. They should retain nothing of what has taken place during those years or anything for which they needed the Savior's forgiveness, and they are to surrender themselves anew to Him as His own. If at this time the children ask about this or that, including things they have sometimes thought about, they should be told as much as they are able to understand at the time. If, however, it becomes clear that they continue in their childlike innocence, one should allow them to remain so and seek only to direct their hearts to the new blessing that they can expect as they change choirs. In the address given to the girls at their admission to the girls' choir, the speaker will remind them of the difference that exists between children and older girls. The girls will be admonished to continue in the grace they received in their childhood years and to hold fast even more faithfully now to the Savior. They are continuing to grow into the age we call, not without reason, the critical years, during which time, as the years pass, human corruption in soul and body becomes more and more evident, and an older girl will increasingly need to be healed through Jesus's wounds. It will therefore be recommended to them that they allow the Savior to grant them a spirit of an open heart, which they will maintain in all circumstances.

§ 19. Now begins the work of a choir helper with such newly received girls. She will wish to introduce them more intimately into her group of girls, and this happens in the following manner. About half a year after their admission to the girls' choir—sooner or later, depending on what seems appropriate— the choir helper will gather the newly admitted girls together and will try to make clear to them the importance of arrangements in the girls' choir and the purpose of the choir. This is

(1)  that such girls will receive more detailed instruction regarding those things that belong to the ordinary course of human nature at their age. They will also be instructed about the ways in which this leads to corruption in body and soul and how defilement of flesh and spirit can arise, as well as how a girl who desires communion with the Savior must guard against these things and must cleanse herself through the power of Jesus's blood.

(2)  The girls will be provided the opportunity, with the Savior and with one another, to be united in the wish to follow their choir path as faithful,

sincere girls completely devoted to the Savior and who will continue to learn how blessedly the power of Jesus's incarnation, merit, and death can be made manifest to girls of upright mind, for their sanctification and preservation.

§ 20. When speaking of things that manifest themselves in adolescent girls during these years in regard to their physical circumstances, following nature's course, and that they themselves (although perhaps one more than another) pay attention to, we include partly the growth of hair around the organs that distinguish them from men, partly the change in their breasts, and finally the onset of their monthly cleansing. It is not thought, however, that the choir helper should explain these points specifically during her discussion with the girls. Instead, she should first direct her talk toward entrusting them to sincerely and boldly discover and rid themselves of any bad matters, thoughts, or actions that may be leftover from their childhood years, things over which the Holy Spirit is now making their hearts troubled. This is provided that they have spoken freely and privately with the Savior about such things. These may be things they saw or heard from others or things that happened to them in secret. She will want to allow them time to do this and then talk with them about it individually. For a second time, she will tell them that in these years, many things can occur which hitherto would have seemed unusual, including thoughts, feelings, and changes in the hidden parts of their bodies. They will need a faithful and sincere heart for this, so that they can talk with their laboress in a timely manner; otherwise, they should tell no one, so that she can advise them, according to the heart of Jesus, to accept themselves properly and so that she can pray for them, that everything they encounter might be sprinkled with the blood of Christ, but that whatever is sinful and proceeds from corruption might be given in Jesus's death.

§ 21. After this they will be spoken to individually, during which time still many a confession from their childhood years will usually appear. Concerning these things, we patiently hear them out, as well as their thoughts and experiences in this and that matter, encourage them to ask if there is something they wish to understand more clearly, and recommend that they keep nothing back that could give them a heavy heart and cloud their spirit. When this Speaking is over, the choir helper brings them together as a group, falls on her knees with them, calls sincerely on the Savior for His absolution for these girls and for everything that is not to His liking that has happened to them, and recommends them to Him and to His spirit for their further direction and grounding in their blessed choir journey.

When the girls then have their covenant's (*Bund*) quarter-hour services, they come and are blessed with the laying on of hands in the presence of their peers, at which opportunity the entire choir renews its bond before the dear Savior and then prostrates itself at His feet.

§ 22. If in the course of time a girl comes and confides in her choir helper that she has noticed the previously mentioned growth of hair or expresses her dislike of it, the choir helper will give her more detailed information, namely, that the wise Creator has so ordered it and that she therefore has no reason to be alarmed or have doubts about it; that He has shown in this way how necessary it is, always to keep this part of her body covered; accordingly, after the Fall of our first parents, He made garments from skins and clothed them. And since He Himself became a man, thus by His holy birth He has blessed this important member in the same way He has blessed all members of our bodies. It should therefore be a girl's concern to treat this part of her body with respect, not to undertake anything frivolous with it, anything that could not come to light or appear without hesitation in the Savior's presence. Should a girl report the other previously mentioned condition—although only a few will be attentive to it—then a choir helper will take the opportunity to remind her that our dear Savior has also especially honored this part of the body, because as a child He sucked at His mother's breast; and she will recommend that a girl conduct herself in a chaste and discreet manner regarding this part of her body.

§ 23. When girls reach the age at which their natural condition tends to change, it will be necessary for the choir helper to give them more detailed information about the change that takes place when their monthly cleansing begins. When this occurs for the first time, and they report it accordingly, the choir helper will take the opportunity to talk with them sincerely and to explain to them that, due to this circumstance and their physical condition, they are now to be counted among the virgins. Because of this important change, therefore, they should place themselves very especially in the care of the Savior, the true physician for body and soul, and should implore Him to sprinkle them with His blood and to bestow on them and preserve in them a pure heart, directed to Him alone. As the most reliable counsel, she will commend them to look up to Jesus daily in His image as reconciler, that their eyes, ears, and other senses can best be protected from everything that is defiled. She will not neglect to tell them at the same time what they need to observe regarding their health, as much as their external circumstances allow, for example, to protect themselves now from extreme cold and heat, as well as from emotional states such as vexation, anger, and so forth, because these can have a doubly harmful influence on their health. It is a good idea for the choir helper to inquire of such a girl from time to time whether she is having any problems with her cleansing and to advise her concerning medical assistance as she thinks fit. If girls accept this particular condition of their nature every time, as coming from the Creator's hand, and commend themselves to Him, then they will receive grace and blessing. At the conclusion of such a Speaking, a girl will be blessed by her choir helper with a laying on of hands and a verse or prayer will be affectionately commended to the Savior in this new stage of her life. It goes without saying that such treatment is not applicable for girls of a secretive nature; it should be made clear to them what kind of blessing they are responsible for bringing upon themselves.

§ 24. Experience teaches that, from the time a girl undergoes this change in her nature, corruption of soul and body awakens in a particular way. Vanity appears, along with an inclination to please others; there also appears the desire to know much, as well as love for the opposite sex and inquisitive thoughts about the married state. To these may be added certain physical impulses, partly brought on by nature but also partly by idle thoughts and fantasies. If, in addition, a lack of innocence appears, which causes some to hold back for a long while before speaking candidly about their condition, there arises in many a lack of trust in the Savior and a timid nature that can cause much distress. In such circumstances it is especially necessary for a choir helper to take pains to gain the girls' confidence and unceasingly to direct them with all their misery to the Lamb of God, who atoned for all our sins on the cross. It would not be advisable to want to explain to them all they are thinking and asking about, particularly when they inquire about this and that regarding marriage. On the contrary, it is better to try to point out to them that this important subject is suitable only for married sisters. She will try to instruct them much more thoroughly in those things that can lead to a clearer insight into their own human corruption, so that they learn to carry their souls in their hands and to use their bodies in a manner pleasing to God.

§ 25. When the time has come for the older girls to be received into the single sisters' choir, which usually takes place at the choir festivals, the choir helper, in talking with them beforehand, will make it her task to go over their girlhood experience with them privately and to entrust to them what pertains to their future course. She will particularly call on each one to ask the Savior in earnest to give her more fully the true treasure of a virgin, to carry herself as though she is engaged to Him, and to renounce joyfully all temporal and earthly things. The more sincere and intimate such a young single sister's association with the Savior has been during her girlhood, the more fully and confidentially she has spoken with her laborer about everything that has happened to her, and the more faithfully she has dealt with the grace she has received from time to time, the sooner she will proceed on her journey in the single sisters' choir in a steady manner and with a serious and chaste demeanor.

§ 26. However, we should observe from our previous experience that for many who are just entering their years as young sisters, there develops a new school of self-knowledge as well as a deeper grounding in grace. For some, unfolding corruption is the cause, in that they approach matters with more reflection and thereby are able to see the subtle depravity of their souls more clearly than before, and they become alarmed, distressed, and embarrassed over it. If a sister faces this in a straightforward manner, she can be helped out of much hesitation and to some extent also out of dangerous ignorance, through one or more Speakings. By means of practical instruction, we can assist her in her entire future journey if she is faithful and, as a poor sinner, seeks pardon for her sins from the Savior.

For others, it begins more with an anxious concern over whether their conversion and redemption is of the right sort and whether they are truly certain of their course. All previous grace seems clouded to them, and they become confused about what they have experienced. For many a one, this goes so far that she feels lost and becomes quite disconsolate about herself. She may carry this matter around with her for a while, weeping in secret, until she trusts herself to speak to her choir helper about it, then dares finally to pour out her heart, perhaps with few words but a flood of tears.

It is then necessary for a choir helper to understand well the Savior's merciful work with such a soul and to witness quietly how He leads this child, possibly blameless from her earliest years, to this level of self-knowledge, so that, with all her heart, she recognizes herself as a sinner deserving of death, but at the same time finds the eternal comfort of mercy and a new assurance of forgiveness for her sins, by Jesus, freely given.

As blessed as this is, and as palpable as the pardon for such sisters generally seems to be, experience shows that such a striking work of mercy does not happen uniformly, but rather the Savior goes this way with one soul and a different way with another. Therefore, in the case of a sister in whom she notices this deficiency, a choir helper would cause harm rather than good, if she herself wanted to lead her into this work of the heart or motivate her to do it. With regard to sisters for whom such an obvious confirmation of their first experience of grace has not occurred in the way previously described, the choir helper would err even more if she did not regard them as well-founded and trustworthy but wanted to think less of them for this reason. She would do better to follow the Savior's direction, which He plainly provides to each soul.

§ 27. However, if a choir helper notices that a young single sister becomes more attentive than before to the depravity of her soul and discloses this in confidence to her, she will do well to take the opportunity to come to her assistance with more detailed information about this. She will make it clear to her that the stirrings perceived in body and soul are not the same. Some can arise for physical reasons, such as an increased flow of monthly bleeding or other similar conditions, and a sister must examine what is good and beneficial for her body and, on the other hand, what is not good and harmful. If there are bodily sensations linked to impure imaginings and fantasies in the soul, or that arise from a forbidden inclination, then these are things that disgrace a virgin of Jesus and are displeasing to the Savior, and a sister who is aware of such things has reason to be alarmed.[13] She should immediately look to Jesus on the cross and seek to be cleansed from this by His blood.

§ 28. A choir helper also has the opportunity to speak with her sisters about a physical condition called the "white Flow" (weißer Fluß).[14] It should be noted that if persons who are otherwise healthy have this, it should be regarded as one of the body's natural changes, the purpose of which is to get rid of excess fluids. But if it is too heavy, or as can occasionally happen, if it appears instead of the monthly cleansing, then a choir helper will not fail to advise a sister that she needs something to maintain her health and that she should avail herself of a wise doctor's advice. It is the opinion of some doctors that if impure desires attain a (certain) level of intensity, they can have an effect on female persons that causes the appearance of this discharge. It can therefore be useful if a choir helper pays attention to whether or not, in one case or another, sinful corruption could play a part. However, presumably this is merely an infrequent occurrence that presupposes previous other physical disorders.

---

13. For contemporary notions of menstruation in the eighteenth century, see Shail and Howie, *Menstruation*. For a discourse on and about masturbation, see Richter, "Wet-Nursing"; and Laqueur, *Solitary Sex*.

14. This white discharge from the vagina was considered to be a harmless part of women's monthly cycle. However, excessive discharge was linked with anemia and also masturbation. See, for example, Kress, *Medicinische-diätetische Gesundheitslehre*, 223–24.

§ 29. Generally, once she is better acquainted with herself, a young single sister will reveal in confidence those thoughts to her choir helper that occasionally occur to her about the married state, or she will consult with her about one thing or another that occurs to her in this regard. It is good for the choir helper to take this opportunity to provide her with a biblical concept of marriage, namely, that it has been instituted and blessed by God and has been ordained in a new covenant as an image of Christ and His congregation; that everything married persons do as children of God, in word or deed, must be in the name of Jesus Christ and in His proximity; that in marriage just as in the single state, people must not serve the desires of the flesh but rather must keep their souls pure through the Holy Spirit and must present their bodies to our Lord Christ as a living, holy sacrifice, pleasing to God. She also creates for her the idea that the conjugal union, blessed by the Creator so that married persons can produce children, is a *respectable* act, which takes place between married persons, accompanied by prayer and proximity to Jesus,[15] and that the impure notions brought into the world by Satan are suppressed by children of God, and the soul must be cleansed of them. When these ideas take root in a sister's soul, then she will abhor every unnecessary thing and, even more, all sinful and inquisitive thinking about this, God's holy arrangement, and she will never allow herself to think about it other than with respect.

§ 30. A choir helper may need to talk about this matter with sisters who have come from the world to the Moravian Church. Particularly in the case of those who have either found themselves deep in temptation or who have otherwise seen and heard much wickedness, she will find that the concepts they have formed about marriage from what they have seen and heard in the world are incorrect. She will desire not only to point this out to them but also to explain clearly to them the way in which children of God think about it and to indicate how the married state is regarded by the Moravian Church.

§ 31. From the beginning a choir helper must direct her attention to this important point: as much as possible, she is to guard wisely against all sorts of seductions in the choir, and when the first signs appear, she will do well to face them earnestly. As pleasing and blessed as it is when a special, warm, and close friendship exists among a group of sisters, a friendship that is edifying as well as grounded in the Savior, it is also important to be on guard lest

---

15. This idea is an interesting departure from Zinzendorf's idea of the marriage union, as outlined in his writings. See Vogt, "Seventeen Points of Matrimony."

beneath this show of friendliness a false relationship should develop. One can find examples of times when a devoted love exists among persons of the same sex, abuses of the flesh and spirit can occur even if it doesn't come to coarse seductions. Conscientious and vigilant room leaders (*Stuben-Vorgesetzten*), observing the sisters' association with one another, will soon become aware of the type and character of their conversations. They should not, however, immediately believe all charges of this kind; rather, they will first seek out those concerned and warn them with love, then carefully inquire into the extent of their relationship. It is especially important to keep watch over younger sisters, so that in their daily association with one another, particularly when dressing and undressing, they observe proper decorum toward one another and do not accustom themselves to a free, playful demeanor.

For sisters living outside the choir house, double vigilance is necessary, so that if things are not going well with them, it may be discovered in a timely manner. The best advice is that one should diligently look out for them and ask them about their progress, since in this way one can observe if there is something wrong in their disposition.

Moreover, a choir helper will make herself very familiar with what the results of the Harmony of the Synods (*Synodalverlaß*) direct concerning the matter of seductions and will consequently communicate with the minister (*Gemeinhelfer*), as circumstances demand.

§ 32. Since a sister must acquaint herself with every type of human corruption if she desires to be steadfast and grounded in proceeding along her path, so this is true with the natural inclination toward the opposite sex, which to be sure becomes particularly active in these very years. A sister, who through mercy has recently gained a pure heart, must constantly be on guard so that no improper inclination, however it may manifest itself, gains a footing with her. Therefore, the single sisters' choir must constantly and earnestly observe the point that all unnecessary association with brethren is to be avoided, not only because of individual human weakness but also because of others' suspicions. When the inclination toward the opposite sex makes itself known in a young sister and intensifies more or less, depending on the nature of her temperament, she will be candid with her laboress about it. The best advice is to pray sincerely to the Savior for such a patient and to offer her sympathetic compassion but not to appear very anxious and alarmed about her condition. Meanwhile, a choir helper will pay attention that this inclination does not turn into true passion. If she fears this will happen, or if the sister has fixated on a certain object in her mind, then the choir helper will do well to communicate with the minister at the right moment so that, in the proper way, a change of location may be considered.

§ 33. What should a choir laboress do if a sister reveals to her that she feels an inclination to marry? This should be handled differently. Generally speaking, such a sister should be dealt with in these circumstances in a motherly and sympathetic manner and should not be discouraged by a display of any dissatisfaction or have her honesty discouraged. If a choir helper is dealing with a sister who above all has an upright heart toward the Savior, then she will try to lead her in love to the point of relinquishing her path and her future destiny to the Savior, in a childlike way. She will also encourage her not to become wrapped up in such reflection, because it could bring with it harmful consequences, or she could at the least unnecessarily ruin her time with it.

If one notices, however, that the inclination to marry is based on obvious and sensual designs, then one will seek to explain to such a person how little hope there would be for her to achieve her purpose with the holy plan for marriage in the congregation. She will be advised to let her heart be cleansed from all vice by the blood of Jesus. If it should happen that young sisters think about marriage before they properly know themselves, then one must necessarily make it clear to them that they are not yet fit for this state, that they would do better to be concerned principally with being joyful in body and soul about the Savior and His merit in their choir.

§ 34. When requests for proposals to marry are made, whether it be for a brother who is going to serve the Savior among the heathen or who otherwise needs a helpmate in his position or for a brother who will marry as a resident in a congregation, this will certainly be one of the most important responsibilities of a choir helper, about which she seeks advice from the Savior to name suitable persons with the greatest possible faithfulness and, from her knowledge of them, to portray them in all truth. She is not concerned with what kinds of persons are named in the conferences on this topic, but she also will not lay aside any proposal advanced by others. And, as she always has before her the best interests of the Savior's affairs, she will never hold back a sister, merely because of her usefulness to the choir house, who could enter into the marriage as a help and blessing for the brother whose marriage is part of the Savior's plan; nor would she propose a sister for marriage because she would gladly be free of this person. But if it should happen that she has reason to fear the choir house is being divested of too many strong and useful sisters, then she is bound to announce her apprehension about this so that it can be given the necessary consideration.

§ 35. A basic rule regarding proposing persons for marriage is this: if a person cannot yet be considered a child of God, she should not be considered for marriage. Besides, we should look at the circumstances of a brother for whom a helpmate is being sought, at the nature of his calling, or his *Plan*, likewise at the nature of his disposition, temperament, age, etc., all of which will be reported to a choir helper.

In the case of nominations to posts among the heathen, we will look to see whether a sister has a willing and faithful heart, devoted completely to the Savior's service; whether she has a peaceable disposition, a cheerful nature, and the gifts otherwise necessary for such a calling. There is great variation among physical constitutions of the sisters; one is more suited to a cold land, another to one that is warm, depending on which can better withstand the cold or heat. This will receive due consideration. A choir helper must be particularly well informed about a sister's physical circumstances and whether she has any bodily defects that make her unfit for marriage. If she lacks such knowledge, a proposal should be delayed for as long as it takes for her to collect more detailed and reliable information.

§ 36. The proposal of marriage to a sister is always made through the choir helper, but there are cases where the congregation helper recommends, or the choir helper requests, to speak with a sister about the proposal made to her, in the presence of his wife or the choir helper.

If it should occur that the promise of marriage comes from both sides, a choir helper should not think that she is no longer involved with the matter, because the sister will leave her choir; rather, the sister remains an object of her prayer and attention particularly during the time of her engagement. She will provide her with the opportunity to speak freely, honestly, and confidentially about everything that may be left over (from her past). She will make a special effort with such a sister, as she changes choirs, to help her renew the covenant to live, not for herself, but for the Savior. Even if she has already talked with her about it, she will once more urge upon her that which previously was brought up concerning marriage. But the special circumstances of marriage, such as the method of conjugal union and similar matters, she leaves entirely to the helpers of the married persons' choir, who will give her the necessary introduction at the right moment.

Following an intimate conversation with her concerning her life to this point, she performs for her the service of foot washing (*Pedilavium*), so that at the end of her journey in the choir, she can provide her with blessed assurance of the Savior's forgiveness. Finally, she will request that the sister be preserved in love for her former choir and that she be accompanied by its blessings. Accordingly, on the day before the wedding, she will be commended to the choir in remembrance and prayer.

§ 37. As each elders' conference must think about the calling (*Destination*) of its brethren and sisters and concern itself with helping to carry out the Savior's mission of peace (*Friedens-Gedanken*), it is also the special duty of a choir helper in her thoughts to bring each of her sisters intentionally before the Savior and faithfully to note what is thereby disclosed to her. She must neglect no opportunity to communicate her ideas and suggestions in the elders' and choir helpers' conference. It is, however, not advisable to talk with the sisters themselves very much about this and to tell them her thoughts about their calling, particularly because one sees also that the Savior sometimes orders a sister's path quite differently from the way one expected.

A choir helper will direct her particular attention to such sisters who distinguish themselves especially in service to the Savior in their choir, and she will seek more and more to awaken their gifts. In doing so, she must not only reflect on those of sensitive and tender disposition who have a self-loving nature and enjoy being cared for but rather more on those who have a mature character, who do not shrink from any work or effort, and who are gladly consumed by love for others.

§ 38. Before every Communion, the choir helper will hold the Speaking with all sisters who are communicants, either alone or with the help of her assistants, or sometimes also in classes. It is assumed at such times that each sister has already examined herself to allow her heart to be cleansed of things that make her unworthy to partake of Holy Communion. The Speaking serves to give each sister the opportunity to speak freely with her choir laborer about her heart and her conduct along her whole life's path. It is not advisable to reserve all sorts of things for the Speaking before Communion to converse about them then thoroughly and in detail, since usually there is not sufficient time for doing so. But if there are things that are incompatible with Christ's intention and love, then they must be settled and laid aside before a sister can go to Communion. And if circumstances make that impossible, then the sister who is at fault or who is not thought ready—or both—will accordingly stay behind from Communion at that time.

§ 39. The classes and companies are a useful way to encourage the association of hearts in a choir and to guide this association onto the right path. Those sisters who fit together well in certain ways are grouped together in the classes, and it is then possible to direct one's conversations with them accordingly. Such opportunities will be used to bring sisters to whatever matters they need to examine in themselves, particularly if the classes are held before

Communion, and that often brings a special blessing. It can sometimes happen, however, that substantial conversations of the heart take place there, and then one sister profits from the grace of another.

In the companies (*Gesellschaften/Sozietäten*) we should take even more care that sisters are compatible, according to their heart, and then the conversation will be directed more closely to their circumstances. A choir helper will be on guard so that the companies in the choir do not get onto a sleepy and careless path. It is necessary for her to hold conferences diligently with those in charge of these companies, to encourage them, and sometimes to pass on to them material with which they can inform their meetings. The chief object is that sisters become more intimately acquainted with one another and that they often experience the most blessed fulfillment of the Savior's promise that, where two or three or more are gathered together in His name, He will be there with them. It is also an opportunity to learn how the sisters think and to note their growth in grace. A choir helper will do well if she occasionally consults with the sisters in charge of the companies about one or another of the sisters.

§ 40. On the correct perception of those sisters who serve in families,[16] a choir laboress certainly needs to have special grace to act wisely in this matter, especially in the case of smaller or greater differences, which can easily arise between married and single sisters in the frequent business they have with each other, either in housekeeping matters or in the matter of the children. The choir helper will not want to interfere too much or too little.

As proper and necessary as it is for her to listen sympathetically to the comments of the married sisters, treating them with all discretion and looking at the matter impartially, and to earnestly exhort her sisters when they are in the wrong, granting them nothing, it is also important for her to remember that she should always treat her sisters as a mother would, and that says a great deal.

A confidential communication to the married persons' choir helper in all such situations that occur between families and the sisters in service to them can settle much and make the matter easier for both sides. She will deal earnestly with the matter of gossiping about their employers or families by the sisters who serve them. She will particularly impress on them that they cannot stand before the Savior if they allow themselves in one way or another to be lured into unfaithfulness in their service. She will sometimes find it necessary to warn sisters in service that, if things do not go as they wish, or if

---

16. Single sisters were often employed as servants in the homes of Moravians.

something occurs that annoys them, they must not threaten (to return to) the choir house or make use of unseemly expressions.

If, through the Savior's grace, she can persuade the sisters to regard all service as service done for the Lord, and to allow no one to confuse them, then all will proceed more easily and blessedly. A choir helper will make herself thoroughly familiar with the recommendations concerning this matter and in general matters concerning sisters serving in families in the Harmony of the Synods (*Synodalverlaß*) and will seek to comply as faithfully as possible.

§ 41. The fact that certain fixed regulations must exist in the choir house is a matter of course. Accordingly, the Unity Elders' Conference has examined and approved the house regulations given to the single sisters by the board of the congregation (*Gemeindirection*).[17] One of the choir helper's main duties, together with the choir warden (*Chordienerin*), is to hold earnestly and stead-fastly to these rules, and with all motherly love and indulgence toward her sisters; and she should be indulgent therein least of all with favoritism toward any person. She can also refer to the fact that the elders' conference is like-minded in this matter, so that sisters do not get the idea that only their labor-esses are strict in observing choir regulations. She will also seek, wisely and where necessary, to support energetically the room leaders in maintaining order throughout the course of the day, for example, in seeing that the sisters arise and go to bed at the proper time, keep themselves clean and neat, do their work well and on time, sit down to a meal properly, pay proper attention to their health, and observe as much as possible the proper exercise of their bodies. The house rules should be read to the choir at least once a year. At this time, the sisters' attention can be particularly drawn to any rule that has been neglected, and it can be recommended that they observe it faithfully.

§ 42. A point of great importance is that the night watches in a choir house be attended to precisely and in a reverent manner. The sisters who perform this duty should therefore be reminded from time to time of their responsi-bility, and it is pleasing if, during a love feast, they are occasionally encour-aged to new faithfulness and concern in this service. It is important that the laboresses, as long as their health allows, not exclude themselves from watches but do what they can.

§ 43. Now we will say something about the care of the sick, because this also requires a choir helper's attention and faithfulness. Not only will she

---

17. "Ordnungen des Schwesternhauses," UA, 7–16.

take notice of everything going on in the sickroom, but she also will stay in daily contact with the nurse, who will inform her each time sisters come to the sickroom. Illnesses can be of various types. Sometimes it is not a matter of many medicines, but rather a good diet and faithful care and nursing do the most good. It often happens that, in her illness, a sister will experience the blessed merciful work of the Holy Spirit. The choir helper then must take a special heartfelt interest in the sister. Circumstances can also occur that one could call a sickness caused by sinful behavior (*Zuchtkrankheit*). The best advice here is, confess your sins, one to another, and pray for one another that you will all get well. Sometimes there are illnesses that the choir helper finds reason to discuss with the doctor; it is advisable that this takes place in a timely manner. If there are serious cases or physical injuries requiring closer review or even an operation and daily dressings, then, according to choir regulation, the helper will be present for the treatment, unless there is a reliable nurse in the choir, approved by the elders. In this case, her presence will be sufficient.

A quiet, reverent, and yet cheerful and unconstrained demeanor should be faithfully maintained in the sickroom. Never should the worst rooms in the choir house be chosen for sickrooms, particularly in large choirs, where they usually are always occupied.

If, during protracted illnesses, sisters fall into debt, they are to be given motherly comfort in this matter. In such a case, the sister will be assisted by the relief fund or, if this is not sufficient, by the house welfare fund (*Diaconie*).

If a sister's home going[18] appears imminent, she will receive a blessing from the choir helper, but one would not want to wait with this until the sick one is so weak that she is not aware of it.

If there are sisters in the choir who are sickly but not yet living in the sickroom, we not only must take their diet into consideration but must also see to it that they are given a separate room for sleeping, if possible, where it is not so cold as in the dormitory. A choir helper will direct her attention constantly to the poor sisters in the choir and will ask from time to time after their requirements, particularly since it is difficult for many to mention their needs themselves.

§ 44. There are many things that give a choir helper and her assistants enough to think about daily and weep over, and to pray about to the Savior, asking for His assistance in their inadequacy and for the guidance of His good spirit. They are concerned that:

---

18. "Home going" refers to death.

daily life in the choir be pleasing, blessed, and cheerful, yet sedate and
grounded;

love and sincerity prevail in all the rooms;

everything appears as simple and straightforward as it is, removed from
all pretense and hypocrisy;

nothing yield to idiosyncrasies such as willfulness, egotism, selfishness,
nor to unnecessary comforts from outside;

further, no spirit of ridicule or condemnation, no slander or such things
be tolerated, nor unfortunate reasoning that does not lead to
improvement.

This gives ample material for conversation in the conferences with the
room leaders and assistants, as well as with the visitors and those in charge of
social gatherings. They will seek to encourage one another and will, with
sincere friendship, always try to be ready to lend a hand. They will be obliged
to admonish one another if the leaders (*Vorgesetzen*) have made a mistake in
one matter or another. To the previously mentioned things, which need to be
guarded against in the sisters' rooms, this should be added: that no free and
careless discussions of marrying take place and that this subject never be
mentioned at all, except with the proper respect.

Further, we can never be too careful in guarding against the inclination,
which all too easily creeps in, to read bad books.[19] To prevent this, a choir
helper will make every effort to find and provide something pleasant and useful to read, to support the sisters in their work, especially in the long winter
evenings.

A choir helper will also keep a close eye out so that no foolishness related
to clothing gains ground among the sisters, and she will deal with any traces
of this in a timely manner.

§ 45. Occasionally there are persons in a choir who know neither the Savior
nor themselves properly and therefore do not have what they could have, in the
congregation or in their choir, but who nevertheless do not wish to leave the
congregation. We bear them patiently and wait, as long as we are certain that
they are not harmful to others, but it is not advisable to permit them to go to
Communion, since life in God is lacking in their hearts. Nevertheless, one
gladly uses every opportunity to set about leading them along life's way. There

---

19. Friedrich Schleiermacher complained bitterly about the censorship of reading materials at
almost exactly the same time. "Bad books" included some of the popular works associated with the
Enlightenment. See also Griffin, *Less Time for Meddling*.

can be those, however, who make life extremely difficult for their poor room-mates (*Stuben-Schwestern*) because of their unsociable character and who are known by the entire choir because of their rudeness. Perhaps we have already tried all sorts of things with them, including trying to free ourselves from them, but they are still with us. At the least, we require of them that when bickering occurs, they apologize to their sisters and make peace with them. Unless they do this, they are not allowed to go to Communion.

We notice with some that they repeatedly bring up former bad things and speak about them in a manner of confession, but not with the pain we would observe in a poor sinner. On the contrary, it seems as if they mentioned these impure things because they continue to be secretly inclined toward them. Finally, we can send such persons away with their oft-repeated confessions and commend to them the blessedness of a pure heart. If there are persons in the choir who, often under a friendly pretext and with a cleverness used by children all over the world, try to teach others their corrupted mental spirit and a free-spirited way of thinking, and whose behavior is otherwise unseemly, a choir helper must have just as sharp an eye on them as she has on those who do harm to others in a coarser manner, because the more subtle this poison is, the deeper the harm that it causes will go.

§ 46. Most important, the hearts of the choir live daily in the pastures of the gospel. Accordingly, a choir helper will see to it that each and every sister diligently makes use of the opportunities in the congregation and choir meet-ings (*Chorversammlungen*). She will summon them faithfully if, out of human weakness and laziness, they become neglectful of them, but her own good example and that of her assistants will surely help the choir more than all reminders and warnings. It is also good if a choir helper quietly investigates whether sisters attend the meetings out of a true hunger and longing for the living bread and carry away from them a blessing or whether some are going more out of habit.

She will also need to be on guard so that no spirit of argument or criticism of brethren who conduct the meetings is permitted, and we expect of the room leaders that they will face this harmful spirit and keep it from thriving among their sisters.

§ 47. One of the most blessed occupations of the single sisters' choir is the singing of lovely sacred hymns. The choir helper will note the inclination toward singing and will support it sweetly, and she can make an important contribution if she sees to it that her sisters diligently learn new verses and that those who have the gift and aptitude for it are trained in appropriate congregational music. The main thing, however, is that their hearts are genuinely filled with thanks and praise for the great forgiveness through the Lord's death, and that they live each day in this, and in response to it their voices will resound cheerfully and with emotion.

§ 48. When sisters travel from one congregation to visit in another, the choir helper will give them a letter to carry along, explaining their visit. Such visitors are to be received in a loving and friendly manner, and care should be taken to see that the visit should bless their hearts. It would also be good for an agreement to be made with each sister wishing to make such a visit, so that she pays for her food fully and other things she needs in the choir house to which she comes. If she is poor, it would be better that she be given what she needs for the trip or that the choir wardens (*Chordienerinnen*) from both locations have an understanding between them regarding such cases. If such a visit is long, she will be advised to arrange to work during her stay.

§ 49. In the matter of single sisters living outside of the congregation, usually a specific sister in the choir will be appointed to serve them. It is also necessary for the choir helper, as much as possible, to take special notice, not only of this sister's work in general but also of the souls themselves. It will be her special concern to become acquainted with those who apply for permission to enter the church, before their request is considered by the elders' conference and brought before the Savior.

Sometimes it happens that single women from the local area are asked to serve in families in the congregations. In such cases, we must carefully ensure that none are proposed for this in whom we perceive neither feeling for the Savior nor signs of an awakening. If afterward they wish to stay in the congregation, which often happens for external reasons, then it can be difficult to get rid of them, or they stay for so long that we finally recommend them for one or another congregation. Even if we immediately recognize satisfactory examples, that "natural" persons have mended their ways and completely become the Savior's while serving in the congregation, we still cannot take a risk with all such persons. Rather, the rule remains that we will look only to those who show hope of flourishing for the Savior.

§ 50. Finally, a word must be mentioned about how a choir helper should conduct herself if she is given a position in another choir where she is not known. She will do well if she first quietly examines everything, noting the choir's procedures in general, before she becomes very active or decides to change or abolish one or another thing that is not clear to her. It will be most advantageous for her if she frequently talks privately not only with her assistants and room leaders but also with other older, experienced sisters in the choir; if she diligently visits the sisters in their rooms and in the places where they work; if she listens more than she talks; if she takes care not to become prejudiced for or against this or that one before getting to know the persons; if she does not listen to complaints about her predecessor but rejoices with all her heart over everything good anyone says about her; and if she lets herself be guided as much as possible by her predecessor's example.

The thorough acquaintance of the heart with her sisters always remains her chief aim, and she will achieve this most easily if she looks around for them in a friendly manner instead of waiting for the sisters to seek her out. She will not require each sister to repeat to her by way of confession old matters she has already talked over thoroughly with her former choir helper. But if she gets the opportunity to have each one narrate her memoir (*Lebenslauf*), she will much prefer that.

Usually she will also find the comments about the sisters that her predecessor made, and she will try to become more familiar with them. Sisters like it when one speaks to them in a natural way and sometimes talks with them about small matters. In this way it can happen that a conversation that was unimportant at the beginning turns toward the most substantial subjects, which can allow a choir helper to become closely acquainted with the heart of such a sister.

If a sister is eager to pour out her heart, it is important not to put this off but instead to give her full attention and listen to her patiently. In general, however, a choir helper will first gain the trust of her sisters when they can feel that she herself is a little, poor sinner-heart who requires new mercy from Jesus every day and who looks unceasingly, out of distress and love, at the Savior. May our dear Savior bestow this on all single sisters' laboresses as their own blessing, for the sake of His holy five wounds.

Amen!

# 2

## THE SINGLE BRETHREN'S CHOIR

### Introduction

In February 1728 a group of single men founded their own dormitory, the single brethren's choir house in Herrnhut, Saxony; here they lived, worshipped, and ate together. Not until 1786, however, were clear instructions for the pastoral care of the single men circulated. In the intervening almost six decades, Moravian masculinity had been first defined according to the concept of "mystical marriage"; however, following the scandals of the 1740s (the so-called Time of Sifting) and the subsequent death of Zinzendorf's son Christian Renatus in 1750, male sexuality had been redefined.[1]

Being a single brother in the Moravian Church involved a complex negotiation among gendered theology, the maintenance of church order (*Gemein-Ordnung*), and economic necessity. The dominant theologization of masculinity throughout the Moravian Atlantic world in the period 1740–70, in the mission field as well as in the town congregations, was one in which the Christ figure constituted an ideal of masculinity for the Moravian brethren, whether they were single, married, or widowed.[2] According to the Moravian theology of the mid-eighteenth century, masculinity was temporal. After the passing of every brother, his earthly form would fall away, and his female soul would then be married to the Eternal Bridegroom. For the Moravian brother, as

---

1. Peucker, *Time of Sifting*.

2. For a closer examination of Moravian masculinity, see Faull, *Masculinity, Senses, Spirit*. For a brief description of the widowers, see Faull, "Savior's Widow." Recent archival work by Scott Gordon on the Christiansbrunn farm near Nazareth focuses on the reality of the economic lives of the single brethren. See "The Lost City of Christian's Spring," Lehigh University, accessed June 29, 2016, https://christiansbrunn.web.lehigh.edu/.

*Fig. 5*   The single brethren's house in Bethlehem was one of the largest buildings in the colonies. Courtesy of the Unity Archives, Herrnhut, Germany.

with the sisters, Jesus was the Eternal Bridegroom in whose arms and side wound he would "go home."

During his earthly life a married brother acted on behalf of Jesus, especially in the conjugal union with his wife. He served as Jesus's vice-regent in marriage. But Moravian men simultaneously possessed feminine souls, which yearned constantly for union with the Eternal Bridegroom.[3] After the death of his wife, a widowed brother was instructed to keep his own upcoming wedding with Christ in his mind and heart and to no longer think of earthly marriage. Eschatologically speaking, especially during the period known as the "Time of Sifting," all brethren were considered to be sisters.[4]

This "gender queering" might not have been as difficult as it might seem for Moravian brethren to have put into practice, as their paradigm, Christ, contained male and female traits. And as the masculinity of Christ was presented in regular daily, weekly, and monthly worship opportunities to every Moravian brother, either as a young man in the single brethren's choir or as a married brother in married persons' choir, we can definitely speak of a normative masculinity within the Moravian Church that was distinct from concepts in European and Euro-American society.

3. See Atwood, "Masculine and Feminine," in Faull, *Masculinity, Senses, Spirit*, 11–38.
4. See Peucker, *Time of Sifting*; and Vogt, "Masculinity of Christ."

Many have argued that this gendered aspect of Moravian piety—the mystical marriage, the worship of the Holy Spirit as Mother, the temporal nature of masculinity—fell away after the death of Zinzendorf.[5] This may have been the case within the texts written for the public, such as Spangenberg's *Idea Fidei Fratrum*, but these privately circulated instructions present a different picture. There was not a complete abandonment of any of these concepts after the death of Zinzendorf. We find references to the "motherly" spirit of the choir helper to the single brethren (§ 13), and Christ is referred to as "my Bridegroom" (§ 25). Indeed, the intimacy in which the choir helper must stand with his charges is defined in feminine and loving terms. He is like a "midwife of faith" (§ 17).

Overall, however, the "Instructions for the Choir Helpers of the Single Brethren" differ substantially in tone from those for the single sisters' choir helpers. As alluded to in the introduction to this volume, the single brethren's choir was the site of many disciplinary problems in both Herrnhut and Bethlehem and also in Salem, North Carolina. Although they comprise only thirty-seven sections, in contrast to fifty for the single sisters, the "Instructions for the Choir Helpers of the Single Brethren" focus far more on the perceived dangers associated with single men living together. Furthermore, the usual path for unmarried men outside the Moravian Church was one that led to increasing (economic) independence: going through an apprenticeship to journeyman to master of a trade or becoming a student at university and learning law, theology, or medicine. The Moravian idea that men should choose to live together in a choir house in the service of Christ rather than seek personal and economic independence was very challenging. Indeed, the opening sections of the instructions define what a single brother is and what the Savior might intend with him. As an answer to the question of why single men should live together, the choir helper is instructed to give the answer: because it helps God's plan. They too, like the single sisters, should be fruitful branches on the vine.

How does a choir helper work with the single brethren to gain their trust, so that each of them can, as it says in section 10, "open a window in their breast" to allow him in? How can he lead the single men to reveal to him their "secret wound," that place within their moral constitution that knows of its own sin and desires to hide it (§ 32)?

According to these instructions, that path is not easy. And it appears to have been made much more difficult by the troubled history of the single brethren's choir. It was the single brethren's choir houses in Herrnhaag and

---

5. See Atwood, "Apologizing for the Moravians."

Herrnhut that were at the center of the Sifting.[6] Even though that happened nearly four decades prior to the composition of the instructions, the church elders were afraid that something similar could happen again if choir helpers were not vigilant. Repeatedly in the instructions, Spangenberg reiterates that the single brethren must be "sour" (like sourdough or leaven) for Christ;[7] they live together to serve God's plan and must have rules to follow so that the many challenges to that plan can be overcome.

Accordingly, the first four sections focus on the justification for the existence of a single brethren's choir house. The choir helper must know the principia for the choir and also the decisions of the Harmony of the Synods as they pertain to the single brethren.[8] In other words, the choir helpers were expected to implement the order agreed on by the synod. Spangenberg's emphasis on the rules of the choir (Haus-Ordnung) belie a troubled past, especially when it comes to weeding out bad influences within the choir. Then, parallel to the "Instructions for the Choir Helpers of the Single Sisters," the following two sections describe the relationship of the choir helper to the elders' conference of the congregation and the Unity Elders' Conference (Unitäts-Ältesten-Conferenz).

In stark contrast to the "Instructions for the Choir Helpers of the Single Sisters," section 9 provides what could be called thirty-eight articles of faith that in fact constitute a summary of the central part of Spangenberg's *Idea Fidei Fratrum*. Clearly the past troubles within the single brethren's choir necessitated that the individual single brother focus on his utter depravity and Christ's torment. By including detailed descriptions of the ideal single brother and reinforcing this model with the inclusion of thirty-eight points that describe the single brother; the nature of his relationship to Christ and God and the Holy Spirit; his relationship between his body and soul; and how, if these points are not heeded, God's wrath will be incurred, the instructions become a spiritual and physical guide for the single brother.

In section 10 Spangenberg instructs the choir helper to ensure that these thirty-eight points are "driven home" with every opportunity in his choir, classes, societies, Speakings, and discussions. In fact, the choir helper must not only repeat these points as often as possible but also ensure that the

---

6. See Peucker, *Time of Sifting*.

7. From the earliest years of the Renewed Church, Zinzendorf employed this image and described his followers as sourdough; they turn everything with which they come into contact into leaven. Zinzendorf called on his followers to be like sourdough: "I infect others as I was infected. I have the nature of sourdough." Zinzendorf, *Litaney zu den Wunden*, 192–93.

8. Other admonitions in the Harmony of the Synods are that single brethren should not skip the Sunday devotions in favor of social gatherings, walks, shooting of pistols in the fields, or loud talk that disturbed the services. See Sommer, *Serving Two Masters*, 64–65n10.

membership of these groupings is not allowed to remain static but rather changes to remove any danger of overfamiliarity between the brethren. All these opportunities to reiterate the thirty-eight points must lead to the moment when single brethren can open up and allow the choir helper to see in (§ 10).

Not only the choir members must follow the house rules; the choir helper himself should follow the rules and not lose sight of the fact that he has been placed in this position by the elders of the congregation and the Unity. Again, this emphasis on defining and delimiting the agency of the choir helper carries with it echoes of the problems of the past.

Sections 13–17 discuss the role of the choir helper in turning the single men to Christ. How does he encourage the men to hear the call of God; how, echoing Saint Augustine, can he help them know that today is the day when they will follow Him? How should the choir helper recognize the brother who desires to lead others astray? The manner in which the choir helper is to work with the single brethren is firm but gentle, loving, and guiding.

In far more detail than in the single sisters' instructions, there then follow two sections that describe the Speaking itself and the acceptance process into the choir. Once the brother has told the choir helper his life story, the latter washes the candidate's feet, and he is accepted into the choir.

Once the brother has been accepted, the choir helper is then instructed to discuss matters of the body with him. Indeed, of all the issues that would most hinder the spiritual growth of a Moravian single brother, excessive attention to the mind and the body, and not the soul, seems to be the most dangerous. In terms of the body, the choir helper describes the wisdom of the Maker in creating male and female bodies in different ways.[9]

In all discussions of the body, the brother is to remember that Christ is the paradigmatic male. The correct and honorable understanding of our human nature stems from the pious regard of Jesus and his humanity. From this a choir helper also derives the respect that one should have for his own and others' souls and organs in his instruction: "The brethren have the honor that Christ assumed the organs that are peculiar to the male sex. He suffered because of them and paid for his sin. He was circumcised on the eighth day and thereby spilled his first blood, just as he did his last drops on the stem of the cross, as a comfort for all his brethren who feel their damnation and sinfulness and take their refuge in Him and wish to be healed through His wounds, including the circumcision wound" (§ 20).

---

9. This is an interesting allusion to the dimorphism and complementarity debate in understanding sexual difference, which Laqueur discusses at length in his book *Making Sex*.

Just as with the single sisters, the single brother has to be prepared for Moravian marriage; he must be spoken with and educated in the theory and discourse of Moravian sexuality. The actual description of sexual intercourse and its practice within the church was reserved for the helpers of the married persons' choir to share after marriage. However, each brother's virginity should be molded to the service of the Savior, and each brother should be a good tree, as "even so every good tree bringeth forth good fruit; but a corrupt tree bringeth forth evil fruit" (§ 13).

Sections 21–23 address the "sin of self-abuse" and are, interestingly, not in Spangenberg's hand in the original manuscript. Reflecting an almost neo-Aristotelian concept of the makeup of semen, the instructions state, "God put a seed in the male sex that consists of the noblest juices of the body and that matures in adults. This is destined for the holy purpose of a husband giving it to his wife" and is therefore not for spilling in night emissions. But how is the adolescent brother to avoid such "illicit sensations in the organs"? How can he avoid the organ's becoming erect and the seed's occasionally leaving it during the day or night? Discussing then physical causes, such as diet or vigorous exercise, the choir helper must also address the possibility that the brother has caused his organ to become erect through fantasies and imaginings. The latter is a "filthy illness" that will prevent him from taking Communion and will bring him spiritual ruin (§ 23). Equally condemned is the single brother who seduces another brother (either boy or grown man) or a sister "to sin in the flesh." Such a brother is considered "to be like a plague" and must be expelled from the choir immediately (§ 24).[10]

Finally the instructions turn to the topic of marriage and attempt to redefine marriage within the bounds of Moravian theology. In sharp contrast to the Pauline instruction that it is better to marry than to burn with lust,[11] the instructions consider that a brother should not marry for fleshly desire. Marriage is not a step to be undertaken lightly or for the wrong reasons; marital relations are not to be seen as sinful but rather as a "respectable activity," conducted in private and accompanied by the thought, "I want only what Jesus, my Bridegroom, wants" (§ 25). In light of scholarly claims that Span-

---

10. In her study of the maintenance of discipline within the Moravian congregations on both sides of the Atlantic, Elisabeth Sommer has shown that the 1780s saw a sharp increase in the number of members expelled from the Salem and Herrnhut congregations. In Herrnhut over a third of the cases that warranted expulsion were for "sexual sins," another third for bad conduct (fighting, curses, frequenting taverns), and, among the remaining third, only two for single brethren who had a "harmful connection." In Salem, North Carolina, of the thirty-seven cases, nearly half were for sexual misconduct. See *Serving Two Masters*, 61–62.

11. "I say therefore to the unmarried and widows, It is good for them if they abide even as I. But if they cannot contain, let them marry: for it is better to marry than to burn." 1 Cor. 8–9 (KJV).

genberg was ridding Moravian theology and praxis of Zinzendorfian over-tones of mystical marriage, this is interesting. Within the private realm of the church, the idea that the earthly husband was merely stepping in for Christ in the marriage bed (as seen in the earlier Moravian marriage concepts) was still very much in practice.

Though Christ is the paradigmatic male for the single brethren, the choir helper is also instructed to emphasize the roles of "pilgrim and militant" that present themselves to the single brethren through regular reading of the mis-sion reports. These missionaries in the field, among the Native Americans and in Greenland and Suriname, serve as vital role models for the single brethren. This work they can do as single brothers, but they would be far more effective if they were married.

Sections 27–30 discuss how a proposal for a marriage takes place; has the single brother someone in mind? Is he wanting to marry for the right reasons? Does he want the choir helpers of the single brethren and single sisters to suggest someone to him? If the choir helper deems that the brother should marry, then his life to date is related to the choir helper and he receives the foot washing as a sign that he is ready to leave this choir and enter the mar-ried persons' choir.

Again, in contrast to the instructions to the single sisters, the single breth-ren's instructions warn the choir helper of the dangers posed to the men of an overly critical mind. Whereas for the single sisters, frivolous reading matter might lead them astray, for the brethren it is the exercise of secular reason. The instructions argue that there are three main impediments to the single brother's Moravian faith; in keeping with the intellectual trends of the late eighteenth-century Enlightenment, they are curiosity, frivolity/carelessness, and freethinking. Friedrich Schleiermacher, a famous nineteenth-century theologian, suffered greatly from these traits while a student at Barby, and his departure from the Moravian Church was occasioned by their exercise.[12] Despite the ban on Immanuel Kant's philosophical books from the seminary, Schleiermacher and his friends Brinkmann and Okely studied them care-fully, absorbing the critical philosophy that called for the exercise of critique and wit and freethinking.

The instructions end with a reiteration of the importance of single breth-ren educating the young boys in how to maintain a consciousness of them-selves as performing a role for Christ. During the meeting of the quarter

---

12. There are many accounts of Schleiermacher's time with the Moravians. The classic account is in Meyer, *Schleiermachers*. See also Faull, "Schleiermacher," in Wilcox, Tice, and Kelsey, *Schleiermacher's Influences*, 293–321.

hour for the renewal of the choir covenant, for example, the choir helper must remind the single brethren that the full purpose of each one of them is "not to live for himself, nor to do the will of his flesh, nor to make reason his guide, but rather to live for the Lord, to be a joy to Him only, to live according to His word in all things, and to allow himself to be led like a child by his Holy Spirit" (§ 35).

§ 1. Depending on differences in circumstances, our Moravian congregations consist of various divisions that are called choirs. The brethren who are not married and who have never lived in a marriage are called the choir of the single brethren and have always been a matter of particular concern to our Savior. He has tirelessly taken their part, and whosoever takes note of His work of grace among them may see that it is concerned with the following, namely,

(1) He desires that every member of this choir is brought through faith to the enjoyment of the holy treasures that He has won by His Life, Passion, and Death through the word of grace that God has wrought among us. He desires that

(2) each person who has come to Him in faith and who has found forgiveness of sins, and thus life and happiness, should be kept in this grace and develop it further to perfection. He should be a fruitful branch on the vine for Him, avoid evil, pursue good, and be renewed and blessed by the Holy Spirit in the image of God, which we lost in Adam. He desires that:

(3) he should attain the purpose that He has set with each and every one that He has accepted in grace. Thus, He needs one brother in one way and the other in another way, and when each person finds himself in the place God has foreseen, that is the best thing for him.

§ 2. If the single brethren can live together in a Moravian congregation, then it is a great help in the achievement of God's purpose with them through our Savior. For it not only removes them from some of the things that could be injurious to them but also gives them an opportunity to be helpful to one another spiritually and also in external matters. Thus, we must thank God from our hearts for the choir houses that He has given the single brethren in our congregations and ask Him that they should fulfill their purpose in all ways. That the brethren who live together in a choir house, or those who belong to the choir even if they cannot live in it, get along well together in external matters and may continue in them without problem, then they need someone to watch over these things, and this person we call among ourselves the choir warden. However, the person who has the task of serving the inner needs or affairs of the soul for the individual, as well as the choir as a whole, is called the choir helper. From time to time it may happen, especially with small choirs, that a choir warden is asked to take over the office of choir helper, or a choir helper is asked to act as choir warden, and then one gives him the name of choir laborer. Someone who takes on both offices at the same time should see himself as a servant of Christ and a servant of the Unity of the Brethren and the congregation in which he lives. The office of warden is no less an office of the spirit than is the office of helper, and if one person fills one or the other or both at the same time, then he must be instructed, lead, and be led by the Holy Spirit if he wishes to be of use and a blessing to the Lord and his choir.

§ 3. Here we want to speak only of those things that are expected of a choir helper of the single brethren. First of all [1], he has to see himself as a servant of Jesus Christ. He has received his position from people, namely, from the Unity Elders' Conference; however, this has happened not merely through their approval but rather according to the instructions of our Lord Jesus Christ.[1] For He is our elder by special grace, and it is His decision whether a brother should be entrusted with this or that office in the Unity of the brethren. Because it is He who puts a choir helper in his position, the latter must always look to Him as his Lord and elder and should plead and petition Him day and night about how he should please Him and meet His purpose in all things. A choir helper may then always be assured of the gracious support of his Lord and Savior because He has called the same to his office. Also he may safely believe that the blessing of the Father in heaven will be with him when it is necessary for him dutifully to fulfill his office. The dear promise of our Lord Jesus Christ, "And whatsoever ye shall ask in my name, that will I do,"[2] is particularly relevant to him. For whenever he steps before the Lord in faith and says to Him in a childlike fashion, "Dear Father, my Lord and Savior, your only begotten Son has recommended me to this office, I have this Grace and the gift, the sense, the strength necessary for this," so He will not ignore any request.

§ 4. A choir helper must:

(2) always bear in mind, that our Lord is the shepherd and bishop of our souls. He has said, "I will take care of my flock. I will seek the lost sheep and bring back the one that has strayed. I will bind up the wounds of the injured and take care of the weak."[3] From this it is clear that He cares not only for the best of His flock, including also every single brethren's choir in our whole

---

1. Choir helpers were selected by the lot; see the introduction to this volume.

2. John 14:13 (KJV). "The Instructions for the Choir Helpers of the Single Brethren" include far more biblical quotations than those for the other choirs. This may well be an indication that there were far more problems in the single brethren's choir than in the others.

3. Ezek. 34:16 (KJV).

congregation, but also particularly for each one of us, according to the demands of the circumstances in which he finds himself. A choir helper therefore is sure that the Lord, our Savior, is the one for whom our souls have made so much trouble, and He has given His life for them and spilled His blood. The welfare of the choir, and of every single soul therein, is of indescribable importance to His heart, and He draws all of them to Him, each one according to His word after He was lifted onto the cross. He is the head of the body, that is, of His congregation, and He is untiring in the care of each of the members of His body. Each choir helper should not see himself in any other way than as a co-worker of Jesus Christ, and that is also the way in which the Scriptures speak of them. At the same time he always pays attention to the Savior's purpose with the whole choir and with each soul, and he follows the path with devotion. If he does this, he will not labor in vain but rather will always find cause to fill his office with praise and thanks through all the pain that he has with the souls.

§ 5. In addition, the choir helper of the single brethren must:

(3) Never forget that he belongs to the Unity of the Brethren and must conduct himself according to their constitution. This he will find in the Harmony of the Synods for the years 1764, 1769, 1775, and 1782, and he must immediately make himself acquainted with this, as the principia for all choirs and also for the choir of the single brethren are recorded there in detail.

From this it is clear that he must abide by the decisions of the Unity Elders' Conference, which has under its purview both internal and external matters in all the congregations of the brethren and its choirs, not least the affairs of the mission and its pilgrims; and by whom he was called to his position and to speak to how he fills it and to give an account of special circumstances in his choir and he must follow their directions directly. In the same way, he is expected to report to the conference on affairs in his choir and on what is to be hoped for and feared in each brother. He especially tells them of his thoughts on a brother who may prove to be dangerous to the others and does not omit to report on those who might be moved to another place or on those who might be more usefully deployed in a brethren's choir among the heathen and among other denominations[4] or on those who could be more usefully employed if married. In short, he is concerned in a heartfelt manner with everything that has to do with the Unity and serves it best and is deeply

---

4. The original here reads "in der Religion." This phrase is used in the synod minutes (1736–60) to distinguish between work done in the Moravian congregations and that done in other denominations.

concerned with this in his prayer and through counsel and deeds, maintaining the notion that when things go well with the Unity of the Brethren then I can enjoy this too; when the Unity sees blessed progress in the business dealings that are entrusted to it by the Lord, then I can also rejoice and thank the Lord our God.

§ 6. The choir helper of the single brethren

(4) must not forget that he is a servant of the congregation in which he lives. Through his office he becomes a member of the elders' conference of the congregation to which he belongs, and whether or not the care of his choir is particularly commended to him, he must, as a member of the elders' conference, observe everything that is useful both internally and externally to the well-being of the congregation, think of everything that might prevent harm or promote utility, and if he is negligent in this then he is not doing things in the proper manner.

In accordance with this, he must make himself well acquainted with the rules to which the congregation has subscribed and which it understands and not only carry himself according to them but also see to it they are followed by each and every one. If he becomes aware of something from outside his choir that is not in accordance with church order (*Gemein-Ordnung*), then he must communicate this to the congregation helper or he can mention it in the choir helpers' or elders' conference. The choirs in a congregation are so closely connected with one another that when there is a problem in one, then the others suffer too, before a single one succumbs to the problem. Every choir belongs to the Lord, and wherever damage occurs, then He and His affairs suffer.

§ 7. A choir helper of the single brethren must listen to the words of Paul at Ephesus: "Therefore take heed to yourselves and to all the flock."[5] He must first take heed to his own self. For if that does not happen then he will not be of much use to his choir.

One assumes of a brother who has been entrusted with the office of choir helper that he is a poor, redeemed sinner. Therefore, it is necessary that he always stay at Jesus's feet as a poor and sorrowful one of the Lord, who considers himself lost in soul and body and who can trust himself to do nothing good and can never forget what he would be if the Savior had not taken pity on him; that he keep Jesus's sacrifice in his mind and heart every day, in which alone redemption and freedom from all sins can be found, and that the grace

---

5. Acts 20:28 (KJV).

found in the blood of Jesus and forgiveness of sins through faith in Him will
be renewed daily; that he will go forward in his intercourse with the Savior in
an ever more heartfelt manner that flows from love, in the manner of the
woman sinner who loved much because much was forgiven of her[6]—for
where the treasure is, there too is the heart; that he will hearken ever more
carefully to the voice of the Holy Spirit, who teaches us, warns us, comforts
us, helps us, strengthens us; that he will always grow in the love to others that
flows from the love of Jesus, etc.

When a choir helper takes care of himself in this way and tries to grow
daily in the grace of our Lord Jesus Christ in his knowledge and tries to
become a joy and honor to Him, then he will always be light of heart and
happy to fulfill his office with all loyalty, and his example will serve as a good
model and illustration for others to follow. He should speak with the congregation helper about the condition of his own heart before Communion and
take note of his advice.

§ 8. Now we will see how a choir helper cares for a choir that has been
entrusted to him. In the teachings of Jesus and His disciples one can find
everything that is useful and necessary for the choir, and for each and every
brother, for the beginning and foundation in God's blessing, and for blessed
progress in this until his happy end and the attainment of eternal life. A choir
helper takes good care that each and every brother has the opportunity to hear
the Gospel both in the congregation and in the choir worship meetings.

If he himself and his fellow workers provide a good example to the other
brethren, then this is more helpful than any kind of enforced rules or laws. At
the same time, it is also necessary, when he finds one or another brother not
adhering to the rules—and he must be vigilant in this—that he speaks to
him in a heartfelt and thorough fashion and points out clearly the damage
that could be done to him. If, just when they should be going to meetings,
brethren find other things to do that they could do just as well or even better
at another time, or if they sit together during meetings and spend the time
talking to one another, then the choir helper has cause to object and put an
end to it with great care. The singing meeting and the liturgies have always
been a great blessing to those who attend them as they should do, and therefore the choir helper is to strongly recommend them to each brother.

§ 9. In the choir meetings everything rests on the fact that Christ is the
foundation, and everything is built on Him. This comes about if we always

---

6. See Luke 7:36–50 (KJV).

stay with what Christ said Himself and what He has taught us through His disciples. It thus becomes clear to us that by nature we are lost in soul and body; this damnation and sinfulness erupts in the shape of bad thoughts, desires, attitudes, emotions, words, and deeds; we are unwilling and unable by nature to do that which is due to God; for this reason all humanity remains under the wrath of God; more wrath is to be expected, but God decided, before He made the world in grace, to redeem us from this pain and sorrow through His Son; that His Son should become Man in holiness and justice and walk on earth for some thirty years; God acknowledged Him and His teachings through great wonders and signs; not only is His holy life an example for us to follow, but He has given us the strength to be like Him in the world; He has taken our sins onto Himself; He became so troubled by this in His soul and mournful unto death, and sweated bloody sweat, that His body was broken and wounded by the whipping and blows, through the crown of thorns and the marks of the nails from the cross; He allowed Himself to be executed horribly and His Side to be pierced and allowed His blood to flow for us for the forgiveness of sins; through this He became the forgiveness of our sins and not just ours but the whole world's; God resurrected Him on the third day and thus showed the world that, through Him, that which was necessary for the redemption of humanity was accomplished; He was on Earth for another forty days after His resurrection, showed Himself to His disciples, and spoke to them about the Kingdom of God; after this He went into heaven and sits at the right hand of God, the Father, and once again took on the heavenly garb that He once had with his Father; it is God's earnest wish and command that humanity believe in this His Son and thereby attain eternal Life; that a poor human being, who is tired of sinning and would like to be saved from it, can become a child of God by believing in Christ, the Savior of all humanity, and will receive a peaceful heart washed in the blood of Jesus; through faith he will partake of the Holy Spirit and gain access to the Father of our Lord Jesus Christ as his dear Father; that he, because so much has been forgiven of him, will now love much and depend on his Lord Jesus Christ; through this faith in Christ, he will become a new creature; he will now keep to his commandments, because he loves Jesus with his whole heart; he will enter into a state of grace through his faith and will become free from the power of sin, and it will never again have power over him against his will; through faith, he will become free from his heart's dependence on the world and its desires and vanities; through faith he will become free from the power of the devil, and the latter will shy away from him and flee if he keeps to the Savior in a childlike fashion; through faith in Christ, our bodies will become temples of the Holy Spirit, and our body's members will be Christ's members; we will therefore maintain all our members in his honor, our eyes, ears, tongue, hands, feet and not use them for sinful purposes; we can and should make our souls pure for untainted brotherly love by keeping to the truth and the Holy Spirit; through love for the Savior we do not therefore permit thoughts, fantasies, desires, and emotions that are not in accord with the sense of Jesus, but rather we should destroy them through His power; one should flee from sin, for which Jesus had to atone on the cross, as though from a snake and avoid all opportunities that could bring us to it; the Savior showed with Peter and his other disciples that he will also accept a person who has fallen into sin with all the grace that He has shown; He bitterly weeps with Peter over his fall; for the love of Jesus, there is no stronger means of protecting oneself from sin than the deep impression of the martyrdom of God that the Savior effected through the Holy Spirit; the heartfelt and trusting intercourse with our Lord Jesus Christ, who is the shepherd and bishop of our souls, is better than anything that one could wish for in this world; we have to give ourselves over like good children to the leadership and guidance of the Holy Spirit so that we may be filled with the fruits of the Holy Spirit, that is with love, joy, peace, patience, etc. (see Galatians 5); the love of His children toward each other is the greatest joy to the Savior and His Father in heaven, and that the opposite is repugnant, even unbearable, to him; we can bring all our cares with pleadings and petitions and thanks before God and need not doubt that we will be heard; we can hope that God will complete the good work that He has started with us in grace, and that He will finally take us to Him in grace; Christ takes a heartfelt part in each and every condition of all brethren; He represents him before His dear Father; He is sympathetic to our weakness and continually petitions on our behalf, etc.[7]

§ 10. These are the principal points that should be remembered in choir meetings from time to time and that should be driven home with grace and wisdom. If this is done with a warm heart and is accompanied by the witness of the Holy Spirit in the heart, it will always bear fruit.

However, one does not only take the opportunity to discuss this material in the choir meetings; discussions can also take place in the classes (*Classen*) and companies (*Gesellschaften*) and during the Speakings with the brethren. In the classes those brethren are brought together who seem to fit best together in a certain manner, and there one can guide the discussion with them to follow a certain direction. In the societies one considers even more

---

7. The German original manuscript contains a long passage of deleted matter here on the matter of the hymns and their role in promoting this vision of Christ.

carefully how the brethren might fit together better according to their hearts, and there the discussion fits their situation even more closely. During the Speaking we are concerned with an individual person, and if a choir helper is acquainted with each person very well, then he can speak with him with appropriate attention. In addition, the occasional visits of the brethren to the choir helper, and of the choir helper to the brethren, should be counted, which together are of great value. The main point is always this: that the Savior has promised to visit those who come together in His name Himself. In this aforesaid matter, the following should be noted: (1) The choir helper does well if he revises the classes and companies from time to time and makes the necessary changes and communicates about this with his closest co-workers and the congregation helper. (2) It is also good that brethren be put into a different company if they no longer fit in the old one. (3) A choir helper must ask for God's help so that the brethren do not find reason to be shy around him or hold back, but rather that they would far more desire to open a window in their breast so that the choir helper can see in.[8]

§ 11. The choir helper must be of one heart and mind with his colleague, the choir warden. They both serve one purpose, although they are distinguished by the fact that the one takes care mainly of external and the other internal matters. If the choir warden is the choir helper's closest aide and the helper the warden's, then it will be very good for both the choir and for themselves. They always have business with the house warden and, if the latter is skillful, loyal, and hardworking, then he can be of help to them on both sides (both in internal and external matters). Because errands are carried out by him, he always has the opportunity to see and hear what is happening in the house and in the rooms. If one can find a brother to fill the office of house warden who has grace and talent, then he might become a choir helper or choir warden. If the choir helper or choir warden suggests someone for the office of house warden, they must always be sure that he also has the trust of the choir, and then the question is asked in the elders' conference if the Savior approves of him for that position. They must also seek reliable brethren for the offices of a guide for strangers (*Fremden-Diener*), master craftsman (*Meister*), room overseer (*Stuben-Aufseher*), and company leader (*Gesellschafthalter*). For this one not only asks that someone has talent and gifts but rather particularly considers how things stand with his heart. For, if it is lacking there, then gifts and talent are not enough. The choir helper stands in close connec-

---

8. This is a recurrent motif in devotional literature and art. See Atwood, "Little Side Holes"; and Hamburger, *Nuns as Artists*.

tion with all these brethren in the matter of their duties as well as in regard to their hearts. If he can manage to speak his mind honestly and simply in the conferences with the company leader, with the master craftsman, or room overseer, and also in-house and other conferences where he is present anyway, then he has achieved much.

§ 12. The Unity Elders' Conference has revised and approved the house rules, which were created by the college of the congregation. These are intended to prevent those bad or inappropriate things that can occur depending on the circumstances of the brethren. Because it pleases the Lord our Savior and is of great profit to the brethren themselves that these things are spoken about, the choir helper and the choir warden keep watch to make sure this happens. If things occur that are not in accordance with this, then the choir helper and the choir warden consider what is to be done. Small things, this and that, can be remarked on with the individual or in the house conference, and he can be brought back onto the right path straight away. Other things have differing consequences and one should speak first to the minister. There it will be decided whether the issues should be brought before the college of overseers (*Aufseher-Collegium*) or the choir helpers' conference or the elders' conference. A further word of wisdom here is that one should extinguish the spark while it is still a spark and not wait until it spreads and becomes a fire. The wardens of Jesus are called watchmen in the holy scriptures. A choir helper must therefore be watchful and take heed of everything, and all brethren in the choir, in particular the room overseers, must please him out of loyalty to the Savior and love for their choir. That a choir helper has to keep to a straight path without thinking of himself is definitely the intention of the Savior, and if this does not happen great harm will result.

§ 13. To take care of all the brethren in his choir, which is the task of the office of choir helper, he must get to know each brother properly. Because the Savior says, "Even so every good tree bringeth forth good fruit; but a corrupt tree bringeth forth evil fruit,"[9] then we can tell clearly by the fruits whether a brother has turned to the Savior or not. That can happen much earlier in a choir house, because we have the comings and goings and the person's daily behavior right before our eyes.

Here we assume that a person who is still a slave to sin has not turned to Christ, for, if he had, then he would stand in grace, and sin could not hold sway over him. One should note here that we are not talking just about bodily

---

9. Matt. 7:17 (KJV).

desires but rather about everything that stands in opposition to Christ. For a person who is prone to hatred and envy, anger and bitterness, greed and enmity, indolence and sloth, pride and gluttony, and drunkenness and other such evil things has not turned to Christ just as much as someone who is a warden of the pleasures of the flesh and depends on them. If the choir helper has to work with a person who has not turned to Christ, then he must try to detect whether he knows and believes that he has not turned to Christ. And if he believes that he has still not turned to Christ, then he looks for the obstacles to his turning to Christ and speaks with him about it in a motherly fashion.

§ 14. A choir helper must take special care with people who have grown up in the congregation. For the most part they have been protected from crass sinfulness and vice through watchful care and, in addition, have acquired by habit much that is suitable for children of God. The deep sinfulness that resides in their soul as well as in their bodies has not yet become so obvious. They have not yet experienced such a marked turning to God as have people who have fallen into crass sinfulness and depravity, but we cannot deny that they have a love for our Lord Jesus Christ and for His children. They are accepted into the congregation and probably go along to Communion. However, many vices appear also with them, so that sometimes one wonders whether this one or that one has really turned to God. A choir helper must serve such brethren with great patience and await the hour at which the Savior will graciously allow that to come to pass that still eludes them. It often happens that they really do fall into things that are clearly evil. The Holy Spirit takes advantage of this opportunity and makes it clear to them in their hearts that they are not better than the people who obviously live in the works of the flesh, about which Saint Paul speaks in Galatians 5.[10] Then they will fall at the feet of the Savior and plead with tears for mercy, and they will receive this also. However, it often happens that the Holy Spirit reveals to them their poverty, misery, and sinfulness through his word without their having strayed into evil beforehand; they cry bitterly about this, bewail their want to the Savior, and are richly comforted by Him.

The following should also be noted: that we must be quite strict with the brethren who have grown up among us as well as show love to them, for if we

---

10. "This I say then, Walk in the Spirit, and ye shall not fulfill the lust of the flesh. For the flesh lusteth against the Spirit, and the Spirit against the flesh: and these are contrary the one to the other: so that ye cannot do the things that ye would. But if ye be led of the Spirit, ye are not under the law." Gal. 5:16–18 (KJV).

think that we could leave them alone and that they would be quite transparent, we would be doing them a wrong. In addition, we know from experience that we must have a doubly watchful eye around brethren who have grown up in the congregation, for we know that they can err into bad things through their air of superiority and lack of understanding more than other brethren who have been brought up outside the congregation and have heard and seen much that is evil. This caution is all the more necessary, as many of our brethren who have grown up in the congregation have not yet gained insight into their naturally sinful state—as mentioned earlier—and thus trust themselves more than they should.

§ 15. The turn toward Christ of one who has not yet turned must be awaited with patience. The Savior waits for the right time for this, and we must do likewise. Always drilling into someone, "Turn yourself to Christ! Turn yourself to Christ!" can have the effect that he takes matters into his own hands, but he will not improve through this, for sure. However, we must warn him not to miss the hour at which God will seek him out. "Today, it seems, today," you will hear his voice, so do not hide your hearts.[11] When the Holy Spirit begins work in the heart, we must recognize it and not hinder its work. The choir helper must also recognize *this* hour, and he must then watch and pray that this grace is not in vain with this person, whose conversion he desires. Now, even if one has patience with an individual who has not yet turned to Christ, that does not mean that one leaves him to do as he wishes. For if he wishes to live in a choir house, he must live not only according to the rules of the choir house but also according to the rules of the congregation, and we must hold to these steadfastly. We must always recognize one who has not turned to Christ immediately and have him in the care of such brethren, so that it is not possible for him to lead someone else astray. However, if this does happen, then he belongs neither in a choir house nor in a congregation. The Savior says, it would be better for him to be drowned in the deepest ocean with a millstone around his neck.[12] Further, nothing could be better for him than to be removed from the choir house and congregation, and in this matter no concern regarding the person himself may hold sway. A matter of this kind can be fully resolved only by the elders' conference and by the college of overseers.

---

11. This passage is redolent with allusions to the conversion of Saint Augustine. See his *Confessions*, bk. 8.

12. Matt. 18:6 (KJV).

§ 16. If a brother has turned to God with all his heart, then the choir helper attempts to acquaint him with the congregation helper and the other brethren of the elders' conference. His candidacy is then considered in the choir helpers' conference, which thereafter brings his name forward to the elders' conference as a candidate for acceptance into the congregation. If he notices a continuous work of grace of the Holy Spirit in a young brother who has grown up in the congregation and finds his heart to be in such state that he may hope for lasting grace, then the choir helper needs to act likewise. If the Savior approves the acceptance of a brother into the congregation, then the choir helper should not desist from showing him clearly and thoroughly what is involved with the congregation and what the acceptance into the same means. For a brother who allows himself to be accepted into the congregation must know that he is being brought together with a people that keeps to the words of reconciliation, "at the hazard of their lives and fortunes," through God's word.[13] He must also consider well that our Lord Jesus Christ is loved and honored in the Unity of the Brethren as our Lord and elder, and the brethren consider themselves bonded, to live not for themselves but rather to live and serve for him alone. In addition to this, the congregations must endure much public shame for the sake of their confession to Jesus Christ, and so he should not shame himself on its account, if he wants to be our brother. If a brother has decided in his heart that he should share his joys and sorrows with the congregation according to the will of Jesus Christ, and is actually accepted into the congregation, then the choir helper must consider himself to be doubly bound to take his part loyally and cordially, so that he can grow in the grace and knowledge of Jesus Christ and enjoy all the blessings that a poor sinner may partake of in the congregation.

§ 17. Regarding the other brethren of whom one can say in unison, we were "like lost sheep, but now we have turned to the Shepherd and Bishop of our souls,"[14] the choir helper should see himself as nothing but the helpmate of their joy. If they bestow on him their love and trust, he thanks God for this and considers it an unearned grace of the Lord. If they tell him something that troubles them, then he looks to the Lord our Savior and tells them what has been granted them as a comfort and lesson through his grace. If they tell him about the grace and mercy their souls have experienced from God, he

---

13. This passage is referring to "Mit Dranwagung Leibes und Lebens," an unusual phrase found in Spangenberg, *Idea Fidei Fratrum*, § 256. I have here used Benjamin LaTrobe's translation of the phrase, in Spangenberg, *Exposition of Christian Doctrine*, § 246, pt. 3.

14. 1 Pet. 2:25 (KJV).

rejoices with them and thanks God with them for this. If someone is in danger of jeopardizing his soul, he warns him lovingly and loyally. If someone has suffered pain, he is sorrowful with him and tries to help him heal. No one in the choir should have reason to doubt his sympathetic and feeling heart toward the circumstances of each and every brother. Each brother must have free access to him, and speaking to him should not be difficult for anyone who is in good standing with the Savior. He must try to be well acquainted with the inner and outer conditions of every brother in his choir, so that he can pray for them when he converses about his brethren with the Savior in a childlike way and be able to give them good advice in accordance with their circumstances, to warn them, to hear them, and to comfort them.

§ 18. Before each Communion, the choir helper usually has the custom of speaking to each communicant separately. It is assumed that each brother has the task of examining himself at this time to cleanse himself of those things that would make him unworthy of partaking of Holy Communion. However, the Speaking has the purpose of allowing each and every brother to talk fully about his heart, his behavior, and his whole walk through life. It is always good if those matters that are not in accordance with Christ's purpose and His love are not ignored when Communion is so close. However, if this has happened then it must be smoothed out and dealt with before one goes to Communion, and if this is not possible then the brother who is at fault, or both brethren, should stay away from Communion.

The substance of the conversation between the brethren and their choir helper is usually this: that they let him know how they stand with the Savior and whether they experience joy at the thought of joining the others for Communion. They then also talk to him about how things have gone since the last Communion in regard to the care of their souls, their bodies, their senses, and their members. If something has occurred that is not in accord with the brethren's love and Christ's intention, then it is reported. If someone has sinned and offended others, it cannot be ignored in the presence of the choir helper, but rather it must be further considered. For example, when the choir helpers' conferences are held after the Speakings with the brethren and sisters in all the choirs, the helper takes the opportunity to talk about the things that are too difficult for him to deal with alone and then, if deemed necessary, the matter is discussed in the elders' conference of the congregation, for it is there that it is announced how many brethren will be going to Communion and which brethren are unable to go this time or are not participating of their own accord. Incidentally, it is quite clear to everyone that anyone who is consciously living in the throes of the flesh should not be taking Communion, for example, in malice, envy, anger, argument, hatred, enmity, gluttony, drunkenness, injustice, deceit, greed, etc.

Whoever is damned by his own heart should not go to Communion without first admitting his sins and receiving a new assurance of the grace of God, for whoever puts himself above this and goes to Communion lightly, or merely out of habit, not only does not receive the blessing that goes with it, but will also be harmed.

The feeble, the weak, the small-minded hearts who still hang on the Savior should be comforted in a motherly way and given encouragement, for they are surely to be welcomed by the Savior, even if they approach Him trembling.

§ 19. If the choir helper determines that a brother who has been accepted into the congregation continues in a childlike fashion to walk in the grace that has been apportioned him, then he puts him forward as a candidate for Communion in the choir helpers' conference, and then in the elders' conference, but not before checking with his closest helper first. If he is approved for this, then he concerns himself more than before with his walk through life. He gives him the opportunity, if it has not happened already, to think thoroughly over his whole life and all the things he has done and left undone and takes the time, if he finds it a good thing, to write a narrative about this or to talk about it thoroughly. If a brother has been raised in the congregation and has never been to Communion, then the minister of the congregation gives him instruction in this. And when the time comes when he truly participates in Communion for the first time, then he is actually addressed beforehand by some members of the elders' conference, and the latter also occurs with a brother who has not been raised in the congregation.

Here we also want to add that when a brother has talked with his choir helper thoroughly about his walk through life thus far and the current state of his heart, then the choir helper accepts him into the single brethren's covenant. At this point he is assured that all that is past is cast off, forgiven, and forgotten, according to the words of the Holy Spirit: "If we confess our sins, he is faithful and just to forgive us our sins, and to cleanse us from all unrighteousness."[15] And he, in return, promises that he has given his heart over to the Savior completely and will guide himself in all things and in all his words, that he will allow himself to be led by the Holy Spirit and that he will keep his body and soul unstained for him. With this intention, the choir

---

15. I John 1:9 (KJV).

helper then washes his feet, and he is recommended to Jesus Christ for the future in a prayer of grace and preservation.[16]

§ 20.[17] At this point the choir helper must give the appropriate instruction to the brother who is to be accepted into the single brethren's covenant; to this end the following should be noted: he attempts to educate him in an understanding and way of thinking about human circumstances that is in accordance with God's word, which is all the more necessary with those who have already stained their soul with impure thoughts and fantasies that have come into the world through the temptation of sin. He gives him a definition of the difference between the two sexes according to the definition from the Bible: the Creator of all things made humans, and he made the man first and afterward the woman with his own hand, and this happened before the Fall. It is he who prepares us in the mother's womb and determines the organs of sexual difference. For this reason, the organs that are peculiar to each sex are actually not impure. Before the Fall, man and woman walked around naked; after the fall, however, God found it necessary to give the human race clothes to cover itself, and in accordance with this ordinance of God a loyal brother promises to keep his organs covered up day and night. He will also avert his gaze if the same of another person should be exposed to him, either of the male or female sex. The correct and honorable understanding of our human nature actually comes from the pious regard of Jesus and his humanity. From this, in his instruction, a choir helper also derives the respect that we should have for our own and another's soul and organs. In this, the brethren have the honor that Christ assumed the organs that are peculiar to the male sex. He suffered because of them and paid for his sin. He was circumcised on the eighth day and thereby spilled his first blood, just as he did his last drops on the stem of the cross, as a comfort for all his brethren who feel their damnation and sinfulness and take their refuge in Him and wish to be healed through His wounds. He also honored the female sex, in that he was conceived in the body of the Virgin Mary through the Holy Spirit and was carried for nine months in her womb and was born into the world through her

---

16. The following passage is deleted in the original: "In diesem Sinn werden ihm dann nicht nur seine Füße gewaschen, sondern er nimmt auch das heilige Abendmahl darauf-das ist dem Leib Christi, der für ihn in den Tod gegeben ist, und das Blut Christi, das für ihn zur Vergebung der Sünden vergossen worden." (In this same way, not only are his feet washed, but he then participates in Holy Communion, that is in the body of Christ, who gave Himself for him into death and the blood of Christ that was spilled for him for the forgiveness of sins.)

17. The handwriting at this point changes from Spangenberg's.

and nursed and was given sustenance at her breast. Whoever has come to Jesus in faith and has received forgiveness of his sins and is taught by the Holy Spirit to gaze into the mystery of the incarnation of Jesus receives a blessing, so that, in accordance with the strictures of the truth, his soul becomes pure and receives a godly understanding of human nature and its purpose.

§ 21. Furthermore, because a single brother also needs to know how to regard his body as something sacred and honorable and, on the one hand, should not live his life according to the law;[18] on the other hand, he should also not give way to the flesh but rather be preserved from the sin of self-abuse. Thus, the choir helper directs the interview also to these following points: God put a seed in the male sex that consists of the noblest juices of the body[19] and that matures in adults. This is destined for the holy purpose of a husband giving it to his wife, and God has thus formed the woman so that she receives this seed and thus becomes pregnant, carries a child in her womb, and brings this child into the world.

It can happen that brethren experience an irregular sensation in the organs that are peculiar to the male sex and that the organ becomes erect and makes cause for complaint and also that the seed that is in it occasionally leaves it during the day or night. What is a choir helper to say to this? In regard to the first matter, the following is to be noted: that such a thing can happen without cause from either the soul or the diet. The cause of this is often a sickliness in the body or, alternatively, if the body is too vigorous or strong. If the brother is not aware of any cause about which he should be ashamed before his Lord, then he should not dismiss it lightly but rather should commend himself with body and soul to the Savior. He should not try to rid himself of this alone, however, and even less should he attempt to rectify everything by touching his body with his hand. In both ways this sensation can become stronger. If, however, the heart and soul fix on another object and gaze at the crucified Savior in particular, then the stirrings (*Regungen*) dissipate by themselves.

It is another matter if similar sensations are caused by an irregular diet. Then a brother should think about the words of the Apostle Paul, "But put ye on the Lord Jesus Christ, and make not provision for the flesh, to fulfil the

---

18. Gal. 5:16–18 (KJV).

19. The reference to Aristotle's notion that semen is concentrated blood is from Aristotle and Peck, *Generation of Animals*. For a discussion of Aristotle and Galen, see Laqueur, *Making Sex*, 38–39; and Foxhall and Salmon, *Thinking Men*, 158.

lusts thereof."[20] He should examine himself to see whether or not he has enjoyed too much rich food or strong drink; whether or not he is working too little; sleeping too much; or, in any other way, is disorderly in his life. For exaggerated alertness can also cause such things. In this case, the choir helper must advise the brother to abstain from whatever is causing him this trouble; otherwise, not only does he make it harder for himself than he needs to, but it can also have other doleful consequences for his body and soul. Sirah says, "Pay attention to what is good for your body."[21] Some people cannot digest any milk products in the evening; with others, it's the coffee; others, wine or strong beer can have the effect of causing disorder in the body. Just as one can give no general rule in this matter, so also a brother cannot follow the example of another but must learn from experience what agrees with him and what doesn't. A choir helper must warn his brethren very carefully about brandy and other similar strong drinks and must take care that these do not find a way into the choir house. Other than this, such sensations arise if one does not keep one's soul pure and gives way to images and fantasies, or encourages them and in this does not listen to the reminders and punishments of the Holy Spirit.[22] Whosoever is aware of this should be afraid, should immediately turn his gaze to Jesus on the cross and seek forgiveness from Him and not call to Him until he is gazed on by Him anew and is comforted.

§ 22. Regarding the other matter, that is how a brother should view the fact that some of his male seed has left him in his sleep or when waking, and what a choir helper should say about this, all comes down to the following:

If such a thing has happened in his sleep, he should never frivolously ignore it but rather ask whether he could have allowed this to happen through some fault of his own. Maybe he did not take care of his soul when awake and allowed just one thought or desire to creep in, or he overburdened his body with food and drink and lived immodestly. If he finds something of this kind, then he should stand before the dear Savior in shame and ask for forgiveness and pray that He grant him new grace to preserve him. However, a brother may encounter this condition, especially in certain years, without being aware of a previous weakness or lack of discipline, either in his soul or in his diet. And it is right and proper that a choir helper takes heed of this, so that he does not cause undue fear in a brother because of his lack of experience.

---

20. Rom. 13:14 (KJV).

21. Sirah 37:30 (Apocrypha).

22. These passages belong squarely in the eighteenth-century debate on the dangers of masturbation; see Laqueur, *Solitary Sex*; Peucker, "Flames of Love"; and Peucker, *Time of Sifting*.

However, it is good if he advises him not to ignore this or to assume, because it has happened unintentionally, that he should not reflect further on it, because the heart can stray and one can become alienated from the Savior because of such an event. However, as experience shows, if during such an occurrence, a brother turns to the Savior as a sinner and sees it as a product of the Fall and draws near to the fount of the wounds of Jesus, then the Savior regards him with friendship, comforts and blesses him, and gives him an opportunity to renew his bond of grace with Him. According to the law of God in Israel, he to whom such a thing has happened must be considered unclean until the evening, when he must bathe himself in water and wash his clothes. Here, the New Testament gives us Jesus Christ, and His blood makes us pure from all sin. It can happen that brethren fall on the idea to petition the Savior that such a thing never happen again to them during sleep; others will doubt their witness to God, as long as this happens to them; others imagine that they have reached a higher degree of piety, if such a thing has not happened to them for a while. But these ideas have no foundation; in fact, they can pave the way to self-justification. And, in such cases, an understanding choir helper brings his brethren back to the free grace of the blood of Jesus.[23]

§ 23. A brother who has a loyal heart, who takes care of his soul, and who is modest in his diet will not lose much of his semen while awake. Occasionally, cases can arise where a choir helper need not conclude that there has been a conscious or intentional sin, at least not with those people who in their natural state have fallen into such outbursts of depravity that their tabernacle has been quite ruined. On occasion it may stem from an illness of the body where someone has brought an extraordinary physical frailty on themselves through a sharp shock or other causes. This happens frequently with failing patients. Also careless, hard riding can cause inexperienced brethren to have an unexpected ejaculation of semen. A brother, to whom something like this has happened, should speak as quickly as he can with his choir helper and the latter then helps him in two different ways: one, he comforts him and attempts to awaken in him childlike confidence in the Savior; he also might advise another brother to take on the services of a specific doctor; he might

---

23. It is significant that the instructions view nocturnal emissions of semen as something natural that allow the brother to see himself as human and in need of grace. Also, if a brother has not experienced them, this does not make him morally superior. This is in direct contrast to the contemporary arguments about nocturnal emissions, the economy of sperm, and the dangers of fantasy; see Laqueur, *Solitary Sex*.

show a third brother how to avoid the cause of such illicit sensations or pun-
ish him for his carelessness. And so on.

Whoever is attached to sinful fantasies or desires and undertakes to spill
his semen himself is doing the will of the flesh and serving sin, and the Holy
Spirit will abandon him. The choir helper must be quite firm with such a
person and may not admit him in this condition to Communion, until, after
thorough examination, he has seen that a true change of heart has taken
place and that he has sought anew forgiveness of his sins in the blood of Jesus
and has received grace and freedom from the same. The choir helper makes it
his special business to make a heart for the Savior even of this one, and, in his
treatment of him, watches carefully for the work of the Holy Spirit in him.
Whoever remains in the service of sin, however, and is its slave, can be
regarded as none other than a soul who has not turned to Christ, not to mention that through this he is ruining his health and himself and is thereby
falling into the most painful and filthy illness.[24]


§ 24.[25] One of the main things a choir helper must take note of and watch
out for in his choir is that the spirit of frankness is upheld and that the brethren do not lose heart and trust to tell him everything. This often happens if
he treats the brethren too harshly and takes things too much to heart that the
Savior does not see in the same way or when they see that he is treating them
with self-love and in a willful fashion or if he continues to deal with matters
even after they have been seriously punished in their hearts by the Savior.
During the Speaking before each Communion with each brother, he must
touch on the particular issue of how they are keeping their soul and body,
even if they do not do this of their own accord, and ask whether something
has occurred with them in this area. However, he must show himself to be
ready to hear each brother at any time if he has something to discuss or an
issue to raise with him, and he must treat each one according to the condition
of his heart. In particular, he should watch over those people who are still
ungrounded and therefore do not yet have clarity in their hearts, so that
impurities do not arise in the choir house through them. Whoever seduces
another person, whether man or woman, whether boy or grown man, to sin
in the flesh, whatever type of sin it might be, he is considered to be like a

---

24. The sin of Onan is described in Genesis 38:6–9. The sickness of "onanism" was almost an
obsession in the eighteenth century, the rise of which has been linked to the changing structures of
social groupings, the rise of print literature and the novel, and increased opportunities for solitude.
See Porter, *Disease*; Laqueur, *Solitary Sex*; and Richter, "Wet-Nursing."

25. Spangenberg's handwriting resumes here.

plague and cannot be tolerated in a choir. We have already been harmed through showing misplaced mercy toward seducers.[26] Oh, how a choir helper must watch out that such things do not creep in the dark into the choir; thus, it is also our rule that whoever detects such a thing in our choir house or in the congregation must not conceal it, so that he not make himself party to another's guilt; rather, he must report such a thing immediately, so that we may immediately impose a ban. Also, a choir helper should make himself acquainted with what is written about seduction in the Harmony of the Synods and communicate accordingly with the congregation helper.

§ 25. It is also the responsibility of the choir helper to see that his brethren receive a truly biblical account of holy matrimony, for this also plays a part in making and keeping their souls pure. The concept of marriage that they have formed before they came to the congregation, from what they have seen in the world, is usually not of the right kind and can become harmful. Therefore, a choir helper must correct this and, at the appropriate time, speak with each brother about this. He should say to his brethren that the sanctification of our bodies and souls is the will of God, and therefore all members of the congregation should keep their souls and vessels pure and unstained; that, just as in the single state, in the married state one must not serve the desires of the flesh but rather keep one's soul pure through the Holy Spirit; one's body should be a living, holy sacrifice that is pleasing to God and dedicated to Lord Christ; that married persons do everything they do in words or deeds in the name and presence of our Lord Jesus Christ. He should say that the married state is one that is created and blessed by the Lord himself and that in the New Testament it is seen as an image of Christ and his congregation; he should say that the sisters and brethren in the married persons' choir in the congregation take care of the business of the Lord with twice the diligence and loyalty, and care for their indebtedness to Him. When these ideas take root in the soul of a brother, then the other images that he may have received through the seduction of sin will fall away, and whenever he thinks of marriage it will be in no other way than in the sense of Christ. The choir helper will find it necessary to speak more specifically about this with some brethren, so that marital relations, on which God has laid His blessing and through which married persons can have children, is considered a respectable activity, which occurs with heartfelt prayer and in Christ's presence and without the

---

26. This line is a reference to the times that a "seducer" was found but not removed from the congregation. See Sommer, *Serving Two Masters*, chap. 3.

presence of anyone else,[27] between married persons who are children of God; and that all impure ideas which Satan has brought into the world and with which he has enchanted his slaves disappear with the people of the Savior; and the soul must be purified of these ideas. A choir helper must also know what his intention is in speaking with his brethren in respect of their person and rank. The main goal with each brother must be that he give himself over in spirit, soul, and body to belong without exception to the dear Savior. "I want only what Jesus, my Bridegroom, wants, I want to be clay in your hands, out of which you may form what you want to your praise." From this comes the second idea: "I want to become a complete person in God at that place, at which God has called me for His pleasure, and enjoy that which, as a single brother, He has won for me through His incarnation, through His meritorious life, through His position as a single brother, and through His martyrdom and death. I want to be like Him; I want my purpose to be like the purpose of the Lamb and so remain unspotted through His martyr's body, soul, and body and spirit on Earth." Oh, when this becomes reality in a single brother's heart, then a hundred and a thousand fantasies and fleeting thoughts disappear and he only looks to how he may please the Lord.

§ 26. Of great advantage to our single brethren is the matter of being pilgrims and militants (*Pilger- und Streitersache*) for Christ. If a brother in the congregation were to see no way before him by which he might serve the Savior and his neighbor, he might become disheartened, and it could arouse in him some vain thoughts about the future. But our choir houses are schools of the Holy Spirit in which He (the Spirit) wishes to prepare the brethren for all sorts of things in His blessed congregations. We have the Savior to thank for giving us such opportunities to use brethren in His service, and he gives the brethren the willingness and encourages them to risk their body and life in the service of the Savior. The most important works of the Lord, among the Greenlanders and the Negroes, among the Indians in North and South America, among the Eskimos, the Lapps, etc., were begun by the single brethren. A choir helper should acquaint himself with this from the *History of the Brethren*;[28] also, he should command each and every brother to appreciate and use the grace that he has experienced to awaken and renew a sinner's

---

27. Spangenberg stresses this absence because of earlier accusations in the anti-Zinzendorfiana that marital relations were performed in the presence of others during the Time of Sifting. Fogleman has most recently used these anti-Zinzendorfian writings in his books *Jesus Is Female* (2007) and *Two Troubled Souls* (2014).

28. Cranz, *Brüder-Historie*.

sense of witness among his brethren. Because, before one looks too far, if this is missing, there will then be a large number of unhappy people who hardly know why they are in the congregation, and so the Savior's great purpose with the people of the brethren, especially with the single brethren, will not be achieved. Just as the elders' conferences in the congregations have to consider what the calling (*Destination*) of each brother is and take to heart the thought of Jesus's peace to help him achieve this, so it is also the duty of the choir helper to be attentive to this matter and to reflect on it, to talk to the Savior about it, and also to put forward ideas and suggestions in the elders' and choir helpers' conferences. This is true for the employment of a brother in the matter of the witnesses and pilgrims (of Christ), his employment in the single brethren's choir, and among the boys and children in the congregation, as well as in the change of choir through marriage or any other kind of change. It is definitely a good thing if a brother is so well prepared in the school of the Holy Spirit in the single brethren's choir that one can think with joy at his marriage, that this is not delayed because of one thing or another but that this is proposed by the wardens of the congregation at the appropriate time and before his own heart and soul think of it and he allows himself unnecessary thoughts, but rather, childlike, he receives it from the hand of the Savior.

§ 27. What then should a choir helper do, when a brother shows signs that he is thinking of marriage and perceives a desire for this within himself? Then he [the choir helper] must take great care that he not be ashamed of his [the brother's] trust and openheartedness but rather he should listen to him fully and give him such information as befits his knowledge of the brother and as is useful. If it is an idle thought (as often happens with people who still lack the true heart and connection with the Savior when they have just arrived in the congregation and often think this way because of false carnal notions gained from the world), then the choir helper takes care to speak to him intimately about the condition of his heart and his other circumstances. If things do not look good in his heart, then he [the choir helper] asks him to become better acquainted first with himself and the Savior before he thinks of marriage and rid himself of everything in him the Savior would not find pleasing. If his circumstances are such that he possesses neither the understanding nor the gift nor the talent to guide and feed a wife and children then he [the choir helper] attempts to make this clear to him in concrete terms. It is a good thing if he allows himself to be spoken to and accepts this advice, and the choir helper checks on him from time to time to see whether he is continuing in his childlike dependence on the Savior. If he learns that thoughts of marriage are not so easily lifted from the brother, then he speaks about this with the congregation helper; at this point, they bring the matter to the elders' conference, according to the nature of circumstances for further consideration. The same occurs if the choir helper himself thinks that a brother should be suggested for marriage.

§ 28. If there are no concerns about the marriage of a brother, but rather circumstances reveal that this is actually advisable and practical, then, in the choir helpers' conference, sisters are considered who might suit him and his circumstances. The matter is then resolved in the elders' conference in the usual way in the congregation, if it does not concern those people, about whom, according to the rules of the synod, one must first speak with the U.A.C.[29] The proposal then usually occurs through the choir helper but also, depending on circumstances, through the choir helper and minister together. However, at this juncture we must remind our choir helpers that they must, on an appropriate occasion, speak with a brother who might be proposed for marriage or who is thinking of it himself about how marriage is conducted in the congregation. As marriage is one of the main events in a person's life on which, to a great extent, the future well-being or woe of a brother depends, it is one of our fundamental tenets that no marriage should take place in the congregation without being assured of the will of our dear Lord. Thus, when a brother is to be married, sisters who suit his inner and outer circumstances are considered carefully in the choir helpers' conference. When such a person is found, questions are then asked in the elders' conference whether the Savior approves that we should suggest that this brother marry this sister. No sister is proposed for a brother unless we have the Savior's approval.[30]

§ 29. In this matter, two points must also be remembered:

(1)  The choir helper should tactfully ask the brother whose marriage is being proposed whether he has someone in mind himself, before he inquires about a sister in the elders' conference. If this is the case, then the choir helper brings this suggestion to the choir helpers' and elders' conferences that the latter may consider whether this is a suitable person for him and also so that the opinion of the Savior can be sought out. If he does not name any sister, then the elders' conference acts as outlined earlier.

(2)  Not only when a proposal is made, but even beforehand (whether or not it is to be repeated), a choir helper should make it quite clear to his brethren

---

29. "U.A.C." stands for Unity Elders' Conference.

30. The Savior's approval is determined through the lot (see the introduction to this volume).

that the lot (without which we can neither intend nor propose any brother or sister for marriage) does not require any brother or sister to accept the proposal or say "yes," but rather each brother and sister can speak their mind if they have thoughts about a person proposed to them, and, on the part of the laborers, no one would take this amiss. But they should talk to the Savior about this and ask to be granted clarity so that it does not occur to them after the event that they acted precipitously and did not follow the workings of the Holy Spirit in their hearts.

If the marriage of such a brother comes to pass through the consent of both parties, then the choir helper of the single brethren should not think that he has nothing more to do because the brother is leaving his choir; rather, especially during the time of his engagement, he remains an object of his prayer as well as his attention, and he should talk with him diligently, so that he enters into his new state with the right ideas, and the blessing that the Savior has devised for him will become his own completely. He gives him the loyal advice to carry himself outwardly in his future state in the manner of the congregation, that is, in the manner of a pilgrim, so that he does not put obstacles in his own way that could hinder him in being ready for the will of the Savior.

With this change in choir, the choir helper especially tries to renew in the brother the covenant he has made to live not according to his own wishes but according to those of the Savior and also in marriage to keep his soul and body unspotted. He has a good opportunity for this when he again speaks with him straightforwardly and from the heart about the matter that was previously mentioned—about marriage, which also has the advantage that he retains a blessed impression of his previous choir and keeps it in the same grace and blessing. The choir helper also offers him the foot washing (*Pedilavium*) after his thorough and heartfelt talk about his walk in the choir to date, so that he can end his walk in this choir with the blessed assurance of the Savior's forgiveness of everything that was not in accordance with His purpose. Finally, the choir helper also suggests that the brother maintain his love to his previous choir and be accompanied by its blessing. Therefore, he is also commended to the choir in thought and prayer before the marriage.

§ 30. However, because there are occasionally people in the choirs either who do not have it in their hearts to turn completely to the Savior or who through the deceit of sin have fallen away from the Savior and into the senses of the flesh, and to whom the thought of marriage occurs for impure and improper reasons, the choir helper must know how he is to behave with such people. He must first attempt to rectify their false ideas, to show them clearly the purpose of the Savior and his congregation in the matter of marriage, and to alert them to the true condition of their hearts in love, and praise God, who has brought forth in many such people the blessed truth that they have turned to the Savior and have still become blessed people of God. That is why a choir helper should not lose faith immediately, when such people pour out their hearts to him, but rather he should treat them with love and sympathy. However, should one of those, about whom one cannot consider marriage in the congregation because of his heart or other circumstances, go so far as to insist on getting married, then he [the choir helper] must declare to him that we cannot forbid him or anyone else from marrying, but that in the congrega- tion no one can be married except according to the rules given by the Lord, but everyone is free to leave the congregation and to get married themselves elsewhere. At this point, however, he should be asked to think clearly about what he is doing and to imagine how easily he could make himself unhappy both in this world and in eternity and could place himself in circumstances that after the fact he could not correct, an occurrence of which we have many sad examples.

§ 31. The choir helper must have periodic discussions with his brethren on another issue, namely, how they should act in their social intercourse with the female sex. A single brother should carry himself with modesty and respect in the presence of all sisters, and actually any woman. On the one hand, he should not act in an affected, shy, or fearful manner, whenever he should or must speak with them; on the other hand, he should not enter into a familiar and intimate discourse with them but rather hold true personally to the established segregation in the congregation. It is therefore a general rule for our single brethren not to accept any intimate confessions of the heart from a woman, nor offer any themselves. A single brother should have love and respect for all the sisters' choirs, but he should keep his eyes and senses away from making any one or the other person the object of his atten- tion, so that he is then led into false thoughts and fantasies that might harm his soul. A single brother, who inclines toward conversation with the sisters, or looks toward them, will feel punishment in his heart immediately (if the Holy Spirit does not withdraw because left unheeded), and if he does not follow this reminder, then it is a sign that his heart is not true and he is in danger of losing his soul.

§ 32. The duties of the choir helper also include bringing the brethren in the choir into intimate intercourse with one another. Whenever intimate friends come together, they like to talk about themselves the most, and if that does not happen, they may think that they have not seen each other. Shouldn't it be the same way among brethren who belong to a choir? Whenever a visit is arranged in a choir so that either the one brother is visiting the other or vice versa, or he is spread between many brethren, this helps a great deal in the brethren getting to know one another and becoming more intimate. Meanwhile, the confessions of past and present sins should not become the stuff of conversation among the brethren, for we know from experience that harm can come from this. Such *special* confessions belong to the choir helper, and he must go to the grave with them, unless others were involved with the bad things, such as with seductions, for example. In this case, however, he tells the brother who is confessing to him that he must not keep such things quiet but rather, for the sake of his conscience, must question further. However, he, the choir helper, must not force a confession but rather must wait for it. If someone has a thorn in his foot, and he is crying out in pain, he will gladly allow it to be pulled out. However, if he has a secret wound that he does not really want to expose and someone rips open his clothes, he will become angry and will not allow himself to be bandaged.

§ 33. A choir helper should make a clear distinction between mistakes and misdeeds and real lapses of loyalty. Loyal hearts always want to be a joy to the Savior, and if something occurs through weakness that they believe might not be a joy to the Lord, then they complain about this from the heart. A disloyal heart knows that it should do this and that, and not do other things. However, it can desire this or that bad thing and has no desire for this or that good thing and thus acts against its better judgment and then develops a bad conscience. It is as clear as day that one needs to deal with the former very differently from the latter. Three things are as bad as the worm that lies at the root of the tree and gnaws at it, and a choir helper must watch for these things so much more vigilantly, as they are generally not held to be as dangerous as those things that are not only no good in themselves but that also pull many other bad things along with them. The first thing is curiosity (*Vorwitz*), the second thing is frivolity/carelessness (*Leichtsinn*), and the third is freethinking (*Freidenken*).

Whenever one has a desire to know things, to see things, or to hear or experience things, which at that time one should not know, hear, see, or experience, then that is what one calls curiosity. This already reveals itself in children, and some parents are so stupid (*thum*) that they are happy when their children ask such curious questions, because they think it comes from the fact that they have such a good mind. If the children grow up this way and do not regard curiosity as something bad, as something one complains to the Savior about and asks him to deliver us from, then it becomes stronger and stronger, and it can go so far that it becomes a passion. We can defend ourselves against thinking about certain things that we would like to know: we get up with them and we go to bed with them, yet they keep coming into our minds. We then turn to reading all kinds of books to satisfy our curiosity, but we get ourselves ever deeper in. This is quite in opposition to simplicity and can incur damage to our souls and those of others. Therefore, one must severely warn those in whom one notices these things. They must, with Christ's power, kill curiosity, which is a fruit of the flesh and not of the spirit, just like other evil desires.

Whenever we speak of frivolity, we understand by this the manner of a person who does not take most things seriously but rather simply thinks, speaks, and acts. Specifically, this person uses all kinds of witty and satirical expressions and witticisms with others, with which he pleases himself and makes others laugh, and in the things he does and does not do, certain matters soon appear that are not appropriate for a child of God. From such frivolity many sinful things can flow with which one can harm oneself and others. If a choir helper notices such frivolity in someone, then he shows him the right way and takes care that others are not affected by it.

Freethinking, discussed here, is when people allow themselves to use reason when thinking about Jesus and his disciples. If, for example, the Savior says that no sparrow falls on the ground without its being the Father's will, etc.; or where two or three are gathered together in my name then I am among them; or, love your enemies, bless also those who curse you; or, pray also for those who injure you and persecute you, and whatever other words there are; then these are words that are true because He said them, and whatever He ordered is good because He deemed it so. Now if someone has doubts about the words of Jesus and is attached to these doubts, he is on a dangerous path and is harmful to the others if he teaches them his reasoning (*Raisonnements*). A choir helper must guard against these things and show these people the danger in which they stand. Books that lead to such things are like the plague.

§ 34. The choir helper of the single brethren also has the responsibility over the young men, boys, and young boys, and for this a quite special gift is needed. For every age has its own particular nature, to which one has to learn to adapt. In everything it is most important, however, that one wins their love and trust, and God can bestow this on him who commends himself to Him in a childlike fashion. Once one has their love and trust, one can expect them to be open and upright and allow themselves to be spoken to and guided. The young boys have their own visitors (*Besucher*) and their own special care. The choir helper of the single brethren takes care to get to know them and speaks to them before they have their prostration (*Anbeten*). We try to keep the young men and older boys under good supervision and employ brethren who have the grace and gift for their improvement to be with them. There are also assistants in their choir who take special care of them, and this work is entrusted to these people not without the recommendation of the Savior. But from time to time, the choir helper of the single brethren speaks to the whole young men's and boys' choir, person for person, and at another time at least to those who go to Communion or who are put forward to be accepted into the congregation or who are among the candidates for Holy Communion. He also diligently holds conferences with their parents and masters and also with the brethren who watch over them, not just those in their rooms (*Stubenwächter*) but also when they go out. He also talks in depth with the assistants in the choir and the brethren with whom they spend time or who are their visitors, and wherever we might fear a temptation, we carefully follow up on it so that it might be squashed at the very outset.

Classes in the teachings of the Gospel according to the holy scriptures must not stop with the young men and boys, and we must take great care to see what good use and blessing comes from this. They must always be reminded to practice reading, writing, and arithmetic and everything they have learned in school, so that they don't forget these things but rather progress in them. We also can identify desires to witness (*Zeugentriebe*),[31] and one would do well not to belittle these, but no young man or boy should think that he should not exert himself in his craft or whatever other skill he is learning because one day he will go among the heathen. For whoever is not true to the small task to which he has been assigned now will not easily become a true warden of Jesus.

§ 35. To celebrate the renewal of the covenant (*Bund*) of the single brethren, their choir helper holds a special meeting, which one calls the quarter hour for the renewal of the choir covenant. Here he speaks about the true purpose of a brother being not to live for himself, nor to do the will of his flesh, nor to make reason his guide, but rather to live for the Lord, to be a joy

---

31. *Zeugentriebe*, best translated as "desire to witness," occurs frequently in the early hymns and sermons to the young men and boys. See, for example, "Vertilge meinen verderbens-wust, bilde mich nach deiner herzens-lust, füll mein ganzes herze mit deiner liebe, erhalt mich beständig im zeugentriebe, öfne den mund." Steinhofer, *Evangelisches Gesang-Buch*, hymn 732.

to Him only, to live according to His word in all things, and to allow himself to be led like a child by his Holy Spirit; the same is spoken about the holy care of the soul and body and all of this because He died for us and spilled His blood for the forgiveness of our sins. If he considers this point alone, namely, the care of the body and its members, then he can awaken people who think themselves complete brethren because they are obedient in this point, whereas in other things, which belong to a well-fashioned being in Jesus Christ, they lag far behind.

The love feasts (*Agapen*) with the whole choir, or with a part of the same, are a wonderful opportunity for fresh encouragement, and a choir helper must have it in his heart that they may always be a blessing through the grace of God. It has quite often happened that a brother whom one has embraced in a heartfelt manner at a love feast has suddenly entered onto the path that had long been wished for and worked on in vain.

§ 36. If there are sick men in the choir, then the choir helper must inquire in detail about their internal and external well-being from day to day and communicate about them with the doctor (*Medico*). When dealing with natural illnesses (*natürlichen Krankheiten*), not only are medicines important, but also a good diet and proper care and attention do the most good. For this reason he must be especially concerned with the proper attention and care of the sick men and the supply of the sickroom.

Circumstances can also arise that one could call illnesses that teach us a lesson (*Zuchtkrankheiten*).[32] If someone hides something in his heart that causes him pain and disquiet, this will also weaken him physically. Here the scriptures say, confess your sins to one another and pray for one another so that you will be well. Medicine does not help in this case, as we know from much experience. If a brother can just find his heart and decide to speak it with words, then soon he is helped. Those in whom one can see the peace of God and the joy of the Lord clearly will carry no trace of such moral illnesses. However, where disquiet in the heart and soul, a low-spirited heart, an unfeeling being, an unsinner-like carriage have the upper hand with a brother, one fears that there is a moral illness; there one sees it, and so we wait for the hour at which the Lord will reach His purpose with him. In the meantime, there occurs a disturbance of the senses because the thing that has caused the illness is exposed to the light of day.

---

32. "Zuchtkrankheit" can be understood as an illness that God has given to individuals to teach them the error of their ways, so that they may come to repentance. It could also be understood as an illness that has come about as the result of a sinful situation.

If one suspects the impending home going (*Heimgang*) of a brother, then the choir helper blesses him and does not wait until the brother is so weak that he does not know what is going on. During the blessing, the choir helper must really believe that the sick man will soon go to his eternal rest, otherwise it would be an abuse of the name of God, or else he must use it with fitting words or verses merely as a faithful prayer for the sick man in view of his passing over into eternity.

§ 37. If one takes all this together, all that is expected of a choir helper in the preceding sections, one can clearly see how important such a position is. If someone dared to fill this position using only his own powers of reason and his previous experience without turning to Christ and seeking grace and help and support from Him, then he would fare badly. However, whoever throws himself at the feet of the Savior, feeling his own unworthiness and incapacity, and holds to Him in faith and gladly hears the advice of his other brethren, he will also receive the necessary grace and gifts from Him and not be shamed.

# 3

## THE MARRIED PERSONS' CHOIR

Introduction

The "Instructions for the Choir Helpers of the Married Persons" cover a whole range of topics and open up the private world of Moravian marriage to the reader.[1] Topics covered include first and foremost the difficulty of the job of married persons' choir helper. The position was always filled by a married couple, usually the minister and his wife, and these two people had the task of acquiring access to the domestic realm of the married couples and families who did not live in choir houses at this point but rather were householders in the congregation.[2] The instructions also provide insight into the way in which a married couple were to engage in intimate relations, nurse their babies, raise their children, deal with their servants, and conduct their marriage. This oversight of the domestic realm was one of the hardest parts of Moravian religious life to oversee and eventually caused the biggest problems with the married householders.

Of course, the Moravian Church was by no means the only religious group that attempted to regulate the domestic life of husband and wife. As Isabel Hull has shown in her investigation of sexuality, law, and the church in the German states of the long eighteenth century, the Protestant Reformation had brought with it a thorough revalorization of married life: "the reformers revalued marriage as the moral crucible tempering human (sexual) nature into godliness and civic responsibility." Understanding marriage as both a microcosm of the ordered state power, in which the husband acts as religious,

---

1. A version of this introduction has appeared in Faull, "Married Choir Instructions."
2. See Smaby, *Transformation*.

*Fig. 6*   August
Spangenberg, by
Johann Valentin Haidt
(1700–1780). Courtesy
of the Moravian
Archives, Bethlehem,
Pennsylvania.

social, and fiscal authority over the wife, children, and wardens, Hull argues
that the positive revalorization of sexuality within that social unit reinforced
the idea that "the capacity for sexual joy was a sign of [God's] goodness and
infinite sweetness (Calvin)." This then promoted marriage and marital acts
into a sphere of "(heterosexual, that is, socially relevant) relational ones, from
the errors of desire and intention to actual public or socially relevant acts."[3]

In addition to this confluence of public and private, British historian
Lyndal Roper has investigated how to reconcile sexuality with "holiness" in
the utopian moments of the Anabaptist and Pietist reformation. Roper
argues for an understanding of sexuality in Pietism as "deriving from a
physical theology in which the body was saturated in moral and religious
significance." To resolve the opposition that had been constructed in the
Catholic Church between the body and the holy, between the sense and the
spirit, some reformers, Anabaptists and Pietists, preferred to "spiritualize
the sexual" within marriage and make the body a gateway for the divine. This
"physical theology" pervades the eighteenth-century Moravian Church, espe-

3. Hull, *Civil Society in Germany*, 17, 20, 21.

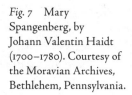

*Fig. 7*   Mary
Spangenberg, by
Johann Valentin Haidt
(1700–1780). Courtesy of
the Moravian Archives,
Bethlehem, Pennsylvania.

cially in Zinzendorf's redefinition of the body and sexuality. Indeed, the practice of the Speakings itself demonstrates such a reformulation of "the place of the body and sexuality in relation to the holy, by purifying marriage of sin and creating a morally perfect relationship."[4]

The promotion of marriage within the post-Zinzendorfian eighteenth century, as revealed in the principia and the instructions, can be read against this larger contextualizing background. The Catholic Church and the more radical Protestant religious groups, such as the Ephrata Cloister or the Shakers, considered human sexuality, as practiced both outside and within marriage, to be a carnal pollution of the divine spirit (Spangenberg himself thought this before he joined the Moravians and Zinzendorf persuaded him otherwise). However, as Roeber has pointed out, the mainstream Lutheran, Anglican, and Dissenting churches in the late seventeenth and eighteenth centuries in Europe and North America recognized the natural sexual drives of human beings as a sign of God's blessing and joy in creation, frequently representing the union with Christ in terms of sexual union through the metaphor of the "mystical marriage."[5]

4. Roper, "Sexual Utopianism," 397, 403, 407.
5. See Roeber, *Hopes for Better Spouses.*

As we have seen in the "Instructions for the Choir Helpers of the Single Brethren," the Moravians were no strangers to the use of the language and imagery of bridal mysticism.[6] What is interesting within the instructions, though, is an awareness of the legacy of Zinzendorfian theology and metaphorical language that so powerfully dominated the lived faith of Moravians in the first half of the eighteenth century. The "Instructions for the Choir Helpers of the Married Persons," like those to the single brethren, retain the notion of Christ as the Bridegroom of the church; however, the most important legacy of Zinzendorf in these texts is the positive valorization of human sexuality.

In a letter accompanying the "Instructions for the Choir Helpers of the Married Persons" distributed to the North American congregations in 1785, the authors and representatives of the Unity Elders' Conference expressed their firm belief that the spiritual health of the Moravian Church in general depended on the spiritual health of the married persons' choir.

> That a congregation can be harmed overall and in all of its departments if things are not well in the married persons' choir has been frequently proven by experience. However, if there is a blessed course in the married persons' choir and the married people reveal themselves in all matters to be wardens and maids of Jesus who direct themselves in their conduct according to God's word and allow themselves to be taught, guided, and governed by the Holy Spirit, then this has an effect on all the choirs; their example brings with it utility and blessing, and by this means the Savior is honored.[7]

The healthy conduct of marriage, according to the principles and concepts of the church, was clearly considered to be crucial to the health of the whole congregation. This same letter, signed by Bishop Spangenberg, Johann Friedrich Koeber, and Johann Friedrich Reichel, alludes to the problems that had arisen in the Moravian Church, when helpers to the married persons' choir had not followed uniform ideas about marriage, especially in the conduct of the monthly Speakings—hence the perceived need for a clear, detailed,

---

6. See, inter alia, Vogt, "*Ehereligion*"; Vogt, "Seventeen Points of Matrimony"; and Faull, "Temporal Men," in Faull, *Masculinity, Senses, Spirit*, 55–80.

7. "Daß eine Gemeine überhaupt, und in allen ihren Abtheilungen, Schaden davon habe, wenn es in dem Ehe Chor nicht gut geht; solches hat die Erfahrung vielfältig gelehrt. Wenn dagegen im Ehe Chor ein seliger Gang ist, und die Eheleute in allen Stücken sich beweisen als Knechte und Mägde Jesu, die sich in ihrem Wandel nach Gottes Worte richten und von dem seligen Geiste sich lehren, leiten und regieren lassen, so hat das einen Einfluß auf alle Chöre, ihr Exempel schafft Nutzen und Segen, und der Heiland hat Ehre davon." Unity Elders' Conference, "Letter to the Holders."

lengthy essay about marriage that expanded on the principia, which had already been drawn up after the 1775 Barby synod.

The earlier "Principia of the Married Persons' Choir" outlined in twenty-nine sections the understanding of the theology of marriage in the Moravian Church. Rather than viewing sex as a consequence of Adam's sin in Eden, Moravians taught that marriage was instituted before the Fall. As such, it has been blessed by God as the unity of not only heart and soul but also flesh; it is a mirror of the relationship between Christ and his church; and its status should be respected both by those exterior to it and also by the parties involved in it. Marital union is a "liturgical action" (*liturgische Handlung*), that is, a matter that God himself has ordained and whose peace and proximity are to be felt each time it is performed by a man and a woman.

A woman's pregnancy should be a blessed time that reminds both her and her husband that God himself in His incarnate form lay beneath the bosom of a woman. In section 23 of the principia the importance of the "godly conduct" of all "Hausväter und Hausmütter" before their children, wardens, and others in their vicinity is underscored: Moravian marriage must be conducted in an "evangelical" fashion. And to this end, to advise the married couples on how this is to be achieved, the instructions were composed; they constitute far more detailed and discursive guidelines to the helpers of the married persons' choir on how to interact with the married brethren and sisters in their care.

As outlined in the introduction, Bishop Spangenberg, in consultation with the other members of the Unity Elders' Conference, drew up the "Instructions for the Choir Helpers of the Married Persons." These instructions are different from the instructions to other choir helpers in that they were to be read by both the husband and wife in the office of choir helper, usually the minister and his wife. Whereas the instructions for the single brethren, single sisters, and widows were only read by one person, the specific choir helper, these instructions reflect the fact that the intended audience is both male and female. It is also likely that Spangenberg consulted his wife, Martha, in the composition of these instructions; the sections in the married persons' choir instructions that discuss pregnancy, childbirth, breast-feeding, and the woman's experience of the first marital union indicate her involvement.

The main theological thrust of the instructions (as the authors themselves argue) comes from Zinzendorf's sermons, delivered in Herrnhaag and Marienborn between 1744 and 1747, which constitute the fundamental expression of Zinzendorf's thoughts on the role of men and women in a Moravian marriage. The married persons' choir was not to be considered in any way a lesser order in the Moravian Church than those of the single sisters and single brethren (in contrast, for example, to the householders in the Ephrata Cloister).[8] On the contrary, Zinzendorf understood marriage to be a service to the church and Christ and therefore defined marriage as a positive (and, for the right brother and sister, a necessary) step in a man's or woman's life. His notion of the "marriage militant," or *Streiterehe*, meant that married women, who did not remain in the town congregation, gave up their children to the nursery as soon as they were weaned so that they could devote all their energies to working with their husband for the church as missionaries or on farms or in trades for the community. The elders decided where the married couple should fulfill their *Plan* and sometimes moved the couple from place to place as they saw fit.

When Bethlehem was first organized into choirs in June 1742, the married people were the cornerstone of both the house congregation (eleven couples) and the pilgrim congregation (four couples). The idea of the marriage militant was carried so far that, in the early years of the settlement, married men and women did not live together in Bethlehem but rather lived with other married men or women in their separate choirs. Attempts were made to ensure that the married couples were able to meet in private once a week. With the dissolution of the General Economy the married couples lived together in their own households.[9]

With the move to householder status, the ability of the choir helpers and the congregation elders to pattern the life of the married couple after the model of Christ and his church was made far more complex. As mentioned earlier in relation to the principia, a marriage consisted of far more than the relationship between a man and a woman. It was a "household economy" that contained within it the children and wardens that helped to run the small farm, the trade shop, perhaps the mill. As a historian of gender, Karin Hausen has pointed out in her research on changing gender roles within family life in early modern Europe that the role of men and women within this economy was clearly prescribed by the needs of the household.[10] And for the elders of the Moravian Church, those needs had to be congruent with those of the church.

The sacralization of "marital union" was both a liberating feature of Moravian eighteenth-century theology and a point of contention.[11] The frankness

---

8. For a discussion of the dispute between the leaders of the Ephrata Cloister and Zinzendorf, see Riley, "Analysis of the Debate"; and Vogt, "*Ehereligion*." For a more general overview of Zinzendorf's position among the Pennsylvania Lutherans, see Vogt, "Pennsylvanischen Synoden"; and Faull, "Temporal Men," in Faull, *Masculinity, Senses, Spirit*, 55–80.

9. For a book-length study of this transition, see Smaby, *Transformation*.

10. Hausen, "Polarisierung," in Conze, *Sozialgeschichte der Familie*, 363–93.

11. See Vogt, "Seventeen Points of Matrimony"; and Peucker, "Blue Cabinet."

and simplicity with which the practice of marital relations is described is quite surprising. For example, in one English-language manuscript in the married persons' choir materials in the Bethlehem archives, the following paragraph can be found:

> The most convenient position for the performance of it [the marriage union] for the wife is to lay down on her back having the middle part of her body raised by a pillow, covered with a double sheet or blanket, spreading her legs so as to make room for the husband to kneel between them and in this position to admit the virile member or genital of the husband into her matrix or opening of the Mother, in which she is to assist by applying her hand to the said member of the husband which is then in an erect state, and directing the same into the virgin-aperture or Mother. This is often in the beginning painful for both and especially for the wife, when it is performed the *first time* and both must use patience; and with tenderness endeavor to assist one another till the proper art of generation can be accomplished by the wife's receiving the manly or generating seed into the inner part of the mother.[12]

However, the very combination of the public and the private as it pertained to the most intimate moments between husband and wife proved also to be the most fraught for the Moravian Church. Attacked from the outside for what seemed to be licentious voyeurism, and from within the church for the intrusion into the private realm of the marital bed, the instructions for Moravian marriage are an important document in the history of sexuality and gender. They reveal a combination of both Zinzendorf's understanding of marriage dating back to the 1740s and Spangenberg's integration of that understanding into the practical running of late eighteenth-century family life.

The instructions are divided into forty-five sections. As with the single sisters' instructions, the first section recounts the history of the choir and its roots in the very beginnings of the Renewed Church in 1722. As the refugees arrived in Berthelsdorf, the institution of marriage was itself a point of concern: some of those already married were worried about their spiritual state and decided to live together no longer as husband and wife but rather as brother and sister. Only after the choir helpers had spoken to each member of the married persons' choir individually did the married couples come to a "true," that is, sacralized, notion of marriage. And this is indeed the justifica-

---

12. Untitled manuscript, MAB. In this description there is no mention of the "sitting method" that is described in the instructions in § 34.

tion for the existence of the choir and for the instructions themselves. It was considered such a difficult task that Zinzendorf himself was the first married persons' choir helper, speaking with each of the married men and a married sister (not his wife) speaking with the married women.

The first ten sections address the origin of the choir, its principles, the difficulties associated with working with married persons' choir members who now can live in households outside the settlement congregations (*Ortsgemeine*), the relationship of the choir helpers within the hierarchy of the church, and the administration of the Speaking and the relation of the memoir (*Lebenslauf*) to the choir helpers.

Sections 11–12 are concerned with ensuring that the married couples love each other and that when there are disagreements between them, the choir helpers have a clearly delineated procedure to follow that prevents the women from aligning themselves against the men. Sections 13–14 address the kinds of questions that should be asked about how the children are being brought up and also how single brethren and single sisters who might be employed in the household are treated. Sections 15–17 again address matters of administration and structure within the choir and the role of any assistants who might work in larger choirs.

Only with section 18 do we come to the thorny topic of marital relations. The Moravian interpretation of marriage is supported by copious references to the Bible and also to Spangenberg's *Idea Fidei Fratrum*. Not all quotations from the Bible are still applicable, however, Spangenberg argues. Some are considered to be particular to Old Testament culture. The nature of marriage is not one that was disapproved of by Christ, argues section 21. And, interestingly, marital separation (*Scheiden*) also exists to protect the well-being of the women.

So how do Moravian brethren and sisters get married? Sections 22–30 address the mechanism of proposal, betrothal, wedding, and consecration of the couple. And once all this is over, the question remains (especially if they don't know each other), how do they grow to love each other?

Sections 31–35 address this. The difficulty of regulating sexuality within the choir is reflected in the amount of text in the instructions devoted to marital relations. Here are the passages that describe in detail how the marriage is consummated, which position the couple might prefer, how the choir helpers prepare the marital bedroom with a chair and towel for the sitting position or a pillow for the recumbent position. Then they are left alone. If the marriage cannot be consummated at that time, then the husband gives his wife a blessing. If the wife experiences pain the first time, then the husband is supposed to stop intercourse and the couple can try again another time. In the morning they have breakfast with the choir helpers and report individually on the success or failure of the wedding night. Married couples were supposed to refrain from public shows of affection and also were to be careful not to engage in marital relations where they might be watched by anyone else (especially their children).

The involvement of the choir helpers in the consummation of the marriage on the wedding night was justified by explaining that this is the way that the marriage can be sanctified and not belong to the "pagan" way of doing things. But both the eighteenth-century contemporaries of the Moravians and scholars since have made much of this marital counseling among the Moravians. Spangenberg was well aware of the scandal this might bring to the church, even in the 1780s.

Sections 36–37 discuss the frequency of intercourse and its important role in the maintenance of a healthy and loving relationship between the husband and wife. Usually, once a week is sufficient, but the couple can engage in marital relations more frequently if necessary for the health of the marriage. Also, the couple should abstain from sexual intercourse when the wife is menstruating, when the couple is feeling distant from God, and on Communion Day, since they should be focusing on that sacrament rather than the marriage sacrament.

Sections 39–40 discuss pregnancy and childbirth, followed by instructions on breast feeding and when to resume marital relations (§§ 41–42). This was a very contentious issue within Moravian congregations, especially within the missions, where other cultural norms held sway. And, indeed, as mentioned in the introduction, a whole separate set of instructions was drawn up for helpers of the married persons' choir in the mission, with the overriding concern that rules not be put in place that would cause the otherwise God-loving couple to sin.[13]

The instructions end with a warning that this is all to be kept very confidential, and the choir helpers may not talk to anyone outside the choir or the church about the content of this document. Once they leave the choir they must pass it on to their successors, which might well explain why this 1786 document is difficult to find in all archives of the Moravian Church.

The relationship that Moravians had to their choir helpers, although difficult, was quite unique. It was difficult, in that husband and wife were discussing the most intimate part of their marriage with someone outside it, but also perhaps positively unique in that the choir helper was a bosom friend

---

13. The "Instructions to the Choir Helpers of the Married Persons in Heathen Places" has not been included in this volume, as it is the subject of future work by the author.

with whom one could be more intimate than with a parent. Also unique is the fact that married women were choir helpers. Women spoke with women about the work of raising a family, whether it was about how long to nurse newborns, how to enforce discipline, or how often to have sexual relations with the husband.

§ 1. The reason that we in the Moravian Church concern ourselves with the condition of married persons stems from the time when the Herrnhut congregation was still young. At that time there were many pious people who had issues with the married state and even thought that true children of God should not marry.[1] And if they were already married they thought that they should live together as brother and sister and not as a married couple, and our brethren even came into contact with such people. Many of the brethren who had lived in the married state before they came to Herrnhut realized that they would have to conduct their marriage differently than they had up to that time and were troubled and downcast, but they did not know what they should do. For others, their married state turned into a state of sin for them to such an extent that they, without speaking to anyone about it, or without saying anything to each other, stopped living with each other as married persons and stopped having married relations with each other.

Once the helpers at that time became aware of this (they were the ones who had taken over the work of the congregation and served the same under the direction of the elders, as the first wardens of the congregation were then called), they considered it necessary to speak individually with each and every member of the married persons' choir, and this was done in actuality. It became clear that only a few brethren and a few sisters had a notion of marriage that was in accordance with the holy scriptures.

However, through the grace of God, two things were brought to light through God's words in the Moravian Church. One was that marriage was an ordinance of God, which He had invented Himself and which was founded and blessed for the good of humanity. The other was that, even after the Fall, a poor sinner could lead and enjoy a marriage that was a pleasure in the eyes of God and that would be a blessing to his heart, if he had turned himself completely to Christ and allowed himself to be taught, led, and guided by the Holy Spirit.

§ 2. The late Ordinary [Zinzendorf], to whom the Savior had granted much grace already when he had entered into marriage, took upon himself to

---

1. Until the mid-sixteenth century, the Bohemian Brethren (the so-called Ancient Unity) considered the married state to be of a lower spiritual state than the single state. For them, marriage was necessary purely for the raising of children. See Atwood, *Czech Brethren*. But Spangenberg's own experience with the Boehmists and Arnoldists might well have provided an even more recent background for this attitude toward marriage.

serve particularly the married persons' choir to understand His purpose with marriage. To serve the sisters in the married persons' choir, sisters were also needed, but he decided that they should not act independently but rather always under the direction of a brother who was chosen and approved for this by the Savior.

Before he entrusted to a brother or a sister all that pertains to the service of the married persons' choir or to this or that member of the same, he gave it great consideration before the Savior.[2] For he regarded this position to be something very important for which special grace and gifts were needed. The brethren and the sisters to whom he confided regarding serving the married persons' choir were very few in number during his lifetime, and many years passed before couples of brethren and sisters were appointed in each congregation specifically for the care of the married persons' choir, because ordinarily the service of the married persons' choir was commissioned to brethren and sisters who already filled another position in the congregation. In the meantime the late Ordinary had already clearly expressed and stated what he had learned and experienced in the school of the Holy Spirit about marriage not only in some homilies for the married persons' choir but also in private conversations, in conferences, and in writing.[3] We have many reasons to thank God in a heartfelt fashion that the principia for the married persons' choir have been so carefully collected and drawn up at our synods since the home going [death] of the blessed Ordinary.[4]

We have spoken with brethren and sisters who were entrusted with these principia for the time being at the synods and have summarized their comments, rather than expanded on them, in a short essay.

This short essay is good and probably sufficient for brethren and sisters who have either heard the considerations at the synods or had other opportunities of receiving an explanation about this in another way. However, because cases arise in which it is not possible to tell brethren and sisters verbally all that is needed to understand this short essay, the Unity Elders' Conference has thought it wise to draw up instructions to teach new choir helpers and to clarify things with the choir helpers who are already in office.

---

2. That is, by the lot.

3. See Vogt, "Seventeen Points of Matrimony," for one example of Zinzendorf's instructions on marriage. The instructions indicate that his thinking may have gone beyond what Vogt has translated. Zinzendorf also saw his role as that of a prophet who believed he was taught directly by the Holy Spirit.

4. The synods of 1764, 1769, 1775, and 1782 were concerned with the codification of much of what had been understood only during Zinzendorf's lifetime. See Faull, "Girl Talk."

O Lord, help us, O Lord, help us to succeed![5]

§ 3. If a married couple is called to the position of choir helper, it is especially necessary that they seal their calling in their heart, for if one comes into
difficult circumstances, then one can say, "Dear Savior, you have assured me
in my heart that you would be with me in this position that you have given
me," and that is a strong support. Then they must think about themselves
before the Lord, for their commission is important and demands that they
promote the aims of the Savior with the choir that has been entrusted to
them and with each married couple who is in it.

They take upon themselves the Apostle's words, "not that we are sufficient
of ourselves to think any thing as of ourselves,"[6] and know with certainty that
God alone will make them able in their office. Thus they must lay themselves
at the feet of the Lord, our Savior, and ask Him from the heart that He may
be with them and give them what they need to fulfill their office in a blessed
fashion. They renew their covenant with Him so that they live, not according
to their own will but according to his, who died for them. And when they
embark on their work and become concerned with their choir as part of their
office, then it should be their daily concern that the Savior should be pleased
with them and their work, and if they have reason to doubt this and their lose
their peace of mind, then they must shed tears at His feet until they know
that He has forgiven them and His peace fills their hearts once again. They
do not rely on their own reason and experience but rather in all circumstances
listen to the word of the Lord and the guidance of His good Spirit,[7] and when
they do not stand in His constant influence and do not allow themselves to be
constantly taught and guided by Him, things will not go well. However, if
they keep themselves to the Word of God in a childlike fashion and without
exception give themselves over to the care of the Holy Spirit, both in matters
concerning their own person as well as those matters that have been entrusted
to them, then, even if they make mistakes and certain omissions, they will
take sure steps and will find reason enough to thank Him for his gracious
support. Then our dear Father in heaven, who loves to bless us, for whom it
is a pleasure to support the wardens of His Son, and to whom our prayers
through Christ are so welcome, will reign over them in grace and show Himself to be the Father of mercy and the God of all comfort.

---

5. Ps. 118:25 (KJV).

6. 2 Cor. 3:5 (KJV).

7. An insertion here at the bottom of the page reads, "for their position is a position of the
Spirit."

§ 4. The position of married persons' choir helper is always given to a brother and his wife together, that they allow the good of the choir to be of heartfelt concern to them, and the brother takes care of especially the married brethren and his wife of the married sisters, each with their own special concerns. The female married persons' choir helper thus has a really important commission and, in this position, can truly serve the married sisters in all ordinary circumstances with good advice, comfort, guidance, admonition, and correction according to the grace the Savior has given her and according to her own experience. However, as soon as a married sister complains to her female choir helper about an incident, or says that she and her husband have had a difference of opinion about the handling of the children or others weighty matters, the female choir helper does not take it upon herself to advise a sister according to what she thinks is right but rather talks about the matter beforehand with her husband, the male married persons' choir helper, and once she has related all this to him in a clear manner and has listened to his thoughts she tells the sister who has sought her advice, and if the male married persons' choir helper finds it necessary to talk to her himself, he does it, as mentioned earlier, in the presence of his wife, so that all misunderstandings can be avoided and all impurities and mistrust may be prevented for the best.

If a female married persons' choir helper takes it upon herself to give advice in serious situations without the knowledge of her husband, or even conceals things that concern not only a married sister but also her husband and hides this from her husband, the married persons' choir helper, then this can have the most sorrowful consequences and make such a sister quite unsuitable for such a position, and then, at the same time, also her husband.

§ 5. If it were ever necessary to have and keep the hearts and trust of the brethren for whose best interest one is called to serve, then this is certainly the case with the position of the married persons' choir helper; for, if the brethren and sisters in this choir have doubts whether or not they can speak freely with their choir helper and tell him everything that it is proper to receive good advice, then the purpose of the married persons' choir helper's position is not fulfilled. If the brethren and sisters are trusting and open in their conversations with the brother and sister to whom has been entrusted the position of married persons' choir helper, then one can through God's grace serve them with good advice that is also right and proper to the issue at hand, and thus everything will proceed in its proper order.

But how do such brethren and sisters, to whom has been entrusted the position of married persons' choir helper, go about winning the heart and trust of their choir? One should not ignore the recommendation of the brethren of the Unity Elders' Conference and the good reports of other brethren who have known them, but these are not enough; Christ is the one who holds the key to all hearts; when he opens the door, then no one can close it again, and no one else can open it again. If He appoints the wardens Himself, then they will be to their brethren what they should be. However, if He does not recommend Himself to those, whom one deals with, not to this or that warden who is appointed to a position, then it is beyond human ability to attain that worth that he should have. For this reason, the brethren who are called to the position of choir helper among the married persons must beg the dear Savior to recommend Himself to them and give them a good report through the work of the Holy Spirit in the hearts of their choir members. It should also be noted that the helpers of the married persons' choir can increase and multiply this trust, that the brethren develop toward them with the support of the Savior and through their conduct. But they can also diminish it, if not completely spoil it, for if they do not prove themselves to be wardens of God in all things, and especially do not regard as sacred the strict confidence that it so highly necessary, then they will be despised and they will lose their credibility completely or partially. It is clearly expected of them that they should be examples for the whole flock, and if they are not that, then they will not receive the necessary credibility in the hearts of others.

§ 6. Helpers of the married persons' choir must fully recognize that they are serving not only their choir but also the congregation to which they belong.

Because of their office they become members of the elders' conference and thereby receive the commission to consider everything that concerns the congregation with application and to be involved as much as possible. If something happens in other choirs where they might prevent harm or do good, then they should not withdraw but rather contribute their part in a loyal manner. They must follow the congregational rules just like all other members with all faithfulness, making no exception.

Since they are ex officio members of the elders' conference, they are also bound by the elders' conference and must allow themselves to be advised, admonished, and instructed by them and obey them.

They must communicate from time to time with other brethren from the married persons' choir who are, like them, members of the elders' conference about the condition of their choir and of this or the other brother and sister in it and profit from their insights and experience.

By this, however, is not meant the confessions that are entrusted to their loyal hearts; those must of course go to the grave with them and no one, whoever it might be, may learn of these through their doing.

Should the helpers of the married persons' choir have concerns with external matters that are under the purview of the college of overseers, then they must take heed with all diligence of that which the college of overseers recommends and act accordingly.

§ 7. In addition to this, helpers of the married persons' choir are to be viewed as wardens of the Unity of the Brethren, and they should never forget this themselves. The Unity Elders' Conference calls them to their position according to the instructions of the Savior, and they have their instructions also from them. If someone should have the misfortune either not to be able to fulfill his position or to be deemed in error in this or that manner, then he is asked to give an account of himself first to the congregational elders' conference, then also to the Unity Elders' Conference. This is because the commission that the Unity Elders' Conference has from the Synod of the Unity means that they must care for all congregations and their choirs and thus also for the married persons' choirs. For this reason, all helpers of the married persons' choir are bound to inform the Unity Elders' Conference from time to time about how things stand in their choir, especially if special circumstances occur there. There has recently been a short outline sent to the elders' conference about how they should best compose their reports, noting especially these certain things. In addition, it is expected of the helpers of the married persons' choir, as of all laborers in the congregations, that they make a good acquaintance with the synodal decisions and allow themselves to be guided by the agreement made before the Lord and all instructions of the Savior.

§ 8. The position of married persons' choir helper is arduous and certainly not easy. The helpers of the other choirs for the most part have all their people together in the choir houses; therefore, it is not difficult to monitor them and to remain with them in steady acquaintance. However, the married persons are frequently scattered, and it requires much time before they can all be visited and spoken with as is necessary.[8] However, if the married persons' choir helper bears in mind that their work is for the Lord, and if they are driven in all their actions by the love of Jesus, who has inflamed their hearts, then all this makes their hard work easy. If in addition to this there is a heartfelt and maternal love for the souls whom they should serve in their position, and if the Holy Spirit makes clear to them that these were bought for them not with transient silver and gold but rather with the dear blood of our Lord,

---

8. One of the main reasons for the instructions is to provide oversight over the married persons.

Jesus Christ, then they will not regret even the bitterest steps. The following is also true for them: through love, the burden that they carry on their backs and that almost crushes our frailty becomes like a light little feather, and one can say, is there anything else for me to carry? They do not forget what the Savior and his Spirit have done for their souls. If they then have to admit that His conduct toward us was merciful, graceful, patient, forgiving fully and daily of our guilt, healing, nurturing and comforting, taking joy and giving blessing and greeting our souls as a friend, then they must feel ashamed if anything threatens to be too much for them. They should also take care of them day and night like a loyal mother who cares for her child untiringly, and this is a good example for brethren who are to take care of souls.

§ 9. Helpers of the married persons' choir need to think about the following points concerning each family in their care, namely,

> How is it with each person, in himself or herself and with his or her person?
> How do the married brethren and sisters behave toward each other, bound as married persons are?
> How are the children kept and raised in each and every house?
> If they have wardens, what is their behavior toward them?
> How are their trade and the circumstances related to the same?
> How does this married couple interact with other brethren with whom they have relations in particular?

Now comes the question, how do helpers of the married persons' choir find these things out from their people?

If they allow the brethren who were in the position of choir helper before them to tell them about what they have noted in each family, this is of great help. But they must not stop at that and only watch through another's eyes. Rather, it is necessary for them to get to know their people themselves, at least because one can assume that this or that matter improves or worsens. The brethren then usually visit their choir helper and if they find that they are welcome then they continue to do this and come to them more often. The choir helper must take good advantage of this time and converse with them as much as they can, not about things that one usually talks about in conversation, but directs their exchange to that which suits their purpose. But they do not leave it at that, that the brethren visit them, but rather that they visit them themselves in their houses. And if they discover that once or twice they have not come at the right time because of circumstances, they should not be discouraged by this, but rather repeat their visit another time. Thereby they have to get to know their brethren, because intimacy increases through this, and they become more familiar to each other.

§ 10. A clear distinction should be made between the efforts of the choir helper to get to know each member for himself or herself, and for his own benefit. For, if the male choir helper or the female choir helper would demand from a brother or a sister, who are now walking a blessed path, a new confession of bad things that have ever happened to them with the pretext of getting to know them more thoroughly, that might not be fruitful. It is, however, quite different if a brother or a sister voluntarily become so intimate with their respective choir helpers that they do not want to conceal those things that are past and long done with, forgotten and forgiven; this may occur without problem.

A choir helper should, however, be aware of the following with each person: whether they belong to those who are to be made blessed and saved through fear or whether they belong to those to whom one should have mercy (Jude 1:22). For whether or not they consort with each person in a friendly and heartfelt manner, this is quite necessary. And whether or not the choir helper does this in the manner of Paul: whosoever becomes angered and I do not burn?[9] I always enter into the fire—it must be so in all circumstances, and this is more necessary with some people than others. Beyond this it should be noted that the choir helper who wants to get to know each brother and sister for himself or herself must concentrate on certain main points. These consist in the fact that one must find out the following:

Does the brother or sister know themselves in soul and body in his or her deeply sinful state? Have they come as poor sinners to Jesus; have they sought and found mercy in his blood; and do they still proceed daily in this mercy? Does God's peace govern them so that their hearts and minds are protected against all that would defile them? Is the love of Jesus master of their hearts, so that they do not love themselves, but Him who died for them? Do they allow the Holy Spirit[10] to teach, guide, and direct them? Do they know their father in heaven, and do they have free access to him in Christ? Do they strive to allow that which is sinful in them to die off and to pursue what conforms to the image of Jesus? If brethren and sisters compose their own memoir, then one can also get to know them through that.

---

9. 2 Cor. 11:29 (KJV).

10. An insertion here at the bottom of the page reads, "who lives in the hearts of God's children."

§ 11. It must be the concern of the married persons' choir helpers to discover how married couples behave toward each other, and they must examine whether each couple is properly familiar with the excellent choir principia given to us through the Savior's grace.[11] Married persons can easily do too much or too little because of the love they have for each other, and, whichever happens, this can lead to harm. Choir helpers will do well to note for each married couple whether or not this is the case. Because if a husband and wife love each other more than they love the Savior, then neither of them is worthy of the Savior. And if a husband does not strive eagerly to be or to become for his wife what Christ is for his congregation, and if a wife does not eagerly strive to be for her husband what the congregation is for Christ, then this is not a marriage in the sense of Christ.[12] Married persons' choir helpers must then accordingly be watchful so that such things might not occur among us. They should also note whether the married state provides married couples with a benefit and blessing for their hearts. For, if it does not, they will need to look for the reason why. It should also be noted whether married couples treat each other in a manner befitting children of God. For, according to scripture, the husband should honor the Savior; and the wife, her husband.

§ 12. When misunderstandings arise between a husband and wife, it is right not only for each person individually to be heard out, but also for the choir helper and his wife to speak with both together so that all partiality may be avoided. For, a husband who is in the wrong must submit to asking his wife's forgiveness and must not think that in doing so he is giving up some of his rights. On the contrary, he is much more likely to be regarded by his wife as a child and warden of God if he genuinely recognizes where he perhaps acted rashly or otherwise erred, and, encouraged by his example, she will be more likely to turn to the Savior as a poor sinner and humbly beg forgiveness for her errors.

If a married sister should come with a complaint about her husband's conduct to the male choir helper instead of to his wife as she should, then the choir helper cannot listen to her without having his wife present, since he cannot know what specific matters she might bring up and also for the reason that if a male choir helper converses alone with another man's wife, suspicion and evil rumors may easily arise.

---

11. See the introduction for a brief discussion of the principia.

12. This notion comes directly from Zinzendorf's "Ehechorreden," recently printed in Breul, *Geschlechtlichkeit*.

If the choir helper and his wife find that such a sister takes back her complaint, then they will consider the matter settled. If not, then the male choir helper must speak with the sister's husband and then with both of them together but also carefully avoid the situation where the sister who has complained might experience any future disadvantage from her husband.

§ 13. The Savior has entrusted the Unity of the Brethren with many fine maxims for the rearing of children. Thank goodness, we have the excellent little book, *Christian Upbringing of Children*,[13] in our hands. One also finds beneficial teachings in the synodal decisions, which refer to child rearing. In congregational conferences with parents, a good education for children is also encouraged. During their visits, married persons' choir helpers have the opportunity to see with their own eyes how the children are cared for in a household. They are also able to inquire when they go to bed and get up, when they undress and dress, when they wake up and fall asleep, when they go to the privy, etc.

If the children are visited and the visitors give a report of this to their conference, then the married persons' choir helpers will become even more familiar with the children.

If they know that here and there something is lacking, they can remedy the bad things with love and promote good order.

It is lovely if they can win the hearts of the children by means of God's grace, so that the children are happy to see them coming and enjoy it when they spend time with them.

§ 14. Much good often comes from brethren and sisters who serve in families, but much bad can also come about. The same can be expected when unfamiliar people work as domestic wardens in a house. If something attracts the attention of the married persons' choir helpers that makes them suspicious, or if married couples have complaints about brethren or sisters who work for them, then it is good to talk with the choir helpers in the single brethren's and single sisters' choir and to settle the matter. But if brethren or sisters make complaints against the married couples for whom they work, then it is advisable for the single brethren's and single sisters' choir helpers to talk with the married persons' choir helpers and in this way remove everything that is interfering or could get in the way of love.

The position of a congregation worker requires that he concern himself not only with matters that concern the congregation as a whole but also with

---

13. Layritz, *Betrachtungen*.

external circumstances and the success of each family. If something in this or that family that concerns their trade and the circumstances connected to it catches the attention of the married persons' choir helpers, they will do well to communicate plainly with the congregation worker about it.

As it is generally necessary for the married persons' choir helpers to converse diligently about their brethren and sisters with the minister as well as with the congregation workers, this should never be neglected. Because the married persons often cannot manage without the help of single sisters and brethren, a constant communication between the married persons' choir helpers and the single brethren's and single sisters' choir helpers is necessary to preserve love and peace.

§ 15. Besides the visits to families of the married persons' choir helpers, the same are also visited by other brethren and sisters chosen for this purpose. These visitors come together afterward in a conference and give a report about what took place during their visits. This proves as useful to the married persons' choir helpers as the classes for married couples, in which one sees and converses with the entire choir in different small groups. Occasionally, changes in the classes are necessary, and agreement about this is reached in a conference in which brethren and sisters from the married persons' choir who belong to the elders' conference are present. In this conference, joint consideration is given to the manner in which consultation for the poor and service to the brethren and sisters who are ill should be carried out. This is not to say that this conference must always be convened if someone who is poor or ill needs to be cared for. It can make whatever arrangement is called for by the situation; for example, a brother or sister is charged with bringing the poor person what he or she needs. It also appoints the brethren and sisters who are to assist the sick people in the married persons' choir. It must also make certain that conferences are held regularly with the alms workers and sick waiters. If instances arise concerning matters of the soul for which married persons' choir helpers need good advice, they will bring them to the choir helpers' conferences of either the brethren or the sisters, depending on whether brethren or sisters are affected. But if there are matters that cannot be discussed with single brethren and single sisters, the married persons' choir helpers will speak about them with the minister, or they will bring them to the conference of the brethren and sisters from the married persons' choir who are members of the elders' conference, or they will notify the Unity Elders' Conference, particularly the helpers' department, yet not without talking first with the minister.

Matters of disorder in the married persons' choir, which go against congregation rules, will be referred to the college of overseers and will be remedied there in all faithfulness. Where a resolution must be made according to instructions from the Savior, the matter will be taken up in the congregational elders' conference.

§ 16. Not only the married persons' choir helpers, but also the college of overseers and the congregational elders' conference, must be watchful that single brethren and single sisters not be permitted to make unnecessary visits to family homes. It is even more important to see that no brother from the married persons' choir be allowed to pass the time sitting with another brother's wife and that no married woman be permitted to do so with another sister's husband. Harm can arise from such behavior, and the sullying of the spirit that tends to result is an abomination to the Lord. And the excuse "We are having a good talk" does not hold up.

We should remember to think about the fact that in all choirs, including among the married persons, assistants may be added. Sometimes one or another brother or sister is found to have unexpected gifts. At other times it becomes evident that they are greatly favored and that other brethren and sisters hold them in high esteem. Faithful choir helpers will notice this and will discuss it in choir helpers' conferences with their brethren and sisters. Attention is given to such brethren and sisters, and they will be assigned something as a test. This will come to the elders' conference, and if the result is that, in proper order, a few of these people become assistants in the married persons' choir, we will be glad of it and give thanks to the Savior for them. The scarcer the people are that one can use, the more needed they are.

If married persons' choir helpers have a male and a female assistant to help with their work, we must ask them to read the synodal decisions carefully and to faithfully follow what is clearly stated therein with regard to how such assistants are to be viewed and how they are to be employed.

§ 17. One person or another may say, "In a choir, one deals with such different persons. One man may lack the feeling of a poor sinner, that is, holy modesty; another is so weighed down by his misery that he cannot even make the effort to find his way to the Savior. One man is so clever in his own eyes that we can tell him nothing because he knows everything better; another is so dull in his understanding that he cannot grasp and comprehend things at all. One man may think that he is evangelic and because of this takes the liberty, which really is more impudence and against Jesus's teaching; another is so anxious that he has scruples about everything and makes things a matter of conscience that are doubtless right and good. One man is always worried unnecessarily about his success and living with his wife and children;

another is careless and instead of living within his income, runs his business recklessly, in the hope that the brethren will help him. Thus one is confronted with many strange things, particularly when one goes into work with people's souls. I would very much like to have a guide for how one should behave toward people in this or that situation."

Answer: We do not want to give anyone instructions for this. Choir helpers must pray about their people, weep and reflect, and let the Holy Spirit teach them what kind of nourishment they should give to each person and what the right time is for doing this. No brother becomes a choir helper by reading the instructions, and it is the same for sisters. The instructions can remind brethren and sisters of this and that, which is what they are meant to do. But the light, desire, and strength, in short everything that matters, one must have from the Savior, and it can be found if one lies at His feet and seeks it from Him with all one's heart.

§ 18. Up to this point, the position of married persons' choir helper in general has been discussed. Now we want to see how married persons' choir helpers should conduct themselves in situations that arise among married persons.

Beforehand, however, we need to note the following: the Unity of the Brethren takes everything it believes and sings and says and does in regard to marriage from the holy scriptures, because we want to be guided by them in all ways, therefore also in our marriage, in our thinking, speaking, and actions. Married persons' choir helpers will do well to become properly acquainted with the teaching of the brethren about marriage, which is available for everyone to see in *Idea Fidei Fratrum*,[14] so that they may be in a position to give correct answers if they are asked about it, something that tends to happen often.

In the Old Testament God gave the people of Israel and their kings and priests many commandments and instructions regarding marriage. They are, however, quite varied in intent, because several commandments and prohibitions about marriage given by God to the people of Israel through his warden Moses are general and apply to all persons. These include everything we read in the eighteenth chapter of Leviticus. For example, there is a strict prohibition against marrying or having sexual relations with a blood relative. Intercourse with a woman during her monthly cleansing is also strictly forbidden. If it is said, how do we know that these commandments and prohibitions of God that we read in Leviticus 18 are meant for all people, then the answer is,

---

14. Spangenberg, *Idea Fidei Fratrum*, §§ 202–5.

God declares in that very place that all the things spoken about are an abomination to Him and that He therefore wants the Israelites to destroy the Canaanites, because they had defiled the land with such abominations. He adds that all people who would do such abominable things in the way they were practiced by the Canaanites should be wiped out.

Other commandments and prohibitions from God concerning married persons found in the Books of Moses apply only to the time of the Old Testament, after which the new covenant of grace through Christ was established. For example, a woman who had borne a son was unclean first for seven days. After that, she had to stay at home for thirty-three more days and was not allowed to come to a service until these days were past. If she had borne a daughter, then she was unclean for two weeks and afterward had to stay at home for sixty-six more days and wait for her period before she received permission to come to a service.

We find a number of such commandments and prohibitions no longer applicable to us. No one should have doubts about them or force them on others.

§ 19. Married persons' choir helpers should bear in mind especially that we find certain places, not only in the Old but also in the New Testament, that concern marriage and that we do not regard as true commandments but merely as concessions and privileges. For example, if a man takes a woman and marries her, and she does not find favor in his eyes simply because he dislikes her, he should write a letter of divorce, put it in her hand, and allow her to leave his house (Deuteronomy 24:1). The Israelites interpret these words as if God, through Moses, had dictated that a divorce be undertaken if the woman did not please her husband. But our Lord Jesus Christ says, No, it is not to be understood in this way. According to God's wish, which he indicated at Creation, a man should not divorce his wife except in the case of adultery. What Moses said in this regard should not be considered a command; he allowed it only because of your hardness of heart. This is the interpretation of Jesus's words: because God knew how hard and wicked your hearts are and that you would torture to death a wife who later displeased you, he gave you the right to divorce to prevent an even greater evil, namely, perpetual enmity, quarrel, wrath, and even murder (see Matthew 19:3ff.).[15]

---

15. According to Sommer, *Serving Two Masters*, the Moravians did allow a form of separation when a marriage was deemed unhealthy in body or soul of one or both people. The *Scheiden* was not a divorce, but the man and woman were sent to separate congregations.

§ 20. In the New Testament there is also a passage that deals with marriage, but it should be regarded as permission rather than as a command from God. Something is permitted, not because it would be most pleasing to God, but rather to prevent things that could lead to more harm. We find the aforementioned place in 1 Corinthians 7:2ff.[16] and we should remember the following as we read it. Paul was dealing with people who had lived in shameful pleasures before their conversion to Christ, which is undeniably proven by 1 Corinthians 6:9–11.[17] Even in this congregation there were many people who had lived in whoredom during the time of their ignorance, and they were not out of danger of falling back into it, which is why Paul so earnestly warned them (see 1 Corinthians 6:13–20).[18] Then Paul says it would be better for them to marry than to go to prostitutes. He does not want to advise that a husband should withdraw from his wife or that a wife should withdraw from her husband. But if this should happen, then it should be only with mutual consent to fast and pray and then only for a limited time. If they did not come back together and behave with each other as a married couple, they could be tempted by Satan for the sake of their impurity. For the rest, he stipulates that a husband and wife belong to each other alone and to no one else. Then Paul adds to the points already mentioned, I mean such things as permission, and not as a commandment. Consequently, the previously cited words of Paul should not be taken as a rule for all children of God, to show them how and why they should begin and conduct their marriage. Although we must say that if they are not misconstrued and taken to have a carnal meaning but are understood and used properly, they contain a good teaching that can be advantageous to everyone. However, it happens unfortunately that people

---

16. "Nevertheless, to avoid fornication, let every man have his own wife, and let every woman have her own husband." 1 Cor. 7:2 (KJV).

17. "Know ye not that the unrighteous shall not inherit the kingdom of God? Be not deceived: neither fornicators, nor idolaters, nor adulterers, nor effeminate, nor abusers of themselves with mankind, nor thieves, nor covetous, nor drunkards, nor revilers, nor extortioners, shall inherit the kingdom of God. And such were some of you: but ye are washed, but ye are sanctified, but ye are justified in the name of the Lord Jesus, and by the Spirit of our God." 1 Cor. 6:9–11 (KJV).

18. In most of the instructions to the married persons' choir helpers, the biblical references are included within the body of the text: "Now the body is not for fornication, but for the Lord; and the Lord for the body. And God hath both raised up the Lord, and will also raise up us by His own power. Know ye not that your bodies are the members of Christ? Shall I then take the members of Christ, and make them the members of an harlot? God forbid. What? Know ye not that he which is joined to an harlot is one body? For two, saith he, shall be one flesh. But he that is joined unto the Lord is one spirit. Flee fornication. Every sin that a man doeth is without the body; but he that committeth fornication sinneth against his own body. What? Know ye not that your body is the temple of the Holy Ghost which is in you, which ye have of God, and ye are not your own? For ye are bought with a price: therefore glorify God in your body, and in your spirit, which are God's." 1 Cor. 6:13–20 (KJV).

generally interpret these words of Paul according to their carnal meaning and thereby set their minds at rest about things that are in conflict with the soul.

§ 21. Let us look at other places in the holy scriptures that make reference to Christian marriage. From these it is completely clear (1) that when one wishes to enter into marriage, it should be done in the Lord (see 1 Corinthians 7:39); (2) scripture says, let us cleanse ourselves from all filthiness of the flesh and spirit, perfecting holiness in the fear of God (2 Corinthians 7:1); (3) abstain from fleshly lusts, which war against the soul (1 Peter 2:11); (4) purify your soul in obeying the truth through the Spirit (1 Peter 1:22); (5) present your bodies a living sacrifice, holy, acceptable unto God (Romans 12:1); (6) know ye not that your body is the temple of the Holy Ghost that is in you, that ye have of God, and ye are not your own? (1 Corinthians 6:19); (7) for ye are bought with a price: therefore glorify God in your body, and in your spirit, which are God's (1 Corinthians 6:20); (8) husbands, love your wives, even as Christ also loved the church, and gave himself for it (Ephesians 5:29);[19] (9) wives, submit yourselves unto your own husbands, as unto the Lord (Ephesians 5:22).

From these and many other places in the holy scriptures, it is clear that conducting a marriage according to the wish of Jesus Christ is an important matter. Because the wardens of Jesus Christ who took care of the Moravian Church from the very beginning made a covenant with one another before the Lord that they wanted in all circumstances to be taught, led, and directed by Him and His word, this particularly concerned the state of marriage. They prayed, wept, and thought about this a great deal; and the wardens of Jesus who followed them and were used by the Lord in the Moravian Church did likewise. For now, matters are handled as follows, but always with the provision that we will change and improve from time to time, as we find necessary.

§ 22. If a marriage is proposed, it will normally be discussed first of all in the choir helpers' conference. We will inquire as to the heart of the brother whose marriage is being talked about. We will consider whether he has the ability to manage a wife and children and to oversee a house.

We consider also whether he would be useful in some other way in the service of the Savior, depending on the grace that resides within him. His disposition, bodily constitution, occupation, family, external circumstances, and whether he will have something in hand at the beginning: all this and other such things will be considered.

---

19. The text quoted is not Ephesians 5:29, but Ephesians 5:25 (KJV).

It is our advice to the married persons' choir helper that, from a distance, he should make an effort to get to know what kind of person such a brother is and then thoroughly discuss his affairs with his choir helper (of the single brethren). Next, the brother's marriage should be discussed in the conference of the sisters' choir helpers. The minister who holds this conference will give the sisters an idea about the brother. Then sisters will be named who are thought to be suitable for him, unless by chance the brother himself has proposed one or another sister, in which case this should by all means be discussed first. The suggestions will then be examined, and if there is doubt about a sister, then another will be named. If it still is not clear to the conference that she is the right person, a third will be named, and so it will continue until minds are at ease with the proposal. If the married persons' choir helpers and their wives do not already know the sisters who are proposed, it is desirable that they now become acquainted with them.

Once the matter has reached this point, it will be placed before the Savior in the congregational elders' conference, but with the difference that communication will first be made with the Unity Elders' Conference, to inquire whether the brother concerned might be used in service to the Savior. Then, unless there is some doubt about it, the congregational elders' conference will lay the question before the Savior as to whether He approves the request for the brother to marry this or that sister. If the proposal has His approval, it will be commended to the Savior, and members of the elders' conference will keep it secret and guard against speaking with anyone about it prematurely.

If the Savior does not approve this proposal, but there is another one, then this next one will also be laid before Him. And so it will continue until the right person is found or there is cause to postpone the matter for the time being.

§ 23. The aforementioned brother will then be told the name of the sister found suitable for him, either by his choir helper or the minister, or by both. It should now be made clear to him that accepting or declining the proposal is dependent on his conviction: he should consider the matter in the presence of the Savior. If he does not yet personally know the sister proposed for him, an opportunity will be created for him to get to know her. If afterward he is not inclined to marry this sister, he will not be persuaded to do so; rather, the proposal will be dropped, and, in the aforementioned manner, at some time or other, another will be considered. But if the brother says yes to the proposal, someone will speak to the sister in question on his behalf, and he will be proposed to her for marriage, either by her choir helper alone or by the minister and the choir helper. Also she knows, and she will be told again, that she is not compelled to say yes to the proposal. She will give her answer after due consideration in the Savior's presence.

If she rejects the offer, the brother who was proposed for her will be told and the proposal is then ended. After that, another sister will have to be chosen in the aforementioned manner; but before another is taken to the lot, the first sister will be told that she is no longer being considered.

If the sister who received the proposal is inclined to accept it, and if she has parents or guardians, it will be necessary first to obtain consent from her dear parents and also to give the news to her guardian.

Either she herself, or the brother who is asking for her hand in marriage, or the minister, or another brother will write to her parents or guardians, if they are not in the vicinity, and without her parents' consent, the marriage will not take place.[20] Occasionally, the parents of a sister have previously declared that they would be satisfied with whatever resolutions would be made on their daughter's behalf by the Unity Elders' Conference or a congregational elders' conference.

In this case everything will be reported to them in detail and they will be asked for their blessed participation. If the parents are nearby, we will talk with them about the proposed marriage between a brother and their daughter before the offer is made to her.

If the brother proposing the marriage still has his parents, he will not fail to communicate with them about it and ask for their consent and blessing.

§ 24. But what does one do if exception is taken to the customary manner of dealing with marriage practiced at this time by the Moravian Church because it departs from the custom of the first church in the time of the apostles? At that time, it depended only on the man who intended to marry as to whom he wanted to take for his wife, and it was up to the parents whether they wanted to give their daughter in marriage to this or that man or wanted her to remain single. A widow, however, was no longer under her parents' control in this way and could take whom she wanted (see 1 Corinthians 7).

The answer then is this: we by no means judge and reject that. Our practice, however, about which we have previously spoken, has the following basis: all brethren and sisters who are true members of the congregation have made a sacred promise to the Savior himself and to one another that they want to be guided in their actions not by their own will, but by the will of

20. One of the frequent charges brought against the Moravians is that they interfered in the parents' right to arrange or at least approve of marriages.

Jesus Christ. A change of choir, when one crosses over from being single to being married, is one of the most important actions one can undertake in life, and each brother and sister wishes that this might happen according to the will of God.

The congregational elders' conference, with the approval of the entire congregation and also of all parents, has the significant task of thinking about what is best for each member of the congregation, and, for those cases that are not determined by the holy scriptures, of asking the Savior by means of the lot whether He approves of this or that proposal. This they do in matters of marriage in such a way so as to allow each brother and sister, as well as their parents, the freedom to accept the proposal or not. They do not ask if such and such a brother should or must take such and such a sister; rather, their question is whether they should request that this well-considered marriage take place. If the elders' conference did not do this but simply left everything to the brethren and sisters or to the discretion of their parents, then the brethren and sisters concerned would be nothing but very unhappy to marry someone according to the Savior's design.

For that reason we want to thank God for his favor in showing us a way that allows our brethren and sisters to be comfortable. We want to commend to Him the fact that we must suffer much ridicule and harsh opinions over it.

§ 25. If situations occur, however, in which people begin to think, we do not want any barriers to our freedom; we want to marry as we please and act according to our impulses and belief, what can be done? Answer: Whoever thinks and speaks in this way clearly indicates that he has forgotten the covenant he entered into with us. We relinquish to him his own will, although with pain and sadness, because we can see in advance that he will suffer even more injury to his soul, as it is evident that he has already greatly damaged it. We will therefore declare to him that he can do what he wants and that he has his freedom. The congregation, however, also has its freedom, and he will not be able to force his will on it in this matter.

We must remember this: if there is a person in the congregation in whom we perceive a sensual disposition or a lack of ability to manage and feed a wife and children and whom we cannot help to get married, this does not mean we should forbid marriage, and whoever interprets it in this way sins.

But if there is a brother in the congregation who wants to marry and who does not lack the grace, talent, and ability to head a household, and if we either stand in his way or want to deny him this with good advice, that would be wrong.

§ 26. But to return to the marriage that has now been approved on all sides; next comes the betrothal. This consists in the brother and sister, who after deliberation before the Lord have resolved to accept each other, coming together with several other persons. In the presence of God and these persons, they will declare that they are inclined to accept each other, and they will give each other their hand as a promise, without a brother laying on his hands. This betrothal is usually held before a small love feast, and if the brother or sister who are to become engaged have parents or grandparents and they can be reached, they are welcome to be present. The newly betrothed sit next to each other and are given the opportunity to tell something about themselves and their circumstances. But we omit the kiss for now. To prevent the brother or sister from being timid, the married persons' choir helpers talk very simply about this with each of them before the love feast.

Their betrothal will be made known to the congregation in the next congregational meeting, and they are commended to the consideration of the Lord. The public notice takes place after this in our usual way, in conformity with the customs of the land.

§ 27. The wedding itself ordinarily takes place in a congregational meeting, and on occasion, the little boys and girls are permitted to be present. For they will hear of it and will perhaps make up more fantastical notions about it if they are not there than if they are.

If strangers are visiting and would like to attend the wedding, this will be permitted, provided that they conduct themselves in an orderly manner.

Because of the mixed audience, the sermon given at the wedding will not go into a specific discussion of marriage. This can be done better at another time; for now it is enough to explain that entering into marriage is an important matter and that abundant grace attends such a change and that the congregation's prayers should be encouraged to accompany the wedding ceremony. The male married persons' choir helper generally leads the bridegroom to the meeting hall[21] and back again, and the female married persons' choir helper does the same for the bride. It is most appropriate for the newly married couple to be seated in the hall so that the bridegroom is on the right and the bride is on the left side. But there are halls where the congregation will not tolerate this well, because they sit opposite the liturgist with sisters on the right and brethren on the left. We will abide by this

---

21. Moravians did not use the terms *church* or *chapel* for their place of worship since they did not consider it to be a separate, sacred place. In German they called it the *Saal*; in English they called it the (meeting) hall.

and allow the bride to sit on the sisters' side and the bridegroom on the brethren's side.

§ 28. The newly married couple is generally very affected by this important change and the prevailing grace of God, and a very special work of the Holy Spirit is being conducted in them. Whoever wants to show them genuine love will pay attention and diligently take care so that nothing is disturbed, even though this could happen with the best intentions.

It is best if the married persons' choir helpers who assist the newly married couple from this time on allow themselves to be led and directed, step for step and from hour to hour, by the Holy Spirit. If the new couple becomes accustomed to paying proper attention to what is taking place in their hearts and to faithfully preserving and making use of the grace they are receiving, they will progress from day to day and will be a joy to the Savior.

After their wedding, the married persons' choir helpers usually go with the new couple into a room, where the sister has the choir ribbon tied on. That this may take place, not in a perfunctory fashion or without reflection, but rather to make a good impression and with sincere prayers to the Savior for all grace needed for the new situation, the choir helper sings some appropriate verses, for example, "Because Your Heart Is with Us, We Do Not Lack for Blessings, Etc."; "That They with New Grace, Etc."; "The Grace of the Lord Jesus Christ, Who Is the Love of His Father, Etc."; and such as these, and while these are being sung, the sister herself unties the emblem of the single sisters, and the choir helper ties the new choir ribbon on for her. The verse "The Entire State of Marriage Depends, Etc." could be misinterpreted, since in it no mention is made of a choir ribbon, so it is better that it not be used for this occasion. When this act, as modest as it seems, takes place close to Jesus and He acknowledges it, a heart often melts from the feeling of grace. At its conclusion, the married couples who are present kiss, including the newly married couple. Their choir helpers talk with them about this beforehand.

§ 29. For the most important reasons, we have done away with ordinary weddings, and whoever wanted to bring them back into the congregation would thereby bring misfortune on himself. But we sometimes hold a small love feast and gladly invite brethren and sisters from the elders' conference and nearest relatives, and we sing lovely verses of blessing to the newly married couple.

Usually, the married persons' choir helpers invite the newly married couple to eat with them, and, now and then, close relatives and several other brethren and sisters will be present. It will usually be arranged that the newly married couple remains with the choir helpers as long as their initiation lasts, so that the helpers can introduce them, through the grace of God, to the excellent principia of the married persons' choir. If the married persons' choir helpers take an interest in them in sincere love and establish an intimate relationship with them, the purpose will be fulfilled. In this way the couple begins to develop a simple, childlike, and candid demeanor toward the brother and sister who have faithfully served them as they entered into their marriage. They will continue in this way as time goes on.

It is just as necessary and blessed in the married persons' choir as in the choirs of the unmarried brethren and sisters that, just as they are, persons are open with their choir helpers and hide nothing from them, because whoever loves the truth does not hate the light, but he comes into the light, according to the words of Christ.

§ 30. Among us, it is customary for the newly married brother, who is given to the sister as husband and head, to be especially blessed for this. Whereas up to this point he had only to think about and be concerned with himself, he henceforth has the duty to direct his wife as well and not only to provide for her bodily needs and nourishment with all faithfulness and according to the wishes of Christ but also to take an interest in her soul and attend to her as is fitting. His wife must recognize him as her husband and head, must love and honor him, follow him, and be obedient to him. So that, from the beginning of their marriage, the newly married couple may enter into this order of God, the brother and sister serving as married persons' choir helpers will take the opportunity to let them know how important this is. They will meet with them separately and will ask one or more other married couples to join them, as they see fit, and, following a brief hymn, the married persons' choir helper or possibly the minister will speak on this subject. He will show how Christ, as head of His congregation, takes an interest in His body and limbs and loves, carries, cares for, and cherishes them. He will explain that, on the other hand, the congregation looks to the Savior as its head, loves, honors, serves, and obeys Him and always keeps in mind that it wants to be a joy and credit to Him. Because the husband in his marriage is now the image of Christ, and the wife the image of the congregation, the same will be expected of them. To this end, a special blessing should be bestowed on the husband, in the name of Jesus Christ, and he should be commended to the Savior, that he might grant him all the grace and talents he will need for his duties. The brother kneels down and prayers are said over him with laying on of hands. The liturgist then raises him up again and kisses him. In conclusion, a verse of blessing is offered, and brethren and sisters kiss. The husband kisses his wife, and she kisses his hand.

If a widower marries, this liturgical observance does not seem to be necessary, but if he begs for a new blessing, we will not deny it to him.

Moreover, it should be noted that this liturgical observance does not take place on the day of the wedding, but on about the second or third day after.

§ 31. A primary concern of the married persons' choir helper is that the new married couple become acquainted with each other and grow fond of each other. If all brethren and sisters in a congregation can become one heart and one soul through God's grace, then a married couple, who convey the image of Christ and his congregation, must especially become one heart and one soul. The natural love that grows between married persons belongs to God's order, and we find it also in the unconverted, if the people do not become inhuman. But above all, for the newly married couple, we wish them the love that is a fruit of the Holy Spirit and that flows from faith in Jesus Christ, because this love endures through all the difficult circumstances married persons can experience. Because it also is linked with the love of Jesus Christ, it deters us from all things that could defile us either in body or spirit.

If newly married persons want to get to know each other, they must have the opportunity to talk with each other. Of course, this can happen even when they are with the married persons' choir helpers, but one must also provide them the opportunity to talk with each other alone, perhaps while they are drinking tea, taking a walk, or at other times. Then one can ask the other how he or she felt about the marriage proposal. They will tell each other about their upbringing, awakening, and receiving of grace, etc., also how they came to the congregation, their experience in the congregation until now, and more such things.

The male married persons' choir helper will speak with the brother in advance and will ask him to speak affectionately and plainly with his wife and to accommodate himself to her, as sisters are sometimes bashful and shy and are unaccustomed to talking about their circumstances with a brother. He will also warn the brother against everything that could originate from either thoughtlessness or a useless curiosity, because if he demonstrates something like this to his wife, it can easily happen that she will lose, if not all, then certainly a lot of, respect for him. For just this reason, the choir helper will remind him that, even with the best of intentions, he should not talk with his wife about things that he actually should confide to no one other than to the faithful ear and heart of his choir helper. He must treat her weakness with consideration and therefore should not press in these early conversations for confessions concerning her previous path.

The female married persons' choir helper will remind the new wife that, rather than being shy toward her husband, she should be childlike, plain, honest, and sincere. Because he is her head and must also be concerned for her soul, she must not be secretive toward him.

§ 32. The sole purpose of all these previously mentioned efforts of the married persons' choir helpers with the newly married persons is to ensure that when they now come together as a married couple and, according to the expression in the holy scriptures, become one flesh, they might receive a true blessing. It is only right that beforehand they be given more detailed instruction about this. The married persons' choir helpers must put before them (1) that before the Fall God created not only the man but also his wife and blessed them with the words, Be fruitful and multiply.[22] Now because this could only happen by means of marital relations, that is, only thereby could the first people be fruitful and multiply, then it is quite evident that, in their innocent condition, God wanted the man to have marital relations with his wife; (2) that the sin that came into the world by means of the Fall so corrupted body and soul that we poor humans, without having a Savior through whom we become new creatures, are not capable in our marriage of undertaking this important act, in which a husband and his wife become one flesh, in an innocence such as the first humans had before the Fall; (3) that our Lord Jesus Christ, however, won for us grace and freedom from sins through His holy life, innocent death, and His blood of reconciliation, and we become children of God through belief in Him, find forgiveness of sins, partake of the Holy Spirit, and become new creatures, so that we can serve him in holiness and righteousness, which pleases Him; (4) that, accordingly, a poor sinner who receives mercy through Christ can henceforth live in a marriage pleasing to God and that the act in which a husband and wife communicate physically with each other, in His name, to His satisfaction, and with a blessing for themselves, can happen through his grace.

Prior to their union, the aforementioned points will be shown to the newly married couple in a discourse from the holy scriptures, and they will be reminded that Jesus Christ, who so revered human reproductive organs that He wanted to be born of the Virgin Mary and allowed Himself to be

---

22. Gen. 1:22 (KJV).

circumcised as a little boy on the eighth day, was also made by God for our sanctification.

§ 33. Furthermore, we must reasonably speak very clearly with the newly married couple if this seems necessary.

They can easily understand that the reproductive organs are used in marriage for propagation of the human race, but they must also be advised that through their use, the most intimate union of a married couple is promoted and that this is in agreement with the Creator's purpose.

Indeed, a married couple's marital union should bring to mind Christ's intimate connection with His congregation, and they should therefore be careful, since their entire marriage journey is to be an image of Christ and His congregation, that nothing should come from this act that would be unlike this image or could discredit it. We can thus assure the newly married persons that, sinful and corrupt in body and soul though they be, if they hold to their faith in Christ, commend themselves to His grace's leading, and come together in His presence with heartfelt prayer and supplication, then He, the Savior, will bless their togetherness.

This act, so misused by many thousands of people, will bring them no harm, but will be accompanied by grace if they avail themselves of it according to His purpose.

The married persons' choir helper will then speak quite clearly with the brother, and his wife will speak with the sister, about the manner of marital union, which can take place while either sitting or lying down. This is because in the congregation, one often deals with persons who know nothing of such things, and they must be regarded as children. In this case, the married persons' choir helper and his wife must talk with the brother and sister just as plainly and intelligibly as a mother talks with her child.

Because these things are considered to be sensitive, people in the world either are ashamed to talk about them in plain words or speak of them using lewd words or making loud jokes. But it is right for us to speak of things made by God's own hand and belonging to his order in a manner fitting for their purpose, before the Lord and with all purity of heart.

§ 34. Once we give the newly married couple an idea about marital union while either sitting or lying down, we will declare to them that both methods are equivalent for us, although we will not deny that, depending on the circumstances, one is preferred over the other, not in and of itself, but because it is more suitable at the time. Sometimes only one method, namely, the recumbent, is possible, for example if the husband or wife is too weak for the seated.

Once the newly married couple has decided on one or the other method, then the female married persons' choir helper makes preparations, with a chair and cloth if they will be seated and with a cushion if they will be lying down.

Something should also be said to the couple about the sister's pain from being opened up and the blood that will result, unless special circumstances exist that are not known ahead of time and that cause it not to be seen.[23]

The newly married couple will then be left alone, with the admonition that they should not act nervously but instead simply, confidently, patiently, and in a childlike manner. They will also be asked not to force anything, but rather, the first time their bodies come together, to let things take their course, even if nothing further ensues, because it can happen, and actually does sometimes, that the brother is not able to have intercourse with his wife when they are to have their first union.

If it does happen that the brother can commune with his wife, he will place his hand on her head and give her his blessing with a few words from a verse. He will give an account to the married persons' choir helper, who then, together with his wife, holds worship with the newly married couple and recommends that, in the future, they mutually commend themselves to the Savior after each union and thank him for his nearness and kindness.

Before they lie down to sleep, either the same evening or the next, they are spoken to about the blessing of sleeping together, and they will be commended to the Savior for that purpose. The next morning, if possible, they will eat breakfast together with the choir helpers.

§ 35. If one asks how it came to be that the introduction to marriage is done with so much concern and at such length in the Moravian Church, this will serve as an answer: The customary way of beginning marriage is more heathen than Christian. What else but harm could result from this? The basis of all that has been discussed up to now is faithfulness to the souls one serves and the desire of those who serve Jesus to make marriage in the congregation an honor and joy to the Savior. We must repeat Paul's words: If we are doing too much, we are doing too much for the Lord.

If we are questioned further: Must everything the instructions say be done for each married couple who are to be introduced to marriage? And must everything be done in the same order as stated in the instructions? Then the answer to both questions would be: no. It can happen that a newly married

---

23. This is an important detail, as for many cultures the sign of blood at first marital intercourse was considered to be necessary proof of the woman's virginity. There is no mention of either such an expectation here or its necessity.

couple will need to make their way to their business shortly after the wedding and will not be able to stay with the choir helpers as long as otherwise would be the case, according to the instructions. Something can also be superfluous for one brother and sister that is necessary for another.

If, however, according to the instructions, we cannot bring to bear with each newly married couple just what we are supposed to, it is obvious that we cannot feel bound to the order in which one thing should follow another. But supposing the choir helpers were able to do everything expected of them by the instructions, then it would not be necessary for them to keep the exact order in which one thing after another is set down.

Choir helpers certainly need to differentiate between the persons they deal with. Some brethren and some sisters would not find it useful if we wanted to hold one liturgical act after another with them, and we would overwhelm them by doing so, because it would be too much for them to comprehend. We are consequently guided by them. It is obvious, however, that choir helpers must not push things, which could be useful, aside and neglect them for the sake of comfort or of finishing something quickly.

Foot washing, which used to be performed for a newly married couple before their first union, has now been abolished after due consideration and is no longer used on this occasion.

Furthermore, the newly married couple will be admonished to speak to no one about this choir introduction to marriage but to keep it all to themselves and to discuss it all the more diligently with the Savior.

§ 36. After a few days, perhaps, we will take the opportunity to converse with a married couple about the future course of their marriage and especially how things stand concerning their union.

The question of how often married persons should renew their marital union is not decreed by the holy scriptures. For children of God, the enticement thereto that arises from nature cannot be the reason why married persons unite with each other, because, in conformity with Scripture, they do not regard marriage as a means to carry out the desires of the flesh. Scripture says, Let not sin therefore reign in your mortal body, that ye should obey it in the lusts thereof.[24]

If married persons neglect to renew their marital union, they generally notice—unless they discontinue it because of age or debility—a decreased tenderness in their love. Hence, it follows that married persons should not fail to renew marital relations. If one marriage partner withdraws from the

---

24. Rom. 6:12 (KJV).

other—we have an example of this: there are wives who do not like having children because to carry, nurse, care for, and raise a child is too difficult for them—this usually has the most miserable consequences and cannot please God, as its source is self-interest, and it is also contrary to the holy scriptures. But to come back to the previously mentioned question, it actually depends on a married couple as to how they want to conduct their marriage with regard to marital relations.

If they ask for good advice from the married persons' choir helpers, it will usually be recommended that they have relations about once a week. They can think about it in advance and look to the Savior with prayer and supplication for his grace. We also have examples of brethren and sisters being advised for important reasons to unite more often than once a week.

§ 37. If a married couple is comfortable renewing marital relations once a week, they can continue doing so in God's name. But they must know that this is to be considered merely good advice and not God's commandment. If a couple thinks it proper to have relations either less often or more frequently, they will now and then give the married persons' choir helpers notice of this.

This is good because we in the congregation like our dealings to be in the light, and we hate secretive conduct. It will also be pleasing to them afterward to know that they are doing this with the good advice and blessing of their helpers.

We need to remember the following, namely, (1) when a wife has her monthly cleansing, it is contrary to scripture for her to have marital relations with her husband. If the cleansing follows a proper cycle, one usually waits from the start until the seventh or ninth day is past. Then when her cleansing is over, the wife can remind her husband about relations, another time the husband can remind his wife. (2) If married persons are not happy in spirit and do not feel the peace of God in their hearts, they would do better to put off their union on that day. (3) The same applies if they are physically ill and not capable of properly undertaking this liturgical act. Here we do not mean small events such as a bit of a headache, toothache, or similar things. (4) On Holy Communion Day, their spirit is so preoccupied by the partaking of the body and blood of Christ that it will be best if they postpone their union until another day.

§ 38. Everyone must be able to see from the behavior of a married couple toward each other that they have love and respect for each other. But the affection of a husband toward his wife and of a wife toward her husband should not be seen or heard by others, as this could give them opportunity for foolish and useless thoughts, because the human heart is so corrupt.

Furthermore, married persons must give consideration to preventing their marital relations from becoming a subject that others find reason to think about. Thus, they will make reasonable arrangements so that their union may be renewed in quiet, unnoticed by others, alone and undisturbed, in nearness to Jesus, with prayer and supplication. Whereas on the one hand the procreation, carrying, bearing, and nursing of children are important matters, pleasing to God when they happen according to his wish, on the other hand the wisdom of God's children requires them to prevent things that could become detrimental if they came before the wrong eyes and ears.

We must also be concerned about the small children around us, because children pay attention to everything parents do and afterward tell other children, and tell them secretly, which always causes harm.


§ 39. If it should happen that God blesses a new wife with a pregnancy, the choir helper will take special interest in her under these circumstances. She will do well to remind her that she should not speak of her situation until she is certain of it, because sometimes one or the other sign can be falsely interpreted as a pregnancy.

There are, however, a number of things to which a pregnant sister must pay attention if she does not want to cause harm either to herself or to her unborn child, and we must talk plainly with her about this.

Sometimes the pregnant sisters will be given a special opportunity for instruction and education, for example on December 25 and on July 2.[25]

She can continue having marital relations with her husband into the sixth or seventh month of her pregnancy, if it can occur without difficulty, and if she and her husband agree, she can suspend relations two or three months before her delivery, and they will do so with a sincere prayer.

Examples occur when a husband or wife, or both, will have doubts about whether to continue to have marital relations once the pregnancy is no longer in doubt. Whether or not it is clear from what was mentioned earlier that they do not have reason for doubts, still we must not strongly urge them to do something that is contrary to their judgment, because a husband has relations with his wife not only so that she may become pregnant but also for the preservation of the tender love between married persons. As long as a person

25. July 2 was the traditional feast day of the visitation of Mary with Elizabeth.

believes that this or that is not good but rather is contrary to God's will, he must not do it, even if his opinion is wrong. And we must hold to this with all our people, without exception.

§ 40. If a woman is delivered of a child before its right time, she will do well to follow the advice of experienced doctors by abstaining from marital relations with her husband during the period from the birth through the remainder of the nine months until the child was to have been born. This is because if she again became pregnant during that time, she could easily have another miscarriage, and the doctors refer to experiences they have made in such situations.

But when the proper time for delivery arrives and labor begins, circumstances permitting, the sister will be blessed either by her choir worker or by her husband, that is, one of them will lay a hand on her head and ask the Savior to be near her with his mercy and to help her. A married persons' choir helper is expected not only to give a sister awaiting delivery necessary reminders beforehand and direct her to the Savior, to whom David bears witness: thou art he that took me out of the womb, etc.,[26] but also to be of comfort and help with the delivery by her good counsel and faithful sympathy in all circumstances that are always difficult and dangerous. Once the child is born, the father can give his blessing, whether it is a baby boy or a baby girl, but if the father does not do this, the choir helper will bless the child if it is a baby boy, and his wife will give the blessing if it is a baby girl. Baptism takes place when the congregation is assembled, and not more than five sponsors are chosen.

§ 41. Oh, what an excellent thing it is if a mother's children can drink from her breast. It is good for the mothers as well as for the children. Married persons' choir helpers therefore do all they can to enable this to happen. If, however, an experienced doctor determines that physical circumstances make this impossible, a mother must submit to giving it up, something that never happens to a faithful mother without pain and sadness. Very good advice concerning the feeding of young children can be found in the lovely little book, Christian Upbringing of Children.[27]

In our congregations we are accustomed to advising married persons to postpone relations until the mother has weaned her child. When she has done so and the monthly cleansing has resumed, the child's father will speak

---

26. Ps. 22:9 (KJV).
27. Layritz, Betrachtungen.

with the married persons' choir helper after he and his wife are in agreement about it and will indicate his opinion. If he wants to resume marital relations with his wife, the married persons' choir helper and his wife meet with him and his wife alone and bestow on them their blessing, with laying on of hands and an appropriate verse. And from that time forward, they behave with each other in their marriage in the manner indicated earlier.

The reason for this directive in the married persons' choir is really a medical one. Some doctors think that when a woman nurses her child, that is enough for her. If she became pregnant, she would have another child to nourish and carry in her womb. Thus, it could happen that this would be too much for the mother and would make her too tired. The child still at her breast could lose something, and the sickness associated with pregnancy could take something away from his nourishment, his mother's milk—or the child in the womb could suffer and come off badly in what is needed for its nourishment and growth. Besides, it is thought that we should permit a wife a bit of rest after the birth of a child, and she should be left undisturbed for the duty of nursing.

Nothing can be said to contradict these reasons, but, in truth, we must concede that they are not always confirmed by experience. In certain lands one can come across many hundreds of married couples who produce a child every year, and the children as well as the mothers are healthy, happy, and hearty.

§ 42. If someone should ask whether we find something to confirm this regulation in the holy scriptures of the Old or the New Testament, we cannot cite such a thing. When a woman of the people of Israel delivered a baby boy, she was required, as previously cited, to wait for seven days, and afterward for thirty-three more days, before she was allowed to come back to the holy place, that is, to the tabernacle or temple. During this time she was unclean, and her husband, according to law, was not permitted to touch her. If she had given birth to a baby girl, she had to wait for fourteen days, and afterward for another sixty-six days, before she was allowed to appear in the tabernacle or the temple (see Leviticus 12). In all this time she was considered unclean and her husband was not allowed to touch her. It is nowhere stipulated, however, that he could not come to his wife and have relations with her from that time on until her child was weaned.

Accordingly, it is considered necessary to say clearly and explicitly to brethren and sisters whom we initiate in this regulation, we are giving you our good advice, based on medical reasons and sincere feeling for you. But it is not a commandment from God. Accordingly, if you both think it would be good for you and would not harm either the mother or the child to resume having marital relations while the mother is still nursing the child, then be straightforward and talk with us about it before beginning, because you will not be sinning. If, however, you resume your marital association and have not let us know about it, and you come to us afterward when the child is weaned and beg for a blessing because you then wanted to begin having marital relations again, that is not truthful and is a misuse of the holy name of God, who will bring misfortune on you.

In such matters, you must not do something with doubt, because if you thought it would be wrong and sinful to have marital relations while the mother is still nursing her child, but you acted in a manner contrary to your knowledge and sought to keep it secret, this would really be sinful. If your wife became pregnant, and it thus came to light that you had had relations with each other, the entire married persons' choir would be looking at you because of this. The Savior would not be glorified, which properly happens whenever a sister in our married persons' choir becomes pregnant.

§ 43. We would like to have good advice from our colleagues about what we should do concerning the current circumstance that while, if not all, then certainly very many, sisters and brethren believe it would be a sin for a married couple to resume intimate relations while the mother is still nursing her child; this is more than plausible. If a married couple nevertheless does so and the wife becomes pregnant, then it will be no different than if they were pilloried by their people. If we then did not allow them to go to Holy Communion, this would strengthen the opinion of all those who consider it a sin for married persons to have intimate relations before a child is weaned, even though this belief is erroneous. But if we do allow them to go to Holy Communion, these same brethren and sisters will think, he and she are going to Communion, even though they are living in sin! God help us!

What can happen in the future if we begin to look more at the words than at the meaning? How should we prevent hidden guilt and guard against scandals?

§ 44. Married persons' choir helpers must not think that everything has been said in this essay about what might be expected of them in any situation they might face. They will always have something to learn at the feet of Jesus and in the school of the Holy Spirit. Various practices will become experience, and experience will bring them hope.

We want to draw attention to the following: namely, (1) if brethren and sisters from outside our congregation should ask, even with the most sincere intention, about our arrangements, practices, and methods, we will not make them known, much less recommend them, and this also applies to the congregations of heathen brought together by the Gospel. Doing the opposite has led to sorrowful consequences. We will show only what is written about them in the holy scriptures. (2) Without strongly urging them, we will encourage married persons who come to the congregation from other denominations to explain confidentially and simply about the course of their marriage. We will take care not to give them instructions or decrees. If it is the desire of their hearts to do whatever they do in the name of Jesus and not to serve sin but to live in righteousness, then we will leave the rest to their insight and knowledge, without constraining their conscience. Unless they are very comfortable doing so, we also cannot advise them to postpone their marriage until they are accepted into the congregation or have been admitted to Holy Communion. If they prove themselves to be children of God, then not the slightest difference will be made between them and the married brethren and sisters in the congregation, with regard to the benediction for renewal of marriage and with regard to all other matters. In all these matters, we need to act with much grace, wisdom, and charity, which each one must request from the Lord.

§ 45. The foregoing instruction certainly contains nothing about which we should be ashamed, because it is based on truth and purity and conforms to the wishes of Jesus. One must nevertheless deal with it carefully so that it does not come into the wrong hands. For plain people, our striving to lead a holy marriage, pleasing to God, is foolishness, and they cannot comprehend it. Other religious people consider it carried too far. We have therefore implored and warned all brethren and sisters who serve as married persons' choir helpers not to let this instruction leave their hands, for Jesus's sake. It must be read aloud to the brethren and sisters from the married persons' choir who are members of the elders' conference, because it is good for them to know what we desire for the married persons' choir and good for them to be of the same mind and to bless our work. But no one except the married persons' choir helper may take a copy of it, and he takes it not for himself personally but because of his work. Therefore, when he dies, it will not go to his heirs but must be put in the hands of his successor in the position of choir helper. This will also be the case if he relinquishes his position or is transferred to another location. He will not keep his copy, even if he made it with his own hand, but he will deliver it to his successor, and if a successor has not yet been designated, he will leave it behind in the faithful hands of the minister.

Furthermore, if one or another choir helper should have doubts about this or that point that appears in the aforementioned instructions, or if he thinks something has been left out that in his judgment should be included, he will be asked to report his thoughts plainly to the Unity Elders' Conference, in particular to the helpers' department. They will be accepted with thanks and will be considered.

# 4

## THE WIDOWS' CHOIR

### Introduction

The "Instructions for the Choir Helpers of the Widows" describe in detail the way in which widows were to be counseled for the health of their bodies and souls during their Speakings, as well as in their daily lives. They provide a clear and fascinating look at the expectations for a widow's emotions and grief after the death of her husband and consider the difference in economic status, as well as the differing emotional needs of the bereaved women that would vary according to the happiness of the marriage that death had dissolved.

Far more scholarship exists on the socioeconomic and historical situation of the widow in the eighteenth century, or on her representation in art, literature, and music, than on her grief. Her emotional condition and her sorrow and likely depression after the death of her spouse usually gain scarce mention, as does the pastoral support given her to help alleviate her mourning. This is surprising, as, according to census records for the United States both now and in the eighteenth century, over 60 percent of married women will be widowed, and the vast majority of them will be alone for twenty years or more after their husbands' deaths. According to Lisa Wilson, in early nineteenth-century Philadelphia, 10 percent of the female population of the city were widows, and half of all married women became widows, usually in their late forties. More than 80 percent of those widows never remarried. Today 75 percent of all married women will become widows, and of them, only a third remarry.[1]

---

1. L. Wilson, *Life After Death*, 1, 2.

*Fig. 8*   Devotional painting of the widows' choir, by Johann Valentin Haidt (1700–1780). Courtesy of the Unity Archives, Herrnhut, Germany.

Maybe one reason for the lack of discussion of the pastoral care of the widow lies in the negative light in which the widow has been historically viewed by society. As Helen Watanabe O'Kelly has pointed out, in the modern period in Europe and North America the widow has most frequently been regarded with pity, suspicion, and fear: pitied for her loss, distrusted for her sexual experience, and feared for her economic agency.[2] The societal expectations of the widow's conduct after the death of her husband define necessary and sometimes contradictory roles of grieving widow and surviving provider for her family.[3] Therefore, it is not surprising that the widow is a figure beset with contradictions, both within representations of her in art, culture, and literature and also in her socioeconomic history. Historical studies of the widow have frequently used her as a foil or "other" to discussions of agency of the married woman. But, as Vivian Bruce Conger goes on to argue, "what ultimately makes widows an important group to examine is that they were among the completing definers and constructors of their society."[4]

Given the number of women in different colonial communities who were widows (over 60 percent of those who were married), historians have argued that men and women were accustomed to the presence of widows in their midst. But little literature is dedicated to the widow. Heeding Jean Soderlund's warning about overgeneralizing from the particular, especially in the case of the Puritan widow of New England, it is still possible to claim that there are some universals in the widow's state.[5] As Thomas McGinn has recently argued, widows represent in all cultures a "problematic category of adult women who are notionally independent of males." On the one hand, one has the example of the wealthy widow whose husband has left her more than the legal minimum share of his estate (in Pennsylvania until the latter half of the nineteenth century this was one-third of the life interest on his property), a business or farm to continue in his stead, and strong male adult children who could help her in this project until she grew too old. On the other hand, widowhood could also bring with it destitution, the almshouse, menial piecework such as sewing and washing, or tasks like rocking the crib for a new mother; widowhood could mean a life supported by the chance charity of strangers, themselves perhaps widows of the first kind, that is, women of means.[6] In her study of the widow in Pennsylvania, Lisa Wilson summarizes the sometimes contradictory experiences of the widow: "the

2. Watanabe O'Kelly, "Dangerous to Know."
3. L. Wilson, *Life After Death*, 5.
4. Bruce Conger, "*Widow's Might*," 3.
5. Soderlund, "Eighteenth-Century Pennsylvania."
6. McGinn, *Widows and Patriarchy*, 2.

grief and emotional loss of the husband, the isolation of mourning, the depression deepened by the glorified memories of an idyllic marriage."

In addition to the necessity of dealing with grief and maybe a new state of poverty, the widow also was no longer a wife. Within the patriarchal structures of colonial society, status was acquired through one's husband, through his wealth, rank, family, and business. The widow now had to find a new role in this society, and for many this led to a preoccupation with the absence of the husband, with his grave, his portrait, and a growing dependence on substances, such as stimulants or opiates, that might obliterate the grief and loss of his death.[7] Where then could the widow turn to gain both spiritual and material support? Most of the historians of gender agree that from the medieval period on, the realm of religion offered some place for agency and solace for the widow. Whether as an anchoress, a Mother Superior, or the owner of a boarding house for widows, widowed women were able to extend their agency and influence to other women in their social sphere.[8]

Fortunately, Moravian widows were much better cared for than their contemporaries. Young men and women, either married or single, made up the bulk of Bethlehem's population in the early years of the settlement. The few widows that there were either remarried or else lived in a log house in the nearby settlement of Nazareth. By the beginning of the dissolution of the General Economy in 1762, the need for a larger choir house for the widows had become pressing. For Moravian Bethlehem prior to 1760, the demographic portrait was somewhat different from that of the general population: there were very few people over the age of sixty.[9] But with the end of the General Economy, these numbers soon changed. According to Beverly Prior Smaby, after 1760, "The majority of adults were either single or widowed, and women predominated. The proportion of people over the age of 60 grew higher than in most other populations," to the extent that in 1766, the synod decided to build a widows' house in Bethlehem. The building was finished and occupied in October 1768 at the same time as a fund was initiated to help those widows in financial difficulties. In three years this society, based on one founded in England by men concerned for the welfare of their wives after their deaths, had grown to a hundred investors and as such constituted the beginning of the Widows' Society of Bethlehem, one of the oldest existing beneficial societies in America.[10]

---

7. L. Wilson, *Life After Death*, 13, 15–18.

8. See Mulder-Bakker, "Age of Discretion"; and Mulder-Bakker, *Lives of the Anchoresses*.

9. Smaby, *Transformation*, 51. See also Gollin, *Moravians in Two Worlds*, 85.

10. Levering, *History of Bethlehem*, 410, 411–12. The other widows' societies that might compete for this title are the Presbyterian Widows' Society, founded by Rev. Francis Allison (1759), and the Episcopalian Corporation for the Relief of the Widows and Children of Clergymen (1769).

In early Bethlehem younger widows frequently remarried, thereby easing the burden on the congregation of their upkeep. If they did not remarry, they would provide services in the congregations where they could (for example, widows were asked to care for aging widowers in other congregations). Widows moved into the choir house when they wanted to spend the rest of their days in peace. The older or more sickly sisters were given a separate room to sleep in, which could be heated in winter. The other widows slept in a dormitory. Widows, when physically capable, were expected to work in the kitchen or laundry or to clean the rooms and care for the infirm.

The actual physical existence of a widows' house was considered to be a gift of grace from Christ, for without the ability to live in proximity, much of the spiritual and physical support the widows gave one another would be impossible. The widows aided one another in their state of bereavement, their own special liturgies sustained their faith, and devotional paintings depicted the widows' own particular relationship to Christ.

In addition to the development of his bridal theology (*Ehereligion*), in the 1740s and 1750s Zinzendorf expounded on a theology of widowhood that was elaborated on in his sermons. By bringing together elements of his bridal theology with the specific situation of the widowed state, Zinzendorf was able to recognize and address many of the "universals" of widowhood and also attempt to resolve the inherent conflict between a widow's worldly experience and her present celibacy. For example, in a sermon to the widows in Herrnhut on October 5, 1747, Zinzendorf refers to them as the "first class in the single sisters' choir, the most noble [class], and the crown of the choir."[11] That Zinzendorf can call widows the crown of the single sisters' choir recognizes their present state of celibacy but also validates their worldly experience.[12] The earthly marriage of the widowed sisters has provided them with a foretaste of the Eternal Bridegroom that remains sealed for the single sisters. This (sexual) knowledge is made sacred by means of Zinzendorf's bridal theology; furthermore, widows are single sisters with more practical experience. With their husbands they have worked for the church (*Gemeine*) and have held an office (*Amt*); thus, even though they have

11. "Die erste Classe im Jungfernchor, die vornehmste und so wie die Crone aus dem Chor," in Zinzendorf, "Seligen Jüngers Rede," UA.

12. "They are no longer single; rather, they have been led toward the coming times by their husbands and bestowed with certain seals and promises of future grace and glory." (Sie sind also nicht mehr ledig, sondern sie sind durch ihre Männer der künftigen Zeit entgegen geführt und schon mit gewissen Siegeln und Pfändern der künftigen Gnade und Herrlichkeit beschert worden.) Zinzendorf, "Seligen Jüngers Rede," UA.

had to give up that position upon the deaths of their husbands, they still retain the memory of worldly experience.[13]

Widows have become virgins again, except that they retain traces of being in the world for Christ. Zinzendorf values the widows so highly that he wishes to make of them a "true elders choir," in that each member should be held in the highest esteem for their age and conduct. The expectation of behavior from the widows that reflects their thoughts, words, and deeds as those of an anointed servant of Christ sets a standard that later is for some too high to keep. Zinzendorf, though, claims that the widows should be regarded as messengers, angels, of their eternal husband, Christ, who has shared with them his wisdom, insight, and grace, and as such the widows should be regarded as a blessing and honor to the *Gemeine*. The Moravian widow's role is thus to infect those around her like sourdough: she is an "angel of the eternal husband" and her sheer proximity should inspire the single sisters to also attain this intimacy with Christ. But this air of experience also had negative consequences for the widows. The ideal widow is the one who is completely content with her Eternal Husband, Christ; who does not feel lonely in her solitude; and who does not consider herself to be abandoned or in need of help or protection.[14] According to Zinzendorf, widows should not regard themselves as "personae miserabiles" but rather as blessed wives of the Savior.

*Principia*

Just as the other choirs throughout the Moravian Church needed a set of principia and instructions that would help define the expectations for spiritual and physical behavior, so too did the widows' choir. The principia of the widows' choir emphasize the transition that the widowed sister now has to undergo. She has to cast off her self-understanding as a married sister

---

13. "They [the widows] are virgins who are following the Lamb and are only different from the other single sisters who do not have their own choir business or office, in that they have more experience, that they are familiar with broader circumstances, that they are more at home everywhere." (Sie [die Witwen] sind Jungfrauen, die dem Lamme nachgehen, und sind nur darinnen von den anderen ledigen Schwestern, die kein eigentliches Chorgeschäfte, kein Amt haben, unterschieden, daß sie mehr Erfahrung haben, daß ihnen mehr Umstände bekannt sind, daß sie überall mehr zu Hause sind.) Zinzendorf, "Seligen Jüngers Rede," UA.

14. "She knows that the husband of the widows is sufficient for her and can honestly say, 'I know that He will not leave me, His truth remains firm with me, no one is ever abandoned, who has been betrothed to the Lord Jesus Christ.'" (Sie weiß, daß der Witwen-Mann ihr allgenügsam ist, und kann mit Wahrheit sagen, "Ich weiß, daß Er mich nicht verläßt, seine Wahrheit bleibt mir ewig fest, niemand jemals verlassen ist, der vertraut war dem Herrn Jesu Christ.") Zinzendorf, "Chorrede an die Wittwen," UA.

through a thorough exploration of her marriage, acknowledging all her sins of omission and inclusion. She has to avoid all that is "frivolous, garrulous, carnal and disorderly" in her new status.[15] While young widows are to commend themselves utterly to the crucified Savior, the elderly should also regard their new status as a "pre-Sabbath" (*Vorsabbat*), a preparation for going home to Christ. The sexual knowledge and worldly experience acquired during her walk through life with her husband, or "Vice Christ," are merely a preparation for her final meeting with Christ.

In the few comments that follow the principia, the authors underscore the fact that the verses that are a subscript for the widows' choir's devotional painting redefine earthly marriage. Furthermore, these comments clarify that not all widows will live in the widows' house. Those who have family or means can choose to live outside, but they should participate in the life of the choir.[16] Members of the widows' choir who are not residents of the choir house can attend services, eat meals, care for the sick, and do laundry, just as those who are residents do.

Interestingly, as a point of comparison, the principia for the widows' choir are preceded by a set of principles for the widowers' choir.[17] The widower, like the widow, once bereaved, is considered to be a type of single person. But he is a single person with the experience of having been Christ's Viceroy in an earthly marriage. His first task, as a new widower, is also to examine the path of his marriage and to ask for forgiveness for all his sins. He is then to carry himself in a priestlike fashion, aware of the role he has played for Christ in his marriage, but at the same time he must be careful not to dwell on the "fantasies and frivolous thoughts and images" in his heart.[18] Like the widow, the widower should think of this time as a *Vorsabbat* and not spend his time dwelling on what has passed but rather look forward to what is to come. Should a widower be called to marriage again, he should accept this call with grace.

---

15. "Alles leichtsinnige, geschwätzige, fleichlich gesinnte und unordentliche Wesen." "Principia," Widows' Choir, UA, 41.

16. "Of those widows who serve outside the choir house, the church expects that they participate in the needs of their choir as their abilities allow and do not remove themselves just because they do not live in it." (Von den Wittwen, die außer dem Chorhause noch dienen, erwartet die Gemein, daß sie an der Nothdurft ihres Chores und Chorhauses nach Vermögen theil nehmen, und nicht etwa darum, weil sie nicht darinnen wohnen, sich denselben entziehen.) "Principia," Widows' Choir, UA, 44–45n9.

17. "Principia," Widows' Choir, UA. Although a set of principles exists, there are no instructions for the choir helpers of the widowers.

18. "Phantasien und unnüzen Gedanken und Bildern in seiner Seele." "Principia," Widows' Choir, UA, §§ 3–4, 39.

The principia of the widowers' choir recognize the difficulty of living with bereavement and old age and, as in the principles of the widows' choir, recommend that the widower look with thanks to the Savior as a role model. Furthermore, like the principles for the widows' choir, these few sections on the widowers employ the tropes of the bridal theology (*Ehereligion*) (the husband as Christ's Viceroy, the husband as the priest of the wife) to distinguish between the sexual experience of the widower and the physical virginity of the single brother. Although the term "virginity" is not explicitly employed to describe the spiritual purity of the single brother, it is clear that the widowed brother has become like Christ again in this aspect as well.

*The Instructions*

While the principia revolve around the central idea of the role of Christ as Bridegroom in the widowed life of the choir member (male or female), the instructions were again intended as a specific guide to the choir helpers who held the monthly Speakings with each choir member.

Although widows in the general population frequently read advice manuals, the Bible, prayer books, and hymns to gain comfort in their bereaved state, the Moravian Church not only implemented what could be termed a form of grief counseling for the new widow but also wrote a specific set of guidelines on how this should be administered. We are extremely fortunate to be able to access this moment in the history of pastoral care. In the very first section of the instructions, the variety of circumstances in which the newly widowed woman finds herself are iterated: some may have had their own household; some may have entered the Moravian community only after being widowed; some may have had children, some not; some have stepchildren who are grown; some may have young children; some may be poor; some are of means; some are of high social standing; some are young and can contemplate remarriage; some are old and cannot look after themselves; some can continue a trade practiced by their husbands, some cannot; some led a happy and blessed marriage, some did not; some served the congregation with their husbands either in the married persons' choir or in the missions; "some have such grace and talents that we can dare to entrust them with one of the jobs in the congregation or in their choir; with others this is not possible, but we can be thankful to God if they simply have a blissful heart and adorn themselves with following Jesus" (§ 1).

The original intention for the establishment of a physical space for the widows (which one can find in almost every Moravian congregation, whether in Germany or in missions) was not only to provide shelter and charity to take care of basic physical needs but also to focus the widows' attention on Christ. Within the choir the women lived communally: they shared a kitchen; they ate together at midday; they shared a dormitory, unless they were sick, in which case they were given their own room, which was well heated in winter. Choir meetings were held in a separate room within the choir house. The widows worked in the house, served in the kitchen, helped with the washing, cared for the sick, tended the garden, and cleaned the household.

The opportunity to live in the widows' choir house was considered to be a state of grace. Occasionally, however, a widow resisted, especially when she had to give up substantial independence. This would lead to the widow not being admitted to Communion until she had "opened her heart" to the choir helper about her path through life thus far (§ 3). It seems from the instructions that for some such transparency was not achieved for many years. Again and again, each complaint of the widow, whether because the choir house demanded she be inactive, or live communally, or give up her children to the school is countered with the advice to reconcile herself to her new circumstances and accept them as a sign of God's hand. The widows' choir helper is advised to be especially gentle with those widows who have led a happy and blessed marriage with their recently departed husband. In addition to empathizing with those who weep and offering consolation, the choir helper also had to acknowledge the difficulty for some widows of relinquishing a household and potential financial and sexual independence.

Not all women who lived in the widows' house were old. Young widows posed a particular problem because they might consider themselves to be lying "fallow" (§ 6). Young widows, depending on the needs of the church, were permitted to remarry quickly to maintain the order of the widows' choir house. Entry into the widows' choir was, of course, occasioned by the death of a husband, an event that may have been anticipated or may have happened suddenly. Unlike other choirs, where acceptance may have been drawn out over several years, acceptance into the widows' choir happened without much ceremony. The helper of the married persons' choir accompanied the new widow to her first meeting at the widows' house, before which the widows' choir helper and a brother who conducted the widows' choir meeting received her from the married persons' choir helper, who then left. To symbolize her change of state, the new widow then removed the married persons' choir ribbon from her cap, and the widows' choir helper replaced it with the ribbon of the widows' choir. The brother would sing a few verses appropriate to the situation, and the choir helper then accompanied her to her first widows' choir meeting. In the memoirs of the widows, acceptance into the widows' choir is spoken of as a mixed blessing. On the one hand, it was a place of refuge and solace, but on the other hand it meant separation from one's children and an external confirmation of one's new solitary state. The instructions warn that this initial time in the widows' choir will be especially difficult.

One of the most surprising entries in the instructions pertains to the treatment of unmarried mothers. Given that the Moravian communities practiced such strict sex segregation, it is quite remarkable to find that the unwed mothers taken into the widows' house were counseled and cared for in a noncondemnatory fashion. In the critical literature that has been written on the status of unwed mothers in the prerevolutionary period, there has been a shift from the dichotomous reading that predominated in the field in the 1970s. According to this older model of scholarship, Nathaniel Hawthorne's nineteenth-century depiction of Hester Prynne in *The Scarlet Letter* (1850) reflected the prevalent moral judgment of unwed mothers; however, this public world of repressive sexual mores was also accompanied by a seething underworld of sexual transgression.[19]

More recent scholarship on colonial American societal attitudes toward pregnancy outside marriage has tended to recognize the enormous differences that exist between communities' beliefs and views on sexuality and women, many of which were based on theological and spiritual interpretations of biblical texts (especially the Old Testament's Song of Songs). Such variances make it unwise to generalize about the universality of, for example, condemnation of premarital sex and pregnancy within the colonial world. Many other factors need to be taken into consideration: religious belief, sex, class, and race, for example, complicate the matter even further. But, as Richard Godbeer has pointed out, in the period that surrounded the French and Indian War and the Revolutionary War, the more general loosening of parental or neighborly stewardship over grown children's sexual behavior and over what was a previously sanctioned practice of "bundling" was accompanied by a general shift away from moral surveillance toward more economic and legal concerns over the issue of children born outside wedlock.[20]

The same political and social disruptions in the colonial world act as the impetus for the Moravian authorities to consider drawing up the choir instructions and the principia for the choirs, and, as Elisabeth Sommer has shown, transgressions from the prescribed moral code were frequent in both German and American Moravian communities in the late 1700s.[21] Given the Moravians' strict segregation of the sexes that was followed in the positioning

---

19. See Cline Cohen, "Sex and Sexuality," 311.
20. See Godbeer, "Courtship and Sexual Freedom"; and Godbeer, *Sexual Revolution*.
21. Faull, "Girl Talk"; Sommer, *Serving Two Masters*, 60–63.

of the choir houses, seating in the meeting hall (*Saal*), the walks that men and women were allowed to take, the separate work spheres that rarely overlapped, and the regulations that surrounded entry into the married state, it is surprising that unmarried mothers were not greeted into the widows' choir with a degree of moral judgment. Rather, the moral demeanor of the "widow" was described as being visible from her physiognomy and physical stature. Moral depravity is manifested physiologically—the stigma of single motherhood can be expressed through a physical deformity, the physical deformity of pride. Rather than attempt to cover up her shame through prideful behavior, the single mother should be humble and thus adopt a stance far more pleasing to the Savior.

As we have seen from the discussions of remarriage of widows and widowers, it was a difficult topic. In the earlier days of the Moravian settlement of Bethlehem, widows were permitted to remarry quickly if they were needed in the mission field or elsewhere. Given the shortage of young women in the colonies at the time, this is not surprising. In the final section of the instructions, the choir helper is given advice on how to address a widowed sister's desire to remarry.

So, even though the widow is the Savior's bride now, as would be suggested by the marriage theology and the words of section 9, there is a clear recognition of the power of temporal desires to undermine any theological stability. If she is to remarry, her exit from the choir is as unceremonious as her entrance: the choir helper and the sister discuss the married state as interpreted by the Moravian notion of the marriage theology, the choir helper performs the foot washing, or *Pedilavium*, and asks the remaining members of the widows' choir for their blessing.

Widows in the Moravian Church of the eighteenth century shared the experience of bereavement and the negotiation of sexual experience with a newly found single state with the widows outside the Moravian Church. This complex tension between sexuality and mourning was in many ways mediated in the Moravian tradition through the employment of the tropes of Zinzendorf's marriage theology and the extensive system of pastoral care and communal life offered by the physical existence of the widows' house and the practice of the monthly Speakings. Far from being cast out or treated with suspicion, the widows of the Moravian Church were considered to be the true elders of the church. Having tasted the pleasures of the Eternal Bridegroom through the priesthood of her earthly husband, the Moravian widow could anticipate her heavenly marriage with joy. Grief at the loss of her temporal husband was mitigated by the knowledge that he had joined the Eternal Bridegroom, who also awaited her. Her physical needs were met through the ministry of the widows' choir, either within the walls of the choir house or within the larger community.

Eighteenth-century Moravian widows also deserve critical attention because for the most part they left behind a memoir (*Lebenslauf*), through which we may read how they reacted to the counseling of their grief. It is clear from the memoirs that have been published from this period that the ministry of the widows' choir was considered a blessing. The walls of the widows' house were seen as a place of peace and security that allowed the widows to enjoy their *Vorsabbat* before they joined their Eternal Bridegroom.

§ 1. When we think about the widows' choirs in the Moravian Church, we find that some of our dear sisters in one congregation or another had their own household before they became widows; others did not live in one of the Moravian congregations before being widowed but instead came into the congregation afterward. Some have no children, either because they never had any or because their children died; others have either their own children or stepchildren, who are either still young or already grown and are either as yet unmarried or already married and themselves have children. Some are poor and receive no help or support from their nearest relatives; others have some means with which they can either partially or totally support themselves, or their relatives can provide them with partial or total support. Some were born into families of high standing or otherwise had a noble upbringing, while others are lacking in this respect. Some are also young and of an age that they can marry again; others are past a suitable age for remarriage; some of them are old and without means; some can live with their children or relatives or can serve in a family; for others, neither situation would be appropriate. Some, in their widowhood, can suitably continue the trade practiced by their husbands and raise their children themselves; for others, this is not possible. Some lived with their husbands in a happy and blessed marriage, but for others, this was not the case. While their husbands were living, some served in the congregation, or in the married persons' choir, or with brethren and sisters and friends outside the community, or among the heathen, and were also deaconesses; others did not have these tasks. Some have such grace and talents that we can dare to entrust them with one of the jobs in the congregation or in their choir; with others this is not possible, but we can be thankful to God if they simply have a blissful heart and adorn themselves with following Jesus.

In dealing with each of our widowed sisters, we must take individual circumstances into consideration. When, for example, a widow's outward circumstances cause concerns, particularly in regard to her children, young and old, then the choir helper makes her maternal and compassionate heart available to her and comes to the widowed sister's aid with advice and comfort, insofar as the dear Savior gives her the grace to do so. We must also not forget that many widows, who belong to the brethren and sister and friends living outside the congregations, join the widows in the congregations, each of them generally living in her own individual situation.

§ 2. In the beginning, the number of widows in the Herrnhut congregation was small, but one of the widowed sisters was appointed to look after the others. The widows did not live together, but instead lived with families. After several years, it became apparent, not only in Herrnhut but also in other congregations where there was a similar situation with the widows, that it would be better if the widows who were able to do so became closer to one another and shared a dwelling. The widows agreed to this, found their own house for this purpose, moved into it together, and managed as well as they were able. A few sisters were then charged with attending partly to the internal concerns and partly to the external concerns of this choir. Because these houses had not been built for this purpose, however, it was difficult to attend to everything in proper order. It was therefore decided, first in one, then in other congregations, to build a choir house for the widows and to furnish it according to the choir's circumstances, and this was done in different places. The idea was not the same as is usually the case with homes (*Hospitäler*) for the aged, whose main purpose is to take care of basic physical needs; rather, the intentions were of greater importance. For the choir houses, we proposed that it would be desirable to see persons in the widows' choir who rejoiced in the Lord, whose hearts were fixed on Him, who did not succumb to the vanities of the world, and whose eyes reflected their happy state of grace. Furthermore, with regard to outward circumstances, the intention was to make life for the widows as bearable as possible.

As there are now several living rooms in the choir house, they are allocated to the sisters in the manner that seems most suitable to them, and each room is under the supervision of one sister, unless one or another desires to and is able to have her own room. The cooking is done for everyone in a kitchen, so that they can dine together at midday; they also have the opportunity to prepare their own breakfast or to heat something up for themselves. Each sister is assisted in the washhouse, as her circumstances require. Sisters who are ill have their own rooms, where they are cared for and waited on. In the dormitory, each sister has her own bed, but those who are old or weak have individual rooms for sleeping that can be well heated in winter. There are separate rooms for taking meals together as well as for choir meetings. It is of course necessary to have sisters serve in the kitchen, help with the washing, and tend to the sick; others need to care for the garden and the household; others need to make sure that everything in the choir house is kept clean and tidy. The choir warden for the widows supervises and consults about all these matters. The choir helper must also be familiar with them and must try to advise and to help everywhere. At the same time it must be remembered that, on account of their circumstances, not all sisters in the widows' choir can live in the choir house, and we will help them as best we can.

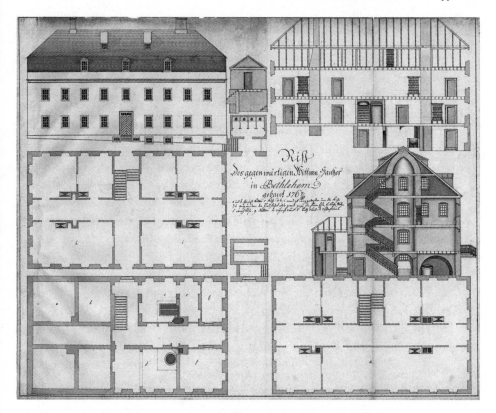

*Fig. 9*  Floor plan of the widows' house. Courtesy of the Unity Archives, Herrnhut, Germany.

§ 3. We regard the widows' choir houses as a merciful gift from our dear Savior, for which we cannot be thankful enough. How difficult it would be for many, if they had to live scattered around the community!

As certain as this is, it is nevertheless essential that no sister be forced to move into the choir house. We should not hold it against her, should her circumstances be such that she continues living in the community, because it is undoubtedly a great change for each sister to leave the busy household she conducted, to enter complete retirement, and to adapt herself totally to the arrangements in a new home. She will have to ask the Savior for special grace, if she wants to follow her path cheerfully and contentedly. It is of great benefit to the sisters who come into the congregation as widows, however, if they move into the choir house right away. A choir helper will have more opportunity to get to know them well, and their own hearts will be more blessed, if they live among their sisters.

Sisters coming to the congregation as widows are usually cheerful about their station in life, because the dear Savior has used it to make a way for them to attain grace, of which they partake in a Moravian congregation, where in peace they can recognize their blessedness. For the most part, each widow has to progress through certain steps, because it is difficult for her to recognize that the Holy Spirit can mercifully work to bring her to a healing knowledge of her limitations and to strip her of her self-righteousness. But we must not cease pursuing a soul with patience and must not press too strongly to convince her of this. We can certainly point it out to her, but we must wait until the Holy Spirit provides the light by which she learns to know herself in her true character. For many, years pass before she understands clearly that she will find her true salvation in living daily as a sinner who finds her way back from every corner and whose heart rejoices in her merciful Savior, who has reconciled her through His suffering and death.

A sister who comes to the congregation a widow will not be recommended for Communion until she has opened her heart to her choir helper and talked in detail about her path up to that time.

The choir helper and choir laborer must be concerned in their hearts with making everything as easy and comfortable as possible for their sisters. There must be order in all things, which together they must maintain with equal regard for all persons.[1]

§ 4. It is the duty of a widows' choir helper to serve the will of God, through His mercy, to achieve His intentions for the whole choir and for each widow. His purpose is this, that the entire choir and each of its members be preserved and led further in the grace that Jesus Christ has bestowed on them. The heart and soul of one and all should be sanctified in the truth and be renewed in God's image through the Holy Spirit. The Savior, who has forgiven their sins, wants to purify each person's weakness with His mercy, and the Holy Spirit wants to fill each with His fruits, which are love, joy, peace, patience, kindness, benevolence, faithfulness, gentleness, purity, etc. A widows' choir helper has an important charge, but she should not lose courage when she prays, weeps, and considers it. She must not forget that it has been entrusted to her, according to the will of God our Savior. In all things which she must do, she can take refuge in Him and can in a childlike way expect from Him guidance and merciful assistance. There is also always a brother in the congregation whose particular task is to assist the sisters' choirs and especially to

---

1. Deleted material in Spangenberg's handwriting is here in the original text.

advise the workers regarding any matters of concern, and this person is nor-mally the congregation helper.

If she needs advice, she communicates with him; she makes it a habit to do nothing in her choir except daily and very ordinary tasks, about which they have an understanding, without consulting him. The choir helpers' confer-ences are also helpful to her, because she has the opportunity to bring any problems and to make use of the experience of other sisters. But if there are matters that require a resolution, and for which it is desirable to have instruc-tion from the Savior, these can be brought by the widows' choir helper to the congregational elders' conference, of which she is a member because of her position. In difficult situations, she has the freedom to turn to the Unity Elders' Conference or to one of its members, particularly from the helpers' department, and to hear their thoughts. At least once a year, she is expected to give a report about her choir, first to the congregation helper, then to the helpers' department of the Unity Elders' Conference.

If a widows' choir helper has an assistant, the assistant shares with her one and the same mission. She should be concerned about the entire widows' choir and each of its members. She must remember to talk with the choir helper about all matters that come to her attention. She is blessed for her office just as the choir helper is, and she also is a member of the elders' confer-ence. An assistant helper in the widows' choir should regard everything in this section that is addressed to the choir helper as though it were addressed to her.

§ 5. When a sister is entrusted with the office of choir helper in a widows' choir, what should she ask of the Savior, and what is first and foremost expected of her?

It is reasonable that she first ask God to take her anew in His hand and make her what she should be, so that she may stand before others as a good example. To this she joins her plea to the Lord that He might cleanse her of everything to which others might object, even if these things are not in and of themselves reprehensible but only appear to be. She should also ask the Lord our Savior to teach, lead, and guide her for the purpose of giving her the spirit of wisdom and understanding, because without Him she will not do any-thing that is good. She also will ask Him for a spirit of mercy and prayer, and because of His presence she will remain constantly in prayer, and thus God will cause her work to prosper. Because she has learned how the Lord leads her with patience, mercy, and grace and because she has learned what com-passion and faithfulness He has shown to her, she now will ask him for a faithful and motherly heart toward each and all of her sisters. If she has such a heart, it will be possible for others to wait patiently until what they wish for comes about.

A choir helper will make herself very familiar with the widows' choir principles, which are contained in the Unity of the Brethren's synod minutes. She will make a copy for herself to have them always at hand so that she can review them.

It can be assumed that a sister who is appointed widows' choir helper will already be familiar with the beautiful widows' choir hymns, which we find in the Moravian hymn book. But when she looks at them again, carefully considering that to which they attest, they will serve to remind her of many wonderful teachings, which provide the widows' choir with guidance for right living.

Much of what is written in the holy scriptures can be a comfort as well as a lesson for widows. A choir helper should be so familiar with Scripture that she is able to point out what is appropriate for each sister, according to her circumstances. Experience teaches that such reminders and grounds for comfort make a special impression when taken from the holy scriptures and used at the proper time and that the Holy Spirit in mercy declares His support in the sisters' hearts. Within herself, a choir helper must be a true poor sinner whose heart enjoys an intimate association with her Savior. She must listen to each sister's request as if she herself were in her circumstances, and she must advise and direct her in as kind and loving a manner as possible. She should treat with particular compassion a sister who had a blessed and happy marriage with her beloved husband and has recently become a widow. No one can hold it against her that she will often feel the pain afresh, that her eyes will sometimes fill with tears. Rather, a choir helper will think of the words: Weep with those who weep!

§ 6. It is undeniable that widowhood is a circumstance calling for consolation; the holy scriptures describe it as such. Yet it is also certain that a sister, if she becomes a widow and relies on the Savior, can have a cheerful and happy heart, even though many things grieve her spirit.

We can and must praise and thank God for showing us admirable examples among our dear widows. A choir helper for the widows will nonetheless almost always need to comfort first one, and then another. All of the sisters, before becoming widows, were mothers of a family, and each had with her husband their own residence, perhaps their own house. Now most of them live with other widows in one room, and it will be difficult for them to become accustomed to this arrangement, particularly because it is inevitable that one will hold something against the others.

A young widow can easily think, Shall I spend my young years in the widows' house and there, as it were, lie fallow? Could I not still be of use for something? And this is often connected with deep pain. It can occur to a widow who is old and ill, Oh if only my dear husband were still living: how much sympathy he would have for me! How much concern he would bear for me! etc. And she does not give this up without pain. A sister who was a worker while her husband lived, and who now is a widow, can often not accommodate to being so inactive, nor to being obliged to do without so many things in which she was formerly blessed to take part. This is all the more painful for her when she cannot imagine that anything will change. In the case of a widow who has all that she needs but still longs for this or that, it can also happen that she will sympathize with herself and will show this. Surely there are many things that can strike a widow with a painful sensation. A widows' choir helper must not think that this is simply a matter of thinking correctly; rather, it is an act of mercy of our Lord Jesus Christ and of His spirit that enables a widow to free herself of whatever hitherto caused her pain. But sometimes when the fog has vanished and the heart has become very cheerful, it can arise anew, which should not be surprising, because the flesh is weak. If we wished to reject immediately everything from a widow who expresses her sorrow and complains about her circumstances, and if we told her that she had foolish notions, we would not gain very much. But if we listen to her sympathetically and admit that this or that could reasonably be difficult for her, she will be much more inclined to pay attention to words of consolation. The remarks of an experienced widowed sister indicate that a widow imagines herself having been forsaken by everyone. Then it is as if she feels sympathy for herself and scarcely trusts herself from time to time to trouble anyone with her concern. For that reason it is necessary to treat her with the utmost compassion and in this way to be a comfort to her.

§ 7. A faithful helper in the widows' choir must become well acquainted with each and every sister who belongs to her choir. She does not cast aside what she hears from those who have frequent contact with a sister and therefore have the opportunity to know her very well, neither does she depend on it, but seeks a personal acquaintance with her. She desires to be a dear friend to each sister and seeks a close association with each one. The most inferior member must not believe that the choir helper loves her less dearly than she loves the most superior member. The poorest member of the choir must know that she has the same free access to her choir helper, as does a sister who is wealthy and distinguished because of her standing. She must not allow herself to become prejudiced against any of the sisters but must inquire and investigate whether a matter is really as it is seems to be.

The widows living in the town must not have reason to think or believe that the choir helper pays less attention to them than to the residents of the choir house.

A choir helper's cordial and humble[2] demeanor toward each sister can certainly inspire trust in her. But everything depends on the Savior's endorsement in grace of a choir helper in the hearts of the sisters she serves, because if this is lacking, her purpose will not be fulfilled. He is only too happy to endorse a choir helper who, in lowliness of heart, prostrates herself at his feet and seeks to take everything she needs to perform her duties from His abundant mercy.

From time to time it happens that a sister is eager to speak completely freely with her choir helper, and, even if she has come at an inopportune time, this sister must not be ignored, because otherwise something could be missed.—A main point here is that the discretion of a choir helper, in whom sisters confide, should never be brought into question, because if this happens, intimacy and frankness will certainly suffer.—When a choir helper makes an effort to get to know her choir sisters, certainly the first thing she would like to know is what is in their hearts. This sometimes requires great patience of a choir helper, because one or another sister may not be able to speak briefly and wants to be heard out. Sometimes she relates her entire life story. It is reasonable to listen, but it is not advisable for a widows' choir helper to urge the sisters to tell her everything that is already settled and buried, because that could do harm.

While a choir helper likes to know, and rightly must know, the condition of each sister's heart, it is also necessary for her to be familiar with each sister's circumstances, for example, whether she is healthy, whether she could work and whether she has work to do, whether she has everything she needs, and other such concerns.

§ 8. On the whole, a choir helper must be very aware of the work of the Holy Spirit in each soul, because He actually takes care of matters, and we are only God's assistants. For example, it can happen that the Holy Spirit leads a sister who has become a widow back to her previous path and shows her various mistakes that became offenses, partly against her husband, partly

---

2. The term translated as "humble" is *herunterlassendes*.

in her household or elsewhere. If she then heartily mourns these mistakes and prostrates herself as a humble sinner at the Savior's feet until He comforts and absolves her, this can have an excellent influence on her for a blessed widow's life.

But if the choir helper wanted to dissuade her from such action and in human fashion speak to her of contentedness before the work of the Holy Spirit had achieved its goal, she would prevent her from receiving a blessing that Jesus's love and faithfulness had intended for her heart. Thus the Holy Spirit can work in such a way that He may show a sister, once she is a widow, how she made mistakes in bringing up her children. If He makes clear to her that she was not a truly faithful mother to her children but rather neglected them, instead of leading them to the Savior and if with His merciful work He brings her to the point of recognizing her own actions and presenting herself as a poor sinner to the Savior, with pain and sadness, then she will find lasting comfort in Him. She would not have received this grace, however, if the choir helper had advised her to put such things out of her mind and not to concern herself further with them, saying that they were over and done with and she could not change anything by worrying.

§ 9. Because in a Moravian congregation we deal with widows who have come to the Savior as poor sinners and have been received by Him in grace, a choir helper can use the proper grounds for consoling them, which one employs with other widows in vain, because they are not proper for them. The widows in our congregations, however, should be full of consolation and should not appear as people who have no Savior and are therefore overcome by grief. For the Kingdom of God is righteousness, that is, a poor sinner is absolved and through Christ receives the forgiveness of sin, which unites the peace of God with joy in the Holy Spirit.

What then are the proper grounds for consolation, which a choir helper can use at all times with her widows? She can remind each widow of the following, from God's Word:

(1) You no longer have your husband, but he has gone home to Christ and will be with Him eternally, in unspeakable joy and blessed light. The multitude of those perfected in righteousness and those of us poor sinners who still manage in our earthly bodies constitute *one* congregation and are joined with one another as members of *one* body, whose head is Christ.

(2) Think of this: Who is the reason you no longer have your beloved husband? Is it not the Lord, who took him to Himself? Does He not have

the right and the power to do with His own what He will? Do not be discontented with His dealings and do not murmur against Him, for to do so is to sin.

(3) All the Savior's ways with us, even if we do not immediately understand them and if they do not seem to bring us joy, are directed toward blessing for us. His intentions are upright and true. If we are His little sheep, led and guided by Him, then we can accept everything that befalls us as coming from His faithful shepherd's hand. A widow can confidently believe: He has peaceful ideas for me, and the path is part of my upbringing for Him and for my perfection.

(4) The Savior comes down to us and sees all our circumstances as an open book before His eyes. He looks upon you as a widow, doing so not with indifference but rather with a tender, compassionate, and sympathetic heart. All our desires are known to Him. By this you can be especially comforted in your present situation, which grieves you so.

(5) Remember what the holy scriptures say: Let us love Him, because He has first loved us. If you do this, then you will also share in the promise: all things must work for good for those who love God. Your beloved husband's death will also work for good for you, and you will be thankful to God that He has taken him to Himself. We then have Him to thank for everything.

(6) Now that your dear husband has completed his course, you are the Savior's widow and you have a special right to Him. He loves you very much— much more than your late husband loved you, and you can associate with Him much more intimately than you were able to associate with your late husband. And in His intimate acquaintance is true happiness.

(7) You are now miserable and forlorn and are therefore privileged before your Heavenly Father, because His eye and heart are directed especially toward whatever is poor, whatever is humble, whatever is despised, whatever is suffering. For that reason He is called the God and helper of widows and orphans. Therefore, Christ's words apply especially to you: whatever you ask the Father in my name, that I will do.

(8) Do not forget that you are a temple of the Holy Spirit. He lives in you and is the guarantee of eternal life. He is the Comforter, which He will prove to you in mercy. Let your heart properly perceive Him, and if you do this and if you genuinely use His grace, then His fruit, which is love, joy, peace, patience, etc., will appear in you.

§ 10. Now these are grounds for consolation for each and all congregation widows. But what does a choir helper do with sisters who have a particular request? If she can help them, she does so. If she cannot help, then she consoles and endeavors to advise them. For example, she will make clear to a sister who would rather have her own room than live with others but does not have the means for this, that we do this out of love for her, since it would be too difficult for her to pay for her own room and the attendant cost of such things as fuel and light. When necessary, she will also have the help and assistance of other sisters, which would not be available to her if she lived alone and had no one to attend to her.

She will listen patiently to a young sister who thinks in advance about what will become of her, but she will indicate to her that she has no reason to be concerned about her future path. The Lord God had in mind from the beginning that He would take care of each and every one of His children, and that He assuredly will do. At the same time, she declares to her that her worry is fruitless and displeasing to the Savior. She should merely tell the dear Savior of her concern in a childlike manner and afterward be quiet and think, I have commended it to Him, He will take care of it in the best way, because He knows what is good for me, and He is more mindful of it than I can be.

A sister who is old and ill is facing her blessed call home. When she comes to Jesus Christ, there is fullness of joy and all need is at an end. Our Lord and Savior suffered infinitely more than we do or can suffer here. With this, the choir helper comforts such dear widows.

If a choir helper is dealing with sisters who were workers before they became widows and are now at a loss because they must do without so much that had formerly been a blessing for them, she will find it difficult to comfort them. It is, however, not good for them to go along discontented with the Savior's directions. They must be shown that they need to reconcile themselves to their circumstances, in which they have been placed, not by any person, but by the hand of the Lord. When their husbands were living, their office called for them to attend conferences, solemn occasions, and festivals. Of course this no longer happens, since the dear Savior has unyoked their beloved husbands. They now have the call commended to widows in the holy scriptures, and they should be untiring in prayer and supplication. If they do this, the Savior will not let them want for happiness.—A widows' choir helper has reason to be very affectionate in her contacts with such sisters. They will be regarded with proper honor in our midst, and we will not forget their faithful service in the house of the Lord, that is, in His congregation. We will occasionally ask for their advice and will gladly use their help here and there when we can, provided that they have the necessary grace and talent and the requisite strength of mind and body for the task.

§ 11. In some persons who have experienced various difficult circumstances and have been affected by many cares, we see with the passing years a certain weakness of spirit; this is often the case in persons of advanced age as well. Lingering physical infirmity can also diminish the mind's vigor. In such cases, it is difficult to pull oneself together and difficult to set aside one's misery or to always curb one's sensitivities, habits, and disposition, which others often find troublesome. A choir helper must employ much love, patience and forbearance in her dealings with sisters who, in spite of their miserable behavior, demonstrate a humble and sincere feeling for the Savior. She must always remember that it is her calling to be a nurse in our congregations, choir houses, and institutions, which are the Savior's homes.

§ 12. A widows' choir helper needs to be concerned and watchful to see that each of her choir sisters is sound in her belief in our Lord Jesus Christ and in her love for Him. Her praying, weeping, and thinking should therefore constantly have as its aim that, in the widows' choir, the sincere love for one another and for all members of the congregation continue growing.

Thus, if she becomes aware that something is missing within or that love has been disturbed by something, then she must not rest until amends have been made. Indeed it is her desire to guard wisely against things that could get in the way of love. Also, because the Savior died that he might procure for Himself His own people, who would be diligent and zealous in good works, she tries in every way to awaken in her choir the willingness to perform loving deeds. There are always opportunities to do loving deeds, and God allows them to come about often, that love might be practiced and tested. There are those who are ill, sometimes in the choir, at other times in the congregation. If one or another sister considers it a kindness to serve someone, then she will not wait until she is requested to do so but will come forward herself.

Many things happen because a widow's willing service is very welcome and is acknowledged with many thanks to the Savior. In his letters, Paul greatly praises such widows, whose loving deeds were prolific. Thanks be to God that the Moravian Church does not lack for such widows; may He give us more such as these!

A widow's first concern is rightly this, that she may have a warm heart for the Savior, but the second is that she may serve in His house, that is in the congregation, and particularly in her choir, wherever there is opportunity for her to do so.

Not only is daily contact necessary for maintaining the relationship among sisters, but classes, social gatherings, and regularly scheduled visits are also intended for this purpose.

§ 13. Without assistants, a choir helper would not get on well, particularly in a large choir. She will be one heart and one soul with her assistant, if she has one. At the same time it is necessary that the two be in complete agreement about the service, not only of the choir in general, but also of each soul in the choir. This cannot happen unless they diligently communicate with each other. It would be difficult for the choir helper as well as for the choir worker if they could not help each other with both internal and external matters, as these are so closely related. Their arrangement must be such that each is the other's right hand and support. Indeed it is very good if, when necessary, the choir worker or the choir helper can take the other's place.

Sometimes the choir helper has one or more assistants. If the Unity Elders' Conference has no misgivings, they are appointed by the congregational elders' conference by means of the lot. The choir helper must faithfully accept her assistants, and when one is assigned a task, she must diligently instruct her beforehand and patiently listen to her report afterward.

Classes are organized to bring together sisters who form a compatible group. One can then speak with them so that each is nourished. The choir helper or her assistant conducts the classes.

Societies are smaller than the classes, making it easier to find sisters who will work well together. Here, a private conversation will be requested, and much depends on the sisters who hold the gatherings. It is good if the choir helper takes the opportunity to make a personal visit to first one, and then another, gathering. Conferences with the sisters who hold the gatherings are absolutely necessary, because they allow a choir helper to learn where hurt may be prevented and where something useful may be done. In this way, she also learns to know better the grace and talent that each sister possesses.

We gladly choose wise and respected sisters as visitors. The choir can be divided among them so that after a while each one makes the rounds to all the sisters and gets to know them. Certain days will be set aside for the visitors to report, in a conference, how they have found things here and there, and the choir helper talks with them about this. It is a great favor if the dear Savior preserves the choir workers in love, so that they keep in mind what will best serve the well-being of their sisters, that they treat one another honestly and with discretion, and that they do not allow anything to arise among the sisters that could lead to conflicts.

§ 14. Congregational rules are printed, and a copy is placed in each room in the widows' house to serve as an occasional reminder of one thing or another. In addition, the widows have their well-considered and undoubtedly necessary house rules. Whoever among the sisters has oversight of a room

(room overseer) is first and foremost expected to seek to preserve love and peace among her sisters. But she must also be concerned that nothing arise among her sisters that is not in accordance with the congregation or house rules. Certain days will be set aside for a conference with these sisters, who are entrusted with supervision of the rooms, so that each might bring what she wishes to mention, and consideration can be given to what help might be offered. So that each one has the opportunity to bring her concerns, a conference will also occasionally be held for the other sisters serving in the choir house, including those who work in the kitchen, the cellar, or the garden, or with the finances, with the washing, in the dormitory, with the sick, or who keep watch at the front door. Strictly speaking, this is a matter for the choir laborer, but the choir helper will do well to take notice of it also and will share her good counsel with the sisters, because honor is also due the Savior in the service of external matters.

Each widow does what she is reasonably able to provide for her own food, but if her earnings, together with what she perhaps has in addition, is not sufficient for her needs, she will receive assistance from the relief fund. This is generally under the choir helper's control, which is fitting, inasmuch as she is the person best acquainted with each sister's circumstances. It is always advisable, however, for the choir helper to choose one sister or several, of unquestionably good character, to help her, and it is generally necessary to write down everything that is collected and disbursed. If she should have on hand too much that is intended for the poor widows, she and her assistant and the choir worker will make a plan as to how and to which sisters it could be distributed. She will present this plan to the elders' conference and, if it is approved, will follow it.

§ 15. If one of the sisters living with others in a room is taken ill, she will be moved to the sickroom. Not only will she receive food to meet her bodily needs, but the choir helper will also give particular attention to how things stand with her heart. For medicine takes effect sooner for a person who is cheerful and blessed in Christ than for one who is not. If a doctor or surgeon should visit a widow who is ill, he should not be left alone, and if the choir helper cannot be present, then the nurse will be there. This is particularly important so that what the doctor or surgeon has to say about diet and medication can be noted exactly. If the widow cannot pay either for the visit of the doctor or the surgeon or for medicine, she will receive assistance from the relief fund.

The choir house and the choir itself are served by various sisters, who must be provided for, and the choir also has other fees. How will the amount

needed to meet these obligations be raised? A distribution is made and each
sister receives a certain amount for her board and a certain amount for room
rent and other fees. The choir helper collects these and then takes care of the
necessary expenses, keeping an orderly account. The curators (*Curatores*) of
the widows' choir review this account, sign it, and then submit it to the elders'
conference. The choir helper takes note of everything and does not withhold
her good advice from the choir worker.

The widows themselves propose the previously mentioned curator to the
elders' conference. If this should happen, the choir helper calls together her
closest assistants, and then also the sisters who supervise the rooms, and
listens to their ideas. When they find one or another brother who is suited
for this position, and if no one has any misgivings, then he is named to it by
the elders' conference. If no objection is offered in the elders' conference, he
is then taken to the lot, and if he is endorsed by it, the position is offered to
him, and if he accepts it, he receives a written instruction for it. Then he
becomes a member of the overseers' conference, representing the widows'
choir, and he speaks for it as often as is necessary. That he be able to do this,
it is of course required that he be familiar with the external circumstances of
the widows' choir and their choir house. If he has no understanding of them,
how can and should he speak for them? A widows' choir helper therefore
properly considers that her curator needs to be aware of what he will be
expected to know. He will also affix his signature to all written transactions
of the widows' choir. His good advice can be useful to the sisters if they by
chance lack for work, because it is always important that work be provided
for them.

If the choir helper wants to use to advantage the ideas of her assistants and
helpers regarding a brother whose name is to be proposed for curator of the
widows' choir, the helpers should also know what the position signifies. It will
therefore be useful to read to them the instructions for the curator of the
widows' choir if they want to hear it, so that their suggestions may serve the
intended purpose.

The curator of the widows' choir can serve as an individual widow's curator, if she so requests. She can, however, choose another curator to take care
of private matters for her.

§ 16. If the sisters are available before Communion, and if the choir is large,
the choir helper asks her closest assistants to help her and divides the work
among them. If in the case of one or another sister something should be found
that is incompatible with the love of God or neighbor, it must be settled or the
sister cannot go to Holy Communion.

A choir helper should also have a sister with whom she is able to communicate confidentially about this or that personal matter. If by chance she does not choose her assistant, the minister's wife can fulfill this role.

As a rule, each sister must be unhesitating in drawing this or that to her attention, since she knows that it will not be held against her.

§ 17. Several necessary remarks follow:

(1) It is a great relief and comfort for the widows' choir helper if she and the other congregation workers get on well together, if she can trustingly communicate her concerns to them, and if they kindly take them to heart.

(2) Acceptance into the widows' choir takes place without much ceremony. When the Savior has placed a sister in the state of widowhood, she comes to a meeting of the widows' choir and, according to accepted agreement, is brought by the married persons' choir helper to the widows' choir helper. A brother also arrives, who is to conduct the widows' choir meeting; otherwise no one else comes, except perhaps the widows' choir assistant, if the choir has one, because even the married persons' choir helper does not remain. Then the widow who is to be received into the choir removes her own choir ribbon, and the widows' choir helper ties the widows' choir ribbon on for her. The brother sings one or two verses appropriate for this change of choirs. Immediately afterward, the choir helper takes her into the choir meeting and sits beside her; the brother who is conducting the meeting commends her to her choir sisters and sings with them one or two verses of blessing for her.

(3) Among the sisters who become widows in the congregation and are still of an active age, there are occasionally persons who need individual care. They have assumed a way of thinking that leads them to believe that now that their husband has died, they should not be subordinate to anyone—everything should go their way. When they then find that, for the sake of order, this cannot work, they become displeased and want to marry again, etc. What should then be done? Experience tells us that nothing can be accomplished in such a situation with a harsh approach. Certainly it is best, if the choir helper demonstrates to such a sister her compassionate and sympathetic heart, putting herself as it were in the sister's place, and if she also advises her simply to give herself up to the faithful hands of Jesus Christ, to adapt to His ways, and to place her hope in His love and faithfulness alone.

(4) If women who in their single state have had children find themselves in the widows' choir, they should be treated wisely and compassionately.

Their demeanor is sometimes striking and is similar to the demeanor of persons whose body and limbs are noticeably disfigured. It tends to occur to them that, for this reason, people they deal with would look down on them. Wishing to guard against this, they assume a manner of dealing with others that may make them appear proud and conceited.

If we find that sisters among the widows who have had children when they were single are presumptuous with others and pace about proudly—which certainly tends to happen, probably with the same intention as in the case of persons whose body and limbs are noticeably disfigured—we must thoroughly enlighten them. That is, we show them that as surely as no true sister would look down on them because of their situation, just as surely would they make themselves contemptible by a peevish, proud, and arrogant demeanor.

On the other hand, if they demonstrate meekness and an afflicted disposition—as the scriptures use the word "afflicted" of persons in a similar situation[3]—in their appearance and entire being, not only would that wipe away others' memory of their situation, but it would also win them love and respect.

§ 18. (5) If a widowed sister who is of an age that she could marry indicates to her choir helper that she would not be averse to marrying, and in fact that she wishes to, the choir helper must not hold this against her but rather must by all means deal with her. Because of course it is better that she talk with her about this than that she express herself to others about it.

(6) If perchance it happens that she should marry again, then the choir helper, if requested, offers to do such things as talk over everything thoroughly with her before the wedding, perform for her the service of foot washing the night before, and commend her anew to the choir for blessing.

(7) If a sister has had little or no education, she will sometimes use words that others who have had a better education find offensive and shocking. She is, however, not aware that her words are so unseemly nor that they are so offensive to others. On the one hand a choir helper must sincerely and earnestly admonish such sisters, letting them know that their expressions and conduct should reflect a heartfelt association with the Savior—regarding this she must stand firm. On the other hand, she must show them love and patience, not scold them for this unseemliness, for it is evident that they do not attach the bad meaning to their words

---

3. The word used is *gedemütigt*, which is translated in the King James Version as "afflicted."

that others tend to. If we were to judge this conduct in a sister who has had little education as harshly as we rightly would in others, we would only make her confused and would accomplish nothing.

(8) We should not prevent the sisters from visiting their families, because we must not hinder their enduing love. Each one must merely take care that her conduct and speech should honor her Lord and Savior. Relevant here is the admonition of the Apostle, 1 Timothy 5:13.[4]

(9) We cannot forbid sons to visit their mothers in a widows' house, nor can we forbid other brethren who have dealings with a sister, but everything must be done correctly. If a sister does not have a separate room for herself, she will have to insist on a small space somewhere else in the house where she can speak with someone. A brother cannot be allowed to come and go freely where several sisters live together in one room.

We herewith conclude this document, which has been drawn up to serve the widows' choir helpers, and wish a thousand blessings upon its use.

---

4. "And withal they learn to be idle, wandering about from house to house; and not only idle, but tattlers also and busybodies, speaking things which they ought not." 1 Tim. 5:13 (KJV).

## GLOSSARY OF TERMS SPECIFIC
## TO THE MORAVIAN CHURCH

*Agapen* love feasts held before Holy Communion

*Ältesten-Conferenz* elders' conference, charged with supervising the spiritual affairs of a congregation or district

*Ältester/in* elder/eldress

*Anbeten* prostration; meeting where worshippers prostrated themselves in adoration

*Arbeiter/in* laborer in full-time employment of the church

*Aufseher-Collegium* college of overseers; in North Carolina, the board of supervisors, later trustees. This board was composed of the brethren of the elders' conference plus several reliable brethren from the married and the single brethren's choirs. It ranked second in authority to the elders' conference.

*Besucher* visitor (official position within choir)

*Brüdergemeine* Moravian Church or Moravian congregation of the brethren; equivalent to *Brüder-Unität* when referring to the church as a whole, sometimes referred to as the "Unity"

*Bund* covenant

*Chor* choir; group in the congregation whose members are of the same sex and marital status, except for the children's and the married persons' choir. According to Peucker, the word comes from the Greek *khorus*, meaning "group." Another etymology claims a root in the French *corps*. Zinzendorf defines the choirs as "orders and groups that are formed by persons of one's gender and marital status" (see "Eventualtestament," 1738, qtd. in Peucker, *Herrnhuter Wörterbuch*, 18).

*Chorarbeiter/in* choir laborer; usually an individual appointed to spiritual leadership within a choir

*Chordiener/in* choir warden/warden. In its broader sense this term was used to designate a church official, including an ordained minister in pastoral service. In the 1740s, however, it more frequently signified individuals in charge of temporal affairs, the wardens or supervisors of a congregation or choir. But in a more restricted sense it could also apply to a sacristan. The official college of *Diener*, the *Diener Collegium*, was as a rule presided over by the warden of the congregation.

*Chorhelfer/in* choir helper; person responsible for the spiritual life of the members of a specific choir. In the eighteenth century, this person was always a member of the choir in which he or she was the helper (even in the children's choir).

*Chorversammlung* choir meeting

*Chorviertelstunde* choir quarter hour; short services for each specific choir

*Classen* classes; group within a choir that fit together well in certain ways (usually according to the degree of spiritual progress) so that their pastoral conversations could be best directed

*Curatores* curators; men appointed as financial and legal advisers and representatives of the widows' and single sisters' choirs in the *Aufseher Collegium* and the *Helfer Conferenz*

*Departement* administrative division

*Destination* calling

*Ehereligion* marriage theology

*Erweckungsprozess* spiritual awakening

*Fremden-Diener* guide for strangers; brother or sister who took care of visitors from outside the congregation and ensured their proper behavior in the Moravian settlement

*Gemein-Arbeiter* minister

*Gemeindirection* board of the congregation; distinct from the board of the worldwide church

*Gemeine* congregation (local) or church (general)

*Gemeinhelfer* minister or pastor of the congregation but not necessarily its stated preacher

*Gemein-Ordnung* church order; rules of the congregation

*Gemeinort* church settlement

*Gemeinversammlung* congregation meeting

*Gesellschaften/Sozietät* companies; small groups of two or three brethren or sisters well suited to meet together with the choir helper for pastoral conversations

*Gesellschafthalter/in* company leader

*Haus-Diener/in* house warden; worker serving the single brethren's or single sisters' choir house

*Haus-Ordnung* rules of the (choir) house

*Heimgang* home going or death

*Hospitäler* homes, especially for elderly widows and widowers

*Kinder-Schwester* sister who works with the children as both a teacher and overseer

*Lebenslauf* memoir; written first-person account of one's own life, frequently framed by the comments of the choir helper

*Ledige Wärterin* single persons' attendant

*Liebesmahl* love feast; informal liturgical meeting in which tea and buns are served to celebrate the communal care of the choir or congregation, always accompanied by music, singing, and announcements

*Meister* master. Especially important in the single brethren's choir, the master was a craftsman or tradesman to the apprentices in the choir and hence added another layer of both supervision and tutelage.

*Ortsgemeine* settlement congregations

*Pedilavium* foot washing

*Pilger- und Streitersache* pilgrims and militants. A central idea of Zinzendorf's theology from the 1730s is that the missions, and Bethlehem itself, were founded to support the "pilgrims and militants" marching onto the fields of battle against Satan and under the command of Jesus Christ.

*Plan* plan; overriding mission or aim of a choir member (frequently fulfilled in the mission field, on a farm, or with children)

*Prediger* ordained minister of the church

*Procurator-Ehe* marriage by proxy, where the earthly husband stands in for Christ

*Saal* hall in which religious services are held

*Singstunde* singing meeting; short service, originated in 1727, during which individual verses of hymns are sung that are connected through a theme or Bible text and form a kind of sermon in song

*Sprechen* Speaking; pastoral conversation, usually carried out individually but also in small groups (especially among the older girls and boys) prior to Holy Communion

*Stuben-Aufseher/in* room overseer

*Stuben-Schwestern* room sisters

*Stuben-Vorgesetzte(r)* room leader

*Stubenwächter* room watch; brother or sister appointed to ensure rules are adhered to in the dormitories

*Synodalverlaß* Harmony (Results) of the Synods; refers primarily to the post-Zinzendorf synods of the 1760s, 1770s, and 1780s and contains various regulations and principles

*Unitäts-Ältesten-Conferenz* Unity Elders' Conference

For a full explanation of terminology specific to the Moravian Church in German, see Peucker, *Herrnhuter Wörterbuch*. See also Crews, *Moravian Meanings*. For an extended examination of the role of offices within the Moravian Church of the eighteenth century, see Wollstadt, *Geordnetes Dienen*.

# BIBLIOGRAPHY

PRIMARY SOURCES

*General Archival Materials*

**Moravian Archives, Bethlehem, Pennsylvania (MAB)**
Bage, Nikolaus Lorenz. Memoir. Memoirs Men Box.
Brunner, Rosina. Memoir. Memoirs Women Box.
Führer, Valentin. Memoir. Memoirs Men Box.
Gregor, Christian. Letter to C. G. Reichel. June 17, 1800. Other Matters. Married Persons' Choir Box.
"In the Married State the Act of Cohabitation . . . ." n.d. Married Persons' Choir Box.
Reichel, Johannes. Letter to the Helpers Conferences of Pennsylvania. February 2, 1785. Married Persons' Choir Box.
Spangenberg, August Gottlieb. "Gutachten des Unitäts-Ältesten-Conferenz die Ehe-Sache in unseren Heiden-Gemeinen betreffend." 1786. Doc. 4. Provincial Helpers Conference Box.
———. "Instructions for the Choir Helpers of the Single Sisters." Doc. 19. Single Sisters' Choir Box.
Unity Elders' Conference, Herrnhut. "Letter to the Holders of the Office of Married Peoples' Choir Helper." April 1, 1785. Doc. 3. Provincial Helpers Conference Box.
Untitled manuscript. Doc. 7. Provincial Helpers Conference Box.

**Unity Archives, Herrnhut, Germany (UA)**
Minutes. General Synod, Barby. 1775. R.2.B.46.1.
Minutes. General Synod, Marienborn. 1764. R.2.B.44.1.c.1.
Minutes. General Synod, Marienborn. 1769. SR.2.B.45.1.
"Ordnungen des Schwesternhauses." N.d. R.4.C.IV.10.a.7–16.
"Principia." Married Persons' Choir. 1769. Supplement 3. Minutes. General Synod, Marienborn. R.2.B.45.1.
"Principia." Single Brethren's Choir. 1769. Supplement 3. Minutes. General Synod, Marienborn. R.2.B.45.1.
"Principia." Single Sisters' Choir. 1769. Supplement 3. Minutes. General Synod, Marienborn. R.2.B.45.1.
"Principia." Widowers' Choir. 1769. Supplement 3. Minutes. General Synod, Marienborn. R.2.B.45.1.
"Principia." Widows' Choir. 1769. Supplement 3. Minutes. General Synod, Marienborn. R.2.B.45.1.
Spangenberg, August Gottlieb. Letter to Sister von Hayn. November 1, 1780. R.4.C.IV.Nr.10.
———. "On the Oeconomie." R.14.A.42.12.
Zinzendorf, Nikolaus Ludwig von. "Chorrede an die Wittwen am 29. Juli, 1755." R.4.C.VI.2.8.
———. "Des seligen Jüngers Rede an die Wittwen in Herrnhuth, den 5. Oktober 1747." R.4.C.VI.2.8.

University of Bristol Special Collections, Bristol, U.K. (UBSC)
Minutes. Provincial Helpers Conference, held with the Labourers of the Moravian Church. September 30–October 13, 1795, Fulneck. Item 53. Box D. GB 003. DM 451.

*Instructions*

"Instructions for the Choir Laborers of the Single Sisters in General and for the Choir Helpers in Particular." 1819. Manuscript. Gracehill Moravian Church Archive, Northern Ireland.
"Instruction zum Gebrauch bey der Einleitung neu getaufter Eheleute in unseren Heidengemeinen." 1786. Folder 4. Provincial Helpers Conference Box. MAB.
Spangenberg, August Gottlieb. "Instruction für die Chor-Helfer der ledigen Brüder." 1786. (In Spangenberg's hand.) R.4.C.III.3.2. UA.
———. "Instruction für die Chor-Helferinnen der Wittwen." 1786. Widows Box. MAB.
———. "Instructions for the Choir Helpers of the Single Brothers." ca. 1785. Folder 19. Bethlehem Single Brothers Box. MAB.
———. "Instructions for the Helpers of the Married Person's Choirs, with Cover Letters from the UEC." 1785. Folder 3. Provincial Helpers Conference Box. MAB.
———. "Instructions for the Helpers of the Single Sisters' Choir, with an Accompanying Letter from the UEC to the Ministers (Gemeinhelfer) and the Choir Helpers and a Separate Letter to the Ministers Regarding the Confidentiality of These Instructions." 1785. Folder 19. Bethlehem Single Sisters Box. MAB.
———. "Instructions for the Laborers of the Married Choir." 1819. Gracehill Moravian Church Archive, Northern Ireland.

*Printed Sources*

Cranz, David. *Alte und neue Brüder-Historie; oder, kurz gefasste Geschichte der Evangelischen Brüder-Unität in den ältern Zeiten und insonderheit in dem gegenwärtigen Jahrhundert.* Barby, Germany: Ebers, 1771.
David, Christian. *Beschreibung und Zuverläßige Nachricht von Herrnhut in der Ober-Lausitz: Wie es erbauet worden, und welcher Gestalt Nach Lutheri Sinn und Meinung Eine recht Christliche Gemeine sich daselbst gesammlet und eingerichtet hat.* Leipzig, Germany: Walther, 1735.
Dober, Johann Martin. *Verfassung der Herrnhutischen Mährischen Brüder-Gemeine.* Leipzig, Germany: Walther, 1735.
Layritz, Paul Eugen. *Betrachtungen über eine verständige und christliche Erziehung der Kinder.* Barby, Germany, 1776.
Richter, Christian Friedrich. *Die Höchst-nöthige Erkennnis des Menschen vom Leibe und natürlichem Leben, oder ein deutlicher Unterricht, von der Gesundheit und deren Erhaltung.* Leipzig, Germany, 1710.
Spangenberg, August Gottlieb. *An Exposition of Christian Doctrine, as Taught in the Protestant Church of the United Brethren, or Unitas Fratrum.* Translated by Benjamin LaTrobe. Bath, England: Hazard, 1796.
———. *Idea Fidei Fratrum, oder kurzer Begrif der christlichen Lehre in den evangelischen Brüdergemeinen dargelegt v. August Gottlieb Spangenberg.* Barby, Germany, 1779.
Steinhofer, Friedrich Christoph. *Evangelisches Gesang-Buch: In einem hinlänglichen Auszug der Alten, Neuern und Neuesten Lieder, der Gemeine in Ebersdorf zu öffentlichem und besonderm Gebrauch gewidmet.* Ebersdorf, Germany: Waysen-Haus, 1745.
*Vier und Dreißig Homiliae über die Wunden-Litaney der Brüder, gehalten auf dem Herrnhaag in den Sommer-Monathen 1747 von dem Ordinario Fratrum. Zu finden in den Brüder-Gemeinen,* n.p., [1747?].

Zinzendorf, Nikolaus Ludwig von. *Antizinzendorfiana: Aus der Anfangszeit, 1729–1735.* In *Nikolaus Ludwig von Zinzendorf: Ergänzungsbände zu den Hauptschriften,* edited by Erich Beyreuther and Gerhard Meyer, vol. 14. Hildesheim, Germany: Olms, 1976.

———. *Litaney zu den Wunden des Mannes.* In *Nikolaus Ludwig von Zinzendorf: Hauptschriften,* edited by Erich Beyreuther and Gerhard Meyer, vol. 3. Hildesheim, Germany: Olms, 1963.

SECONDARY SOURCES

Aristotle. *Generation of Animals.* Translated by A. L. Peck. London: Heinemann, 1943.

Atwood, Craig D. "Apologizing for the Moravians: Spangenberg's *Idea Fidei Fratrum.*" *Journal of Moravian History,* no. 8 (Spring 2010): 53–88.

———. *Community of the Cross: Moravian Piety in Colonial Bethlehem.* University Park: Pennsylvania State University Press, 2004.

———. "Little Side Holes: Moravian Devotional Cards of the Mid-Eighteenth Century." *Journal of Moravian History,* no. 6 (Spring 2009): 61–75.

———. "Spangenberg: A Radical Pietist in Colonial America." *Journal of Moravian History* 4 (2008): 7–27.

———. *The Theology of the Czech Brethren from Hus to Comenius.* University Park: Pennsylvania State University Press, 2009.

———. "The Union of Masculine and Feminine in Zinzendorfian Piety." In Faull, *Masculinity, Senses, Spirit,* 11–38.

———. "The Use of the 'Ancient Unity' in the Historiography of the Moravian Church." *Journal of Moravian History* 13, no. 2 (2013): 109–57.

Augustine. *Confessions.* Vol. 1, *Books 1–8.* Edited and translated by Carolyn J.-B. Hammond. Cambridge, Mass.: Harvard University Press, 2014.

Breul, Wolfgang. *Geschlechtlichkeit und Ehe im Pietismus.* Leipzig, Germany: Evangelische Verlagsanstalt, 2014.

"A Brief History of Moravian Theological Seminary." *Moravian Theological Seminary.* Accessed September 9, 2016. www.moravianseminary.edu.

Broomhall, Susan, and Jacqueline Van Gent, eds. *Governing Masculinities in the Early Modern Period: Regulating Selves and Others.* Farnham: Ashgate, 2011.

Bruce Conger, Vivian. *"The Widow's Might": Widowhood and Gender in Early British America.* New York: New York University, 2009.

Cline Cohen, Patricia. "Sex and Sexuality: The Public, the Private, and the Spirit Worlds." *Journal of the Early Republic* 24, no. 2 (2004): 310–18.

Crews, C. Daniel. *Moravian Meanings: A Glossary of Historical Terms of the Moravian Province, Southern Province.* Winston-Salem: Moravian Archives, 1996.

Duden, Barbara. *The Woman Beneath the Skin: A Doctor's Patients in Eighteenth-Century Germany.* Translated by Thomas Dunlap. Cambridge, Mass.: Harvard University Press, 1991.

Engel, Kate Carté. *Religion and Profit: Moravians in Early America.* Philadelphia: University of Pennsylvania Press, 2009.

Falckner, Daniel. *Falckner's "Curieuse Nachricht von Pennsylvania": The Book That Stimulated the Great German Emigration to Pennsylvania in the Early Years of the XVIII Century.* Translated by Julius Friedrich Sachse. Philadelphia: printed for the author, 1905.

Faull, Katherine. "Girl Talk: The Role of the 'Speakings' in the Pastoral Care of the Older Girls' Choir." *Journal of Moravian History,* no. 6 (Spring 2009): 77–99.

———. "The Married Choir Instructions (1785)." *Journal of Moravian History,* no. 10 (Spring 2011): 69–110.

———. "Masculinity in the Eighteenth-Century Moravian Mission Field: Contact and Negotiation." *Journal of Moravian History* 13, no. 1 (2013): 27–53.

————, ed. *Masculinity, Senses, Spirit*. Lewisburg: Bucknell University Press, 2011.

————, trans. and ed. *Moravian Women's Memoirs: Their Related Lives, 1750–1820*. Syracuse: Syracuse University Press, 1997.

————. "Schleiermacher and Transcendentalist Truth-Telling: Ethics, Gender and Speech in Nineteenth-Century New England." In *Schleiermacher's Influences on American Thought and Religious Life, 1835–1920*, edited by Jeffrey A. Wilcox, Terrence N. Tice, and Catherine L. Kelsey, 293–321. Princeton Theological Monograph Series 205. Eugene: Pickwick, 2014.

————. "Speaking and Truth-Telling: Parrhesia in the Eighteenth-Century Moravian Church." In *Self, Community, World: Moravian Education in a Transatlantic World*, edited by Heikki Lempa and Paul Peucker, 147–67. Bethlehem: Lehigh University Press, 2010.

————. "Temporal Men and the Eternal Bridegroom: Moravian Masculinity in the Eighteenth Century." In Faull, *Masculinity, Senses, Spirit*, 55–80.

————. "'You Are the Savior's Widow': Religion/Sexuality and Bereavement in the Eighteenth-Century Moravian Church." *Journal of Moravian History*, no. 8 (Spring 2010): 89–115.

Fogleman, Aaron Spencer. *Jesus Is Female: Moravians and the Challenge of Radical Religion in Early America*. Philadelphia: University of Pennsylvania Press, 2007.

————. *Two Troubled Souls: An Eighteenth-Century Couple's Spiritual Journey in the Atlantic World*. Chapel Hill: University of North Carolina Press, 2014.

Foucault, Michel. *History of Sexuality*. Translated by Robert Hurley. New York: Pantheon Books, 1978.

Fox, Christopher, Roy Porter, and Robert Wokler, eds. *Inventing Human Science: Eighteenth-Century Domains*. Berkeley: University of California Press, 1995.

Foxhall, Lin, and J. B. Salmon. *Thinking Men: Masculinity and Its Self-Representation in the Classical Tradition*. London: Routledge, 1998.

Gillespie, Michele, and Robert Beachy, eds. *Pious Pursuits: German Moravians in the Atlantic World*. New York: Berghahn Books, 2007.

Gilman, Sander L. *Disease and Representation: Images of Illness from Madness to AIDS*. Ithaca: Cornell University Press, 1988.

————. *Making the Body Beautiful: A Cultural History of Aesthetic Surgery*. Princeton: Princeton University Press, 1999.

Godbeer, Richard. "Courtship and Sexual Freedom in Eighteenth-Century America." *Magazine of History* 18, no. 4 (2004): 9–13.

————. *Sexual Revolution in Early America*. Baltimore: Johns Hopkins University Press, 2004.

Gollin, Gillian. *Moravians in Two Worlds: A Study of Changing Communities*. New York: Columbia University Press, 1967.

Griffin, Frances. *Less Time for Meddling: A History of Salem Academy and College, 1772–1866*. Winston-Salem: Blair, 1979.

Hahn, Hans-Christoph, and Hellmut Reichel, eds. *Zinzendorf und die Herrnhuter Brüder: Quellen zur Geschichte der Brüder-Unität von 1722 bis 1760*. Hamburg: Wittig, 1977.

Hamburger, Jeffrey. *Nuns as Artists: The Visual Culture of a Medieval Convent*. Berkeley: University of California Press, 1996.

Hamilton, J. Taylor, and Kenneth G. Hamilton. *History of the Moravian Church: The Renewed Unitas Fratrum, 1722–1957*. Bethlehem: Interprovincial College of Christian Education, Moravian Church of America, 1967.

Hausen, Karin. "Die Polarisierung der 'Geschlechtscharaktere': Eine Spiegelung der Dissoziation von Erwerbs- und Familienleben." In *Sozialgeschichte der Familie in der Neuzeit Europas: Neue Forschungen*, edited by Werner Conze, 363–93. Stuttgart: Klett, 1976.

Hull, Isabel V. *Sexuality, State, and Civil Society in Germany, 1700–1815*. Ithaca: Cornell University Press, 1996.

Hutton, James E. *A History of the Moravian Church*. London: Moravian Publication Office, 1909.

Jensz, Felicity. *German Moravian Missionaries in the British Colony of Victoria, Australia, 1848–1908: Influential Strangers.* Studies in Christian Mission 38. Leiden: Brill Academic, 2010.

Jones, Colin, and Roy Porter. *Reassessing Foucault: Power, Medicine, and the Body.* London: Routledge, 1994.

Kress, Otto. *Medicinische-diätetische Gesundheitslehre nach den gesetzen der natur und dem baue des menschlichen organismus. Mit besonderer rücksicht auf die krankheiten der höheren stände, ihre ursachen und ihre heilung populär dargestellt.* Dresden: Klemm, 1864.

Laqueur, Thomas. *Making Sex: Body and Gender from the Greeks to Freud.* Cambridge, Mass.: Harvard University Press, 1990.

———. *Solitary Sex: A Cultural History of Masturbation.* New York: Zone Books, 2003.

Levering, Joseph Mortimer. *A History of Bethlehem, Pennsylvania, 1741–1892: With Some Account of Its Founders and Their Early Activity in America.* Bethlehem: Times, 1903.

Lloyd, George. "'Speaking' in the Moravian Church: An Inquiry into the Historical and Religious Significance of This Practice and Its Implications for Pastoral Care and Counseling." D.Min., San Francisco Theological Seminary, 1983.

Lost, Christine. "'Kinder in Gemeinschaft bringen': Zu Konzept und Praxis der Kindererziehung in der frühen Brüdergemeine." In *Das Kind in Pietismus und Aufklärung: Beiträge des Internationalen Symposions vom 12.-15. November 1997 in den Franckeschen Stiftungen zu Halle,* edited by Josef N. Neumann and Udo Sträter, 95–110. Tübingen: Franckeschen Stiftungen Halle im Niemeyer, 2000.

———. *Leben als Lehrtext: Lebensläufe aus der Herrnhuter Brüdergemeine.* Herrnhut: Herrnhuter, 2007.

McGinn, Thomas A. J. *Widows and Patriarchy: Ancient and Modern.* London: Duckworth, 2008.

Meyer, Dietrich, and Hans-Christoph Hahn. *Bibliographisches Handbuch zur Zinzendorf-Forschung.* Mülheim: Blech, 1987.

Meyer, E. Rudolf. *Schleiermachers und C. G. Brinkmanns Gang durch die Brüdergemeine.* Leipzig, Germany: Jansa, 1905.

Miller, Derrick R. "Moravian Familiarities: Queer Community in the Moravian Church in Europe and North America in the Mid-Eighteenth Century." *Journal of Moravian History* 13, no. 1 (2013): 54–75.

Mulder-Bakker, Annette. "The Age of Discretion: The Role of the Wise Old Widow in Medieval Society." Paper presented at the Centre for Research into Gender and Culture in Society conference, "The Merry Widow: Rethinking Widowhood in History, Culture, and Society," Swansea University, Wales, July 7–9, 2007.

———. *Lives of the Anchoresses: The Rise of the Urban Recluse in Medieval Europe.* Translated by Myra Heerspink Scholz. Philadelphia: University of Pennsylvania Press, 2005.

Peucker, Paul. "Gegen das Regiment von Schwestern: Die Änderungen nach Zinzendorfs Tod." *Unitas Fratrum Zeitschrift für Geschichte und Gegenwartsfragen der Brüdergemeine* 45–46 (1999): 61–72.

———. *Herrnhuter Wörterbuch: Kleines Lexikon von brüderischen Begriffen.* Herrnhut: Unitätsarchiv, 2000.

———. "The Ideal of Primitive Christianity as a Source of Moravian Liturgical Practice." *Journal of Moravian History,* no. 6 (2009): 7–29.

———. "'Inspired by Flames of Love': Homosexuality, Mysticism, and Moravian Brothers Around 1750." *Journal of the History of Sexuality* 15, no. 1 (2006): 30–64.

———. "In the Blue Cabinet: Moravians, Marriage, and Sex." *Journal of Moravian History,* no. 10 (Spring 2011): 6–37.

———. "Selection and Destruction in Moravian Archives Between 1760 and 1810." *Journal of Moravian History* 12, no. 2 (2012): 170–215.

———. *A Time of Sifting: Mystical Marriage and the Crisis of Moravian Piety in the Eighteenth Century.* University Park: Pennsylvania State University Press, 2015.

Porter, Roy. *Disease, Medicine, and Society in England, 1550–1860.* Cambridge: Cambridge University Press, 1995.

———. *Rewriting the Self: Histories from the Renaissance to the Present.* London: Routledge, 1997.

Porter, Roy, and Lesley A. Hall. *The Facts of Life: The Creation of Sexual Knowledge in Britain, 1650–1950.* New Haven: Yale University Press, 1995.

Ptaszyński, Maciej. "Between Marginalization and Orthodoxy: The Unitas Fratrum in Poland in the Sixteenth Century." *Journal of Moravian History* 14, no. 1 (2014): 1–29.

Rau, Robert, and Elizabeth L. Myers. "The Physicians of Early Bethlehem." *Transactions of the Moravian Historical Society* 11, no. 1 (1931): 56–61.

Reichel, Gerhard. *Die Anfänge Herrnhuts: Ein Buch vom Werden der Brüdergemeine; Zur Erinnerung an die Gründung Herrnhuts am 17. Juni 1722.* Herrnhut: Verlag der Missionsbuchhandlung, 1922.

Říčan, Rudolf, C. Daniel Crews, and Amedeo Molnár. *The History of the Unity of Brethren: A Protestant Hussite Church in Bohemia and Moravia.* Bethlehem: Moravian Church in America, 1992.

Richter, Simon. "Wet-Nursing, Onanism, and the Breast in Eighteenth-Century Germany." *Journal of the History of Sexuality* 7, no. 1 (1996): 1–22.

Riley, Jobie E. "An Analysis of the Debate Between Johann Conrad Beissel and Various Eighteenth-Century Contemporaries Concerning the Importance of Celibacy." PhD diss, Temple University, 1974.

Roeber, A. Gregg. *Hopes for Better Spouses: Protestant Marriage and the Church Renewal in Early Modern Europe, India, and North America.* Grand Rapids: Eerdmans, 2013.

———. "The Waters of Rebirth: The Eighteenth Century and Transoceanic Protestant Christianity." *Church History* 79, no. 1 (2010): 40–76.

Roper, Lyndal. "Sexual Utopianism in the German Reformation." *Journal of Ecclesiastical History* 42, no. 3 (1991): 394–418.

Schings, Hans-Jürgen. *Melancholie und Aufklärung: Melancholiker und ihre Kritiker in Erfahrungsseelenkunde u. Literatur des 18. Jh.* Stuttgart: Metzler, 1977.

Shail, Andrew, and Gillian Howie. *Menstruation: A Cultural History.* Basingstoke, England: Palgrave Macmillan, 2005.

Smaby, Beverly Prior. "'No One Should Lust for Power . . . Women Least of All': Dismantling Female Leadership Among Eighteenth-Century Moravians." In Gillespie and Beachy, *Pious Pursuits,* 159–75.

———. "'Only Brothers Should Be Accepted into This Proposed Council': Restricting Women's Leadership in Moravian Bethlehem." In *Pietism in Germany and North America, 1680–1820,* edited by Jonathan Strom, Hartmut Lehmann, and James Van Horn Melton, 133–62. Farnham, England: Ashgate, 2009.

———. *The Transformation of Moravian Bethlehem: From Communal Mission to Family Economy.* Philadelphia: University of Pennsylvania Press, 1989.

Soderlund, Jean. "Women in Eighteenth-Century Pennsylvania: Toward a Model of Diversity." *Pennsylvania Magazine of History and Biography* 115, no. 2 (1991): 163–83.

Sommer, Elisabeth W. *Serving Two Masters: Moravian Brethren in Germany and North America, 1727–1801.* Lexington: University Press of Kentucky, 2000.

Tobin, Robert Deam. *Doctor's Orders: Goethe and Enlightenment Thought.* Lewisburg: Bucknell University Press, 2001.

———. *Warm Brothers: Queer Theory and the Age of Goethe.* Philadelphia: University of Pennsylvania Press, 2000.

Uttendörfer, Otto. *Zinzendorfs christliches Lebensideal.* Gnadau: Verlag der Universitäts Buchhandlung, 1940.

———. *Zinzendorf und die Jugend: Die Erziehungsgrundsätze Zinzendorfs und der Brüdergemeine.* Berlin: Furche-Verlag, 1923.

Van Gent, Jacqueline. "Side-Wounds, Sex, and Savages: Moravian Masculinities and Early Modern Protestant Missions." In Broomhall and Van Gent, *Governing Masculinities*, 189–208.

Vogt, Peter. "*Ehereligion*: The Moravian Theory and Practice of Marriage as Point of Contention in the Conflict Between Ephrata and Bethlehem." *Communal Societies* 21 (2001): 37–48.

———. "The Masculinity of Christ According to Zinzendorf: Evidence and Interpretation." *Journal of Moravian History* 15, no. 2 (2015): 97–135.

———. "Zinzendorf's 'Seventeen Points of Matrimony': A Fundamental Document on the Moravian Understanding of Marriage and Sexuality." *Journal of Moravian History*, no. 10 (Spring 2011): 38–67.

———. "Zinzendorf und die Pennsylvanischen Synoden 1742." *Unitas Fratrum* 36 (1994): 5–62.

Watanabe O'Kelly, Helen. "Sad, Bad, Dangerous to Know? Representations of the Widow in Literature and Art." Paper presented at the Centre for Research into Gender and Culture in Society conference, "The Merry Widow: Rethinking Widowhood in History, Culture, and Society," Swansea University, Wales, July 7–9, 2007.

Wilson, Lisa. *Life After Death: Widows in Pennsylvania, 1750–1850*. Philadelphia: Temple University Press, 1992.

Wilson, Renate. "Moravian Physicians and Their Medicine in Colonial North America: European Models and Colonial Reality." In Gillespie and Beachy, *Pious Pursuits*, 65–82.

Wollstadt, Hanns-Joachim. *Geordnetes Dienen in der christlichen Gemeinde dargestellt an den Lebensformen der Herrnhuter Brüdergemeine in ihren Anfängen*. Göttingen: Vandenhoeck und Ruprecht, 1966.

# INDEX

*Typeset by*
COGHILL COMPOSITION COMPANY
*Printed and bound by*
SHERIDAN BOOKS
*Composed in*
ADOBE JENSON PRO AND COPPERPLATE LIGHT
*Printed on*
NATURES NATURAL